Discourses on Art

The Library of Liberal Arts
OSKAR PIEST, FOUNDER

DISCOURSES ON ART

With Selections from *The Idler*

Sir Joshua Reynolds

Edited, with an Introduction, by

STEPHEN O. MITCHELL

Associate Professor of English, Syracuse University

The Library of Liberal Arts
published by
The Bobbs-Merrill Company, Inc.
A subsidiary of Howard W. Sams & Co., Inc.
Publishers • Indianapolis • New York • Kansas City

Sir Joshua Reynolds: 1723–1792

Discourses on Art was first published as a single work in 1797.

6148

Copyright © 1965

THE BOBBS-MERRILL COMPANY, INC.

Printed in the United States of America
Library of Congress Catalog Card Number: 65-26523
First Printing

~☜🄸 Contents

DISCOURSES ON ART

The advantages proceeding from the institution of a Royal Academy.—Hints offered to the consideration of the professors and visitors;—that an implicit obedience to the rules of art be exacted from the young students;—that a premature disposition to a masterly dexterity be repressed;—that diligence be constantly recommended, and (that it may be effectual) directed to its proper object.

The course and order of study.—The different stages of art.—Much copying discountenanced.—The artist at all times and in all places should be employed in laying up materials for the exercise of his art.

The great leading principles of the grand style.—Of beauty.—The genuine habits of nature to be distinguished from those of fashion.

defects.—Simplicity. Its excess disagreeable.—Rules not to be always observed in their literal sense: sufficient to preserve the spirit of the law.—Observations on the prize-pictures.

Illustrations

✦ Introduction

THERE can be no question about the lasting importance of Sir Joshua Reynold's *Discourses on Art*. They are not only an accurate reflection of a painter's mind, a natural outgrowth of his own intellectual needs; they are also a critical, historical, and philosophical monument, an indispensable guide to the theory underlying a sort of art that has since been largely submerged or converted to commercial ends. The *Discourses* are a product of their age as well as of their author; for any true insight into eighteenth-century English art, or understanding of the Neoclassical movement, they are of major significance.

1

When Reynolds was born in Plympton, England, in 1723, the reign of George I was drawing to an end. It was a year after the death of the great Marlborough; Newton, Swift, and Defoe were still alive. Reynold's father, a learned and amiable, but unworldly, clergyman, was headmaster of the local school, and most of Reynolds' early academic training was accomplished through his father's efforts. In a rural countryside where £20 could support a single man for a year, his family was in comfortable circumstances. His father's side was composed of pious and moderately successful members of the minor gentry; one of Reynolds' two uncles held a fellowship at Oxford, the other at Cambridge. We have less information about his mother: it is known that she was born Theophila Potter, granddaughter to Thomas Baker, a well-known mathematician of the time. She seems to have had a passive and unobtrusive personality, obscured by the demands of bearing and raising children; her general background, however, was similar to her husband's. Thus, Reynolds' early youth was spent in an atmosphere of quiet, secure respectability.

His early education, although not exceptionally thorough, was adequate and typical of his time. His parents' home was filled with books, and spontaneous lectures on various academic topics were common. In school Reynolds followed the classical tradition of the day, studying Ovid with some care, as well as Pope and Dryden, Shakespeare and Milton. By contemporary standards, Reynolds' education shows unexpected flaws: even in an age when spelling was regarded as a matter of minor importance, his was splendidly original; his ordinary mathematics, too, was weak. But Reynolds, who throughout his life retained a remarkable drive toward self-improvement, later balanced these omissions by his thorough reading, and by his acquaintance with the literary world of contemporary London. Yet he was never a natural scholar; his later successes as a writer—indeed, all of his successes— are attributable to great self-control, good health, and unflagging vitality. He was a self-made man, in every good sense of the phrase.

Reynolds' artistic career begins with the usual stories of early drawing, including charcoal figures on whitewashed walls and cartoons on school exercises; on one of the latter his father wrote, "This was drawn by Joshua in school out of pure idleness." More significant to the expansion of his artistic horizons were a number of books: Padre Pozzo's *The Jesuit's Perspective* (1707), an English translation of Felibien's *Tent of Darius Explained* (1707), and Jacob Cats' *Book of Emblems* (1637). None of these bears any resemblance to our present art books, but their severe black-and-white plates were valuable in an age when book illustrations were not expected as a matter of course. Their subject matter is representative of the writings on art that were then current: Pozzo concerns himself with the technical aspects of perspective, Felibien with architecture, and Cats with the portrayal of the universal through the particular. Also of great importance to Reynolds was Jonathan Richardson's *Essay on the Theory of Painting*. Richardson's criticism is not highly original and his style is rather ponderous; but his precepts, typical of the period, adumbrate some of the things Reynolds was to say much more clearly a few years after. His introduction, for example, states that "The great Business of Painting I have often said and would fain inculcate, is to relate a History, or a Fable." [1] A few pages further on he argues that painting is "one of the means whereby we convey our Ideas to one another." [2] We find various forms of this view in Reynolds, and it may possibly be traced to Richardson.

For a time Reynolds' father considered making him an apothecary, an area in which Reynolds always showed some curiosity; but at the age of seventeen, he was bound apprentice to Thomas Hudson, a commercial portrait painter who, as it happened, was Jonathan Richardson's son-in-law. Thus in October, 1740, Reynolds went to London to begin his formal artistic training. It was not training as we know it, however. Both the ends and the spirit of Hudson's painting were severely practical; he was, in effect, operating a portrait factory, painting the head himself and sending the rest out to specialists in drapery and background. The results were satisfactory portraiture, not great art, and the entire business was quite justly regarded as a trade. (See first illustration.)

Despite this severely confining practicality, Reynolds did benefit from his training, strictly utilitarian as it was; besides, for someone with his energy and talent, city life itself and the contact with the great and near-great that it made possible were as valuable as more liberal, formal study would have been. Genius stimulates genius; during these early London years, Reynolds moved on the fringes of one of the world's most brilliant intellectual societies. Although it may have lacked the color and social grace of European court society, or the peculiar vigor of colonial America, it made up

---

[1] Richardson, *Essay on the Theory of Painting* (London, 1715), p. v.
[2] *Ibid.*, p. 2.

for any such lack by intellectual excitement and mobility. After centuries of existence as the capital of a small, at times unnoticed, country, London was on its way to becoming one of the world's great cities, and Reynolds participated in the ferment.

Also valuable to the young Reynolds was Hudson's collection of prints and drawings. At this time there were no public galleries, no academies, and few schools; accurate color printing was not yet known. Thus the student of painting had to content himself with what he could find, either at home or abroad, either studying copies which were often inaccurate or begging permission—not always forthcoming—to see the original. Hudson's collection served the apprentice rather as museums and color reproductions might serve today.

Reynolds did not stay with Hudson for the full four-year term of his apprenticeship, but left before three years had fully passed. There was no open break with Hudson, but there are signs of restiveness on Reynolds' part, and it is certain that he already knew all that Hudson could teach him. Reynolds' next few years were rather aimless and inactive: his father died in 1746, and until 1749 he moved between London and Devonshire, supporting himself by some scattered portrait painting. Of this period Reynolds later said it was "so much time thrown away . . . of which he ever afterwards lamented the loss."

In 1749, however, things changed abruptly, when Reynolds became acquainted with Augustus Keppel, in later life Admiral, commander of the H.M.S. *Centurion* on a mission to the Mediterranean. The two men took an immediate liking to each other, and it was decided that Reynolds would receive free passage to the Mediterranean and Italy—an arrangement that, in the comparative freedom of the eighteenth century, was not at all unusual. Thus with money borrowed from his sisters, and through the unwitting kindness of the lords of the Admiralty, Reynolds sailed for Italy, which at that time was still considered the home of all true art. The trip was broken by a long stay in Minorca, during which Reynolds supported himself by painting a number of commonplace portraits, most of which have vanished, and amused himself by riding about the countryside. After this interlude, he continued on to Italy; in February, 1750, he arrived at Leghorn, on his way to Rome.

Italian art at this time was basking in the remains of its past glory, both of the classic period and of the Renaissance. The English went there in great numbers, because of their vaguely classical education and because it was expected of them; but since they remained closeted with English friends, few learned anything about the language, people, or culture of Italy. More often than not, the Italian tour was merely a ritual gesture, a confirmation of preconceived opinions. By contrast, Reynolds spent his time in reading, in drawing, and in studying—especially, as the *Discourses* show, Michelangelo and Raphael. He was accumulating inner resources, breaking away from the limitations of Hudson and from the unexacting demands of provincial taste. Such experiment is reflected in his success at caricature and the extensive drawings in his notebooks. Reynolds did very little copying of the accepted Renaissance masters, and then only that which seemed to be the source of the entire painting's artistic merit, but he was constantly at work. His pocket notebook for the period records expenses "at the library"; he was continuing his education, reading Shaftesbury, Pliny, Cervantes, and Vergil.

It is here that Reynolds' talent must have started to flower; yet any close record of the Italian years is impossible. There are few serious portraits during this time and the extant records are inadequate for any substantial discussion. A number of biographers have conjectured that Reynolds managed to enjoy himself with pleasures of the town, but such speculations do not obscure the fact that the post-Italian Reynolds was, in effect, a mature artist. His early work is hardly to be distinguished from that of Hudson or any other successful but unimaginative painter of the period: these portraits show us human icons, people apparently untroubled by emotion, depicted in a hard, dry, and metallic manner. But the artistic riches and personal freedom that Italy gave to Reynolds seemingly brought about a personal renaissance. After Italy, his painting is distinguished by an endless series of fine portraits. In them we recognize and sympathize with living people, subject to all the passions; their likenesses come to life through an attitude and expression corresponding to character or circumstance. Mothers appear kind, leaders wear authority, squires look solidly prosperous. Further, much of Reynolds' painting is distinguished by an air of suggested but not intrusive movement. His figures either seem about to move or to have just come to rest, and he carefully avoids the stop-camera technique of frozen or posed activity. Possibly less to Reynolds' credit are his difficulty in seeing forms accurately, his taste for borrowed technique, and his apparent carelessness about background and detail as long as they suited his subject. But even a major painter has his defects. The best of Reynolds' art—the art he explains and defends in the *Discourses*—centers about people, not things; its vitality stems from its success in capturing an illusion of life.

Reynolds left for home in August of 1752; he arrived in London in October, and went at once to Devonshire to see his family and friends. After a short stay in the country, Reynolds returned to London to make his own way. He was thirty years old, and unknown; yet against all expectations he was immediately successful. The reasons for this success were not only his undoubted talent and the new life and vigor with which the Italian trip had infused his painting. Energy and willingness to work also contributed to it: pictures were completed and sent out on time, not left waiting about for weeks on end.

One work of this period is a portrait of Reynolds' early benefactor, Keppel. He is shown stepping ashore after the *Maidstone,* his most recent command had been wrecked— still manly, still brave, still in full possession of his own fate and, by implication, the fate of great events. The painting is a happy combination of the peculiar demands of portraiture with those of aesthetics. (See illustrations.) It was a good advertisement for the young painter, and may well be entirely by Reynolds' own hand. We know that the picture was so important to him that at one point he scrubbed out the entire surface and started again.

Reynolds' success was substantial; he was soon able to fix his prices at the level of his former master, Hudson. He painted, among others, the Dukes of Beaufort and of Devonshire, the Earl of Huntingdon, Lord Cathcart, and a number of less illustrious members of London society. His method was essentially that of others of his day: he made free use of subordinate painters, including Giuseppe Marchi, who followed Reynolds back from Italy, and James Northcote, who was to achieve his own more limited success. Yet Reynolds' popularity was founded on his own ability, which transcended these somewhat mechanical methods.

At about this time, no doubt as a result of his success, Reynolds' intellectual life expanded greatly. Even though he had 120 sitters in 1755 and 150 in 1758, he found time to cultivate the friendship of Edmund Burke, David Garrick, and Oliver Goldsmith, as well as Dr. Samuel Johnson, who probably had a greater influence on Reynolds than any other single man. Reynolds had a distinct penchant for those literary men who had undeniable talent, and who were familiar with the world of polite letters.

He had also started his own extensive collection of paintings. Toward the end of his life, he seems to have regarded this more as an investment than anything else; his last trip to the Continent (1785) was to buy pictures as a speculation. Yet Reynolds' wide popularity never induced him to regard his own painting as simply a livelihood; to the end he retained an interest in art for its own sake. In 1760 he moved to Leicester Square, then a fashionable address. Reynolds made several changes in the house, which had been built in 1690: he added a gallery and painting rooms, thus in effect constructing a physical plant for the production of portraits and the training of apprentices. His popularity continued, and his life followed the pattern of most successful artists

and scholars: long hours of work, a careful attention to money
matters, a certain amount of conviviality. He drove an elaborate coach, which was, after all, good publicity, and in 1764
founded the famous Club whose original members were Goldsmith, Johnson, Burke, Reynolds, and five others. Even when
the number of members was eventually increased to thirty-
five—by which time it included most of the intellectual and
artistic leaders of the period—the Club remained a product
of Reynolds' mind and tastes. It is during these middle years
that we get a clear picture of the successful Reynolds managing the complex, large-scale business of portraiture with
relative ease, and simultaneously engaging in the wider intellectual life of his time. The essential pattern is that of
Reynolds' Italian years: hard work, study, and a desire to
better himself as an artist and as a man.

In 1773 Reynolds was given a D. C. L. from Oxford. This,
and all it signified, became more and more important to
him as the years passed. In the 1767 portrait of Reynolds
painted by Angelica Kauffman, one of his closest friends, he
is shown with books, papers, and manuscripts, not with the
tools of his trade; and in his 1773 self-portrait, he wears his
doctoral robes with the dignity of an established scholar.
These portraits reveal the Reynolds of the Academy and of
the *Discourses,* the man who, out of the established security
of his artistic career, produced one of the best statements
ever made of the Neoclassic critical position.

2

The founding of the Royal Academy, the immediate source
of the *Discourses,* was a rather haphazard affair, reflecting the
confused state of English artistic life at the time. In these
middle decades of the eighteenth century the arts were blos-
soming with new life. It was the period of Pope, Johnson, and
Fielding: Adam Smith was working out the principles of
his economic system, and Voltaire was shocking and delight-

ing all Europe. Only English painting was having difficulty.
George I and George II were exceedingly bad patrons, and
the established Church, despite its relative wealth and influence, was artistically quiescent. Thus, the two traditional
sources of patronage—king and church—were withdrawn, and
what interest there was came from the nobility and the newly
augmented and flourishing middle class. Or else interest came
from those with utilitarian ends, people who needed a sign
painted, a copy made, or a picture concocted to go with the
decor. English painters were on the verge of becoming
adjuncts to the decorator or builder, rather than autonomous
creators. Indeed, there was at this time a tradition, carefully
fostered on the Continent, that the English were "face painters"—that is, they could paint only portraits. At this time
there was no clear idea in England of art as art—as an extension of personality, a way of seeing the world. It was a
commodity, the product of a semiskilled trade; therefore, the
average painter felt more or less compelled to flatter the
subject or patron, and to bend to the whim or wishes of
whoever paid the bill. Reynolds was able to purify this low
and servile idea of art, distilling it into the advice: ". . . never
to lose sight of the general idea of perfection in each kind" [3];
but in the hands of an average artist such a precept sinks into
simple flattery. This concept of art is reflected in the existence
of specialists, of journeyman painters; there was even a subset
of artisans who painted only dogs. There were "artists" who
painted signs, coaches, or plaster, and, even less reputable,
those who filled awkward architectural spaces and hid cracks
in the wall, by providing hasty reproductions of an Italian
master. And it had to be an Italian, for the classic fashion
was in full sway. Most of the people buying pictures had made
the Italian tour; they at least pretended to a classical education, and wanted to be in step with their neighbors.

Pictures, then, were *things,* subordinate and vaguely utilitarian objects. Gainsborough, to cite the best-known example,
left at his death a number of unsold landscapes, and Hogarth,

3 Discourse 3, p. 32.

being neither Italian nor subject to the dictates of popular taste, was never much in the fashion in the best circles. Finally, English art was handicapped by shockingly bad crafts-manship. Skills and techniques now considered a matter of elementary training were ignored, or else gained only at the expense of unusual individual effort. In some English country houses or at rural auctions we can still see examples of such bad art: pictures with entirely faulty perspective, lacking all sense of composition, muddy in color, were common. In a sense these pictures deserved the inappropriate frames and improper lighting to which they were subjected; their sole purpose was to testify to the local squire's affluence and to record his estimable image for posterity.

In such an artistic climate, it is little wonder that painting had reached a point where Reynolds, in his first discourse to the newly formed Academy, could say wryly: "One advan-tage, I will venture to affirm, we shall have in our Academy, which no other nation can boast. We shall have nothing to unlearn." The time was ripe for a place where artists might exhibit, and see the work of others; teach, and learn. An Academy, or so it was thought, would ensure the social and artistic progress of the next generation of painters; it would be a place where the fine arts could be regularly cultivated. Ideally, such an Academy would have its own building, re-ceive assistance from the king or from some other member of the royal family, and support professorships in various skills. Most important, however, a standard would be set and a common goal agreed upon. In 1753, a twenty-one-member Academy was proposed, but the scheme lacked backing and soon died. In 1759, however, at an annual artists' dinner, the assembled body decided to hold an exhibit in 1760, to be sponsored by polite society. It took place in the large, light room maintained by the Society for the Encouragement of Arts, Manufacture, and Commerce, a group devoted to the improvement of English commercial and industrial life; the social approval of this group contributed to the exhibition's success. The exhibit was crowded, nonselective, and not always visible. Pictures were haphazardly arranged and hung at quite impossible heights from the floor. But despite all its faults it was a great success, and performed a highly valuable service for English painting: for the first time, the public could see and compare a variety of pictures over a period of several months.

There was friction the next year, however, between the artists and the sponsoring society over who exactly could exhibit. The artists withdrew; calling themselves the Society of Artists, they held an exhibit at less elegant quarters in Charing Cross where, at one shilling per catalogue, they made £650, a good indication of public interest. Another portion of the original exhibitors formed a splinter group under the name of the Free Society of Artists of Great Britain, and held an exhibit in the original room. They were successful enough to build a gallery in 1778, but their good intentions were unsupported by either talent or patronage, and the gallery closed the next year.

The Society of Artists grew stronger and stronger, and achieved a royal charter in 1765; but in 1768 internal conflicts arose over who should govern the group, and the directors were ousted. The best of the painters left along with them, and petitioned George III for sanction to form another group. This sanction was soon granted; on December 10, 1768, the Royal Academy of London came into being, including in its membership Benjamin West, William Chambers, and Francis Cotes; Sir Joshua Reynolds, the most eminent English painter of the day, was its first president.

Whatever the value of academies and schools in general, this one was enormously helpful; it provided models and scholarships, as well as lectures, the most important of which were the *Discourses* delivered in conjunction with the ritual of prize-giving and recognition of merit. Far from merely adorning the day with graceful rhetoric, the *Discourses* were intended to teach and to provide useful insight; they were essays in practical aesthetics, given by a working painter. He himself says:

The knowledge which an artist has of his subject will more than compensate for any want of elegance in the manner of treating it, or even of perspicuity, which is still more essential; and I am convinced that one short essay written by a painter, will contribute more to advance the theory of our art, than a thousand volumes such as we sometimes see; the purpose of which appears to be rather to display the refinement of the author's own conceptions of impossible practice, than to convey useful knowledge or instruction of any kind whatever. An artist knows what is, and what is not, within the province of his art to perform. . . .[4]

3

What it is that Reynolds teaches is at first somewhat hard to discern, especially today when so many people are devoted to private expression and individual taste. When Reynolds tells us he "would chiefly recommend, that an implicit obedience to the *rules of art,* as established by the practice of the great masters should be exacted from *young* students,"[5] we are at first put off by a seeming rigidity; the term "rules of art" has overtones of sterile imitation and dull academic exercise. But Reynolds' rules are something altogether different. We must remember that his aesthetic theory was classical, traditional, and moral; his first premise is that the end of art is ethical growth: "instead of endeavouring to amuse mankind with the minute neatness of his imitations, the painter must endeavour to improve them by the grandeur of his ideas."[6] Faced with the choice between art as pleasure and art as moral improvement, Reynolds always opts for the latter: "Whatever abstracts the thoughts from sensual gratifications, whatever teaches us to look for happiness within ourselves, must advance in some measure the dignity of our nature."[7]

[4] Discourse 15, p. 226.
[5] Discourse 1, p. 8.
[6] Discourse 3, p. 27.
[7] Discourse 9, p. 142.

This first precept is the controlling idea for all that follows. It is not, of course, a new idea—it occurs from Plato on. Reynolds' importance lies in his explicit statement, in readable and graceful form, of things that are scattered throughout eighteenth-century critical doctrine. He reinterprets a vast, confused mass of borrowed dicta and tradition to assemble a powerful and coherent defense of Neoclassic art, that is, of art as Reynolds and subsequent academicians saw it.

Art, then—and portraiture more than any other genre— aims at ethical growth, a growth that is to be achieved by the viewer when he grasps the concept of the ideal, the reality hidden away beyond the accidental imperfections of birth, age, or particularity; art allows us to see the world and human beings as they truly are and hence gives us a standard for our individual lives, an insight which produces the virtue of freedom from the particular and the sensual. "The beauty of which we are in quest is general and intellectual; it is an idea that subsists only in the mind." [8] Or, "Whatever abstracts the thoughts from sensual gratifications, whatever teaches us to look for happiness within ourselves, must advance in some measure the dignity of our nature." [9] Oddities in an individual, for example, are omissions or errors; "true" portraiture or ideal representation will show the universality of the original, in its essential being. This one premise leads us to a number of other ideas. The portrait painter's flattery of the sitter, for example, might be excused as a search for the true inner man. Also, art may neglect the nonhuman world, or at best subordinate it to man, since even the most interesting landscape, unless clearly related to human life in some manner or capable of allegorical interpretation, will lead to ethical growth only in exceptional circumstances. "Figures must have a ground whereon to stand; they must be cloathed; there must be a background; there must be light and shadow; but none of these ought to appear

[8] *Ibid.*, p. 142
[9] *Ibid.*, p. 142.

to have taken up any part of the artist's attention." [10] Landscapes and all nonhuman representation may show technical skill in matters of line, color, form, proportion, or anything else, but they are not praiseworthy in their own right. They remain a "lower rank of art."

Yet there is a paradox or contradiction in Reynolds' critical position. He is the great exponent of classicism and of a traditional, ethical aesthetic, but apparently he came to find morality and truth insufficient criteria for aesthetic merit. In the later discourses, Reynolds attempts—often without much clarity or success—to insert feeling into his classical and highly rational theory. In his need for some principle of aesthetic satisfaction other than ethics, and later in his comments on genius, Reynolds is a precursor of the Romantics. This ambivalent quality is evident in Reynolds' idea of the Sublime.

During the eighteenth century the concept of the Sublime underwent a number of fluctuations, moving from the earlier intellectual tradition found in Longinus to Edmund Burke's heavy stress on emotion. In Longinus, the Sublime is treated as that which is always pleasing, whose generality is nearly irresistible, and which applies to all men. It is a quality which comes from the artist's soul, a quality whose greatness and universality attracts our admiration and respect. Burke, however, in his essay on *The Sublime and the Beautiful* (1757), clearly regards the Sublime as something based on the emotions, in particular, terror. The Sublime is an emotion generated in the observer, springing from his inability to comprehend. Hence, the sea, the mountains, the storm are all sublime. Reynolds takes a middle course between these two. He accepts the mystery and suddenness inherent in Burke's view, but at the same time he keeps Longinus' intellectual qualities. Thus Reynolds tells us: "The sublime impresses the mind at once with one great idea; it is a single blow. . . ." [11] Years later, in his last discourse, he nearly repeats himself:

10 Discourse 4, p. 41.
11 Discourse 4, p. 48.

"The sublime in painting, as in poetry, so overpowers, and takes such possession of the whole mind, that no room is left for attention to minute criticism. The little elegancies of art in the presence of these great ideas thus greatly expressed, lose all their value, and are for the instant at least, felt to be unworthy of our notice." [12] Clearly enough he is steering a middle course between the immediacy of an emotional state and the reserve of Longinus. In so doing he not only explains a common Neoclassic critical term in his own way; he also foreshadows the more emotional theories of art found at a later period.

Another of Reynolds' important terms is "taste." In the early part of the century those critics who followed Shaftesbury regarded taste as innate, unlettered feeling, some immediate reaction to beauty or its absence. But by the middle of the century the word was badly blurred, and had come to mean any number of things. Reynolds, however, rejuvenated the concept, maintaining that although taste does draw on novelty, excitement, and the evocation of personal or conventional associations, it is fundamentally the ability to distinguish right from wrong, good from bad. "The natural appetite or taste of the human mind is for *truth*." [13] It is at one and the same time an intellectual sense and an artistic one, going back to Reynolds' predication of an aesthetic based on reason. "It is the very same taste which relishes a demonstration in geometry, that is pleased with the resemblance of a picture to an original, and touched with the harmony of musick." [14] It follows that, for Reynolds, taste comes first of all from thought, from reason, and from philosophy; in short, from intellectual activity, not from an inherent emotion. "It is reason and good sense therefore which ranks and estimates every art." [15] In these terms, taste is the ability to distinguish what is generally good, that is, of the highest moral value:

12 Discourse 15, p. 235.
13 Discourse 7, p. 97.
14 *Ibid.*, p. 97.
15 *Ibid.*, p. 105.

"Nor can those works which remind us of the poverty and meanness of our nature, be considered as of equal rank with what excites ideas of grandeur, or raises and dignifies humanity; or, in the words of a late poet, which makes the beholder *'learn to venerate himself as a man.'* " [16] Consequently the first principle of taste is the imitation of nature—not just any nature, of course, but that ideal nature which has the power to please and instruct. In the day-to-day world, admittedly, distorted ideas and unusual experiences have a temporary importance; but sound taste should be able to rise above such vagaries and to distinguish that which gives general and lasting pleasure. This can be accomplished by the study of important works by previous artists (in Reynolds' case, Michelangelo and Raphael), and by acquaintance with other arts, in particular, poetry. "Every man," says Reynolds, "whose business is description, ought to be tolerably conversant with the poets, in some language or other; that he may imbibe a poetical spirit, and enlarge his stock of ideas." [17] Further on he advises, "Reading, if it can be made the favourite recreation of his leisure hours, will improve and enlarge his mind, without retarding his actual industry." [18] Genuine taste is a full effort of the mind brought to bear on the work of art, whereby the ideal and the general are perceived in the work at the same time that it is compared to other works of art.

This notion of taste leads naturally to the question of rules. For Reynolds, these are a generalization of the solutions to various aesthetic problems arrived at by generations of mankind: "The great use of studying our predecessors is, to open the mind, to shorten our labour, and to give us the result of the selection made by those great minds of what is grand or beautiful in nature." [19] Rules are not a restrictive set of mechanical procedures, but guides to a moral end. In

[16] *Ibid.*, p. 105.
[17] *Ibid.*, p. 93.
[18] *Ibid.*, p. 93.
[19] Discourse 6, p. 80.

Reynolds' hands, they become a way of study, a discipline: "Study therefore the great works of the great masters . . . consider them as models which you are to imitate, and at the same time as rivals with whom you are to contend." [20]

Something should be said here about Reynolds' conception of genius, since "The highest ambition of every artist is to be thought a man of genius." [21] In general, Reynolds equates genius with the ability to step beyond the bounds of mere technical competence. It is the ability to grasp and then portray the universal and ideal. In the eleventh discourse, for example, he singles out what he calls mechanical genius. "This genius consists, I conceive, in the power of expressing that which employs your pencil, whatever it may be, *as a whole;* so that the general effect and power of the whole may take possession of the mind, and for a while suspend the consideration of the subordinate and particular beauties or defects." [22] Further on this same general ability is applied to landscape painting:

> A landscape-painter certainly ought to study anatomically (if I may use the expression) all the objects which he paints; but when he is to turn his studies to use, his skill, as a man of genius, will be displayed in shewing the general effect, preserving the same degree of hardness and softness which the objects have in nature; for he applies himself to the imagination, not to the curiosity, and works not for the virtuoso or the naturalist, but for the common observer of life and nature.[23]

After this, however, Reynolds seems to remember his duties as a president giving a pedagogical address. "I should be very sorry," he says, "if what has been said should be understood to have any tendency to encourage that carelessness which leaves work in an unfinished state. . . ." [24] A few lines down he claims, "To give a right direction to your industry

20 *Ibid.,* p. 91.
21 Discourse 11, p. 159.
22 *Ibid.,* p. 160.
23 *Ibid.,* p. 167.
24 *Ibid.,* p. 171.

has been my principal purpose in this discourse." [25] Still, despite these cautious afterthoughts, Reynolds' general idea of genius shows through as that of an innate ability, and since he operates in a Neoclassic milieu, we assume it is the innate ability to seize that which is most general and most representative.

This brief review of Reynolds' major ideas has so far omitted mention of his limitations: beneath the genial surface, the urbanity and good sense, of the *Discourses* lie several problems. It may be objected, for example, that Reynolds is too intellectual, or that he is proposing an aesthetic theory by which all art, not just his own kind of art, must be judged; or else that he is too general, too frequently failing to grasp the specific problem at hand. But all such complaints ignore the two essential aims of the *Discourses:* first, to provide pedagogical advice suitable to all levels of skill; second, to formulate a general theory for English painting. More serious objections arise when we examine Reynolds' relation to Italian painting. There is evidence of conflict between his private taste and his standards for the academic art that he promoted; a clear disjunction exists between his desire for an English school of painting and his own strongly Italianate bias, and, similarly, between his admiration for Raphael and for Michelangelo. For official reasons—that is, because Raphael fits the Neoclassic conception of art—Reynolds, like scores of other critics, praises him frequently and thoroughly. But throughout the years Reynolds tended to perfer Michelangelo, the man of genius who stepped beyond the rules and precedents; it is worth noting that he closes his *Discourses* with Michelangelo's name.

4

Many years before the *Discourses* appeared Reynolds was, so to speak, preparing them; they are a logical product of his personality and goals. We may understand their origin if

[25] *Ibid.*, p. 171.

we examine Reynolds' life as that of a literary amateur, one who was always interested in letters but never professionally concerned with them. Goldsmith dedicated *The Deserted Village* to Reynolds in 1770; twenty-one years later, Boswell dedicated to him the greatest biography in the English language, the monumental *Life of Johnson.* From his earliest days in London, Reynolds was attracted to the literary world; the *Discourses* recommend the "conversation of learned and ingenious men" [26] as part of the artist's education, and, as we have already seen, he urges the aspiring painter to read poetry as an aid in forming his taste.

Reynolds' first published work appeared in September, 1759, and can be traced to his tie with Johnson. During this time Johnson was engaged in writing, or arranging for others to write, *The Idler,* a series of periodical essays similar to the *Tatler* and *Spectator* papers of an earlier day. Number 76 of this series, which discusses the foolishness of critics who judge only by their own rules, was written by Reynolds, as were Numbers 79 and 82, published in October and November of 1759, which discuss the Grand Style in painting and the true idea of beauty. In these three short essays, collected and reprinted as a single essay in 1761, Reynolds outlines many of the ideas which appear in the *Discourses.* He tells us that "what may be an excellence in a lower class of painting, becomes a blemish in a higher," and that "To distinguish beauty, then, implies the having seen many individuals of that species." [27]

In 1769 Reynolds delivered the first of his discourses. He was never at his best before an audience, having not only deafness (hence the inability to judge his volume or correct his pronunciation) counting against him, but also poor enunciation and a distinct Devonshire accent. A less happy combination can hardly be imagined; yet his first lecture was received with approbation. The first discourse was printed in January of 1769, at the request of the Royal Academy; it was reviewed

[26] Discourse 7, p. 93.
[27] Samuel Johnson, *Works* (Oxford, 1925), IV, 375.

in both the *Gentleman's Magazine* and the *Monthly Review*, and was translated into German and French. After this sound beginning, the *Discourses* attracted no wide critical attention, but the book sold rather well (Reynolds received £62 as his share) and in due course Italian (1778), German (1781), and French (1787) editions appeared. They were not always well received but, much more important, they were noticed and read. Not every reader of the translations could be expected to agree with Reynolds, the established English painter; yet he was paid the supreme compliment of being taken seriously as a writer and critic, on the basis of his first book.

The discourses continued to be given. They were printed and widely read; and, to Reynolds' satisfaction, they were accorded serious consideration. Rather more specific topics are taken up in the last discourses, and the ninth is unexpectedly brief, but their general tenor has been set and their critical bias remains the same. By 1790 Reynolds was physically worn; although only sixty-seven, his eyes were failing, and in 1791 he gave his last discourse, fittingly enough on the subject of genius, a topic which had always fascinated him.

5

A final word needs to be said about the significance of the *Discourses*. They represent different things to different people and are liable to various interpretations; but we might best assess their value in terms of their contribution to our historical and our critical understanding. Regarded as a historical document, the *Discourses* represent a turning away from standards narrowly limited to the visual arts, toward an interest in general critical principles. Not only does Reynolds recognize that poetry and the plastic and representational arts are related; he also realizes that poetry is the more flexible and general of the two:

> Poetry having a more extensive power than our art, exerts its influence over almost all the passions; among those may be reckoned one of our most prevalent dispositions,

anxiety for the future. Poetry operates by raising our
curiosity, engaging the mind by degrees to take an interest in the event, keeping that event suspended, and
surprising at last with an unexpected catastrophe.

The painter's art is more confined, and has nothing
that corresponds with, or perhaps is equivalent to, this
power. . . .[28]

At the same time that Reynolds is moving toward a more
general critical theory of art, he also turns his back on the
narrow formalism of much eighteenth-century criticism and
practice. He urges pursuit of the ideal and acknowledges the
inspiration of genius. In many ways his chief theme is "that
the mind should be elevated to the idea of general beauty,
and the contemplation of general truth." [29] Artistic rules and
the doctrine of imitation—deadly concepts in the wrong
hands—become, for Reynolds, tools to explain his own practice. But he frequently ignores the rules, relying on imagination and emotion for his critical judgment. In this
judgment, it is true, we may often feel that he is mistaken,
as when he condemns Hogarth for using his genius on "low
and confined subjects" [30] or pities Dürer for being born in the
wrong country. But against such relatively minor errors can
be set his careful re-examination of eighteenth-century
critical standards, and his willingness to expound upon his
own theories of art. Reynolds' aim is to explain and teach,
not to codify or destroy; thus his continual effort to grapple
with the critical terms then current. His idea of the Sublime
may be obscure, and we may find that he contradicts himself
in discussing genius; yet he is willing to try, and in so doing
he generates a kind of standard against which the ideas of
others may be measured.

The *Discourses* are also invaluable in the area of criticism,
since they contribute greatly to our understanding of
Reynolds' own work and of eighteenth-century art in general.

28 Discourse 8, p. 119.
29 Discourse 9, p. 142.
30 Discourse 3, p. 36.

After even a cursory examination of Reynolds' painting, we understand that such a self-provided insight is important and even necessary: according to our own background and experience his works are variously good, imitative, dull, dated, quaint, or obscure. His best art is timeless; but consider, for example, the portrait "Mrs. Siddons as the Tragic Muse," which shows Mrs. Siddons, a famous actress of the day, seated on a throne flanked by two allegorical figures, and looking into the distance. It is not a good picture; the idea and the execution are trite, and Mrs. Siddons herself looks somewhat stage-struck. Yet such a portrait is more understandable if we are aware of Reynolds' belief in the ability to learn technique, and his belief in the importance of general ideas. In short, the *Discourses* explain much that we find dated and obscure in his work, and many of his limitations and failures.

And the *Discourses* illuminate not only Reynolds, but others of the period. Gainsborough is given high praise, although not quite for the reasons we might expect: "It is to the credit of his good sense and judgment that he never did attempt that style of historical painting for which his previous studies had made no preparation." [31] These and other comments go far in explaining the worldly success or failure of a number of people. Hogarth's relative lack of recognition is easily comprehensible if we understand Reynolds' critical standards, as is the complete failure of Blake, who came nowhere near to meeting the social and cultural ideals that Reynolds represented. In the *Discourses* we can examine the public workings of a mind acquainted with all ranks of polite society, and friendly with a significant portion of the literary world of the day. Reynolds' reasons for rejecting Hogarth were comparable to those of his entire circle, and in his love of the Italian masters he shares (although with more understanding) the tastes of English society during this period. Too frequently major artists leave nothing but their art and, at best, a mass of unsorted papers, so that all evidence bearing on their intellectual life is lost. Reynolds, by contrast, left us a body of

[31] Discourse 14, p. 216.

criticism and opinion which we know to have been highly regarded in the eighteenth century, and consequently, to reflect the tastes and opinions of his day.

In a still more far-reaching sense, Reynolds helps us to understand eighteenth-century literary practice, and the subsequent revolt against Neoclassic norms. His stress on generality does much to explain the practice of a Pope or a Johnson, whose aim is to portray the ideal. At the same time, Reynolds' paradoxical ideas of genius, his inability to exclude emotion from his aesthetic, illuminate what Wordsworth is about, and why the Romantics felt themselves to be in revolt against a dead tradition. Reynolds is first and last a man of his day; even in his mistakes, he lends us insight.

S. O. M.

◈ Selected Bibliography

Reynolds' Works and Letters

The Works of Sir Joshua Reynolds. Edited by EDMUND MA-
LONE, ESQ. London, 1797.

The Works of Sir Joshua Reynolds, . . . The Second Edition.
3 vols. London, 1798.

The Letters of Sir Joshua Reynolds. Edited by FREDERICK W.
HILLES. Cambridge, Eng.: Cambridge University Press,
1929.

Three letters to *The Idler,* Nos. 76, 79, and 82. *Universal
Chronicle,* September 29, October 20, and November 10,
1759. These are more generally available in Reynolds'
Works, or in *The Works of Samuel Johnson.*

*Portraits by Sir Joshua Reynolds. Character Sketches of Oliver
Goldsmith, Samuel Johnson, and David Garrick, together
with Other Manuscripts of Reynolds Recently Discovered
among the Private Papers of James Boswell and now
First Published.* Edited by FREDERICK W. HILLES. New
York: McGraw-Hill, 1952.

Discourses on Art. Edited by ROBERT R. WARK. San Marino,
California: Huntington, 1959.

Works That Reynolds May Have
Read in Preparing the Discourses

BURKE, EDMUND. *A Philosophical Enquiry into the Origin of
Our Ideas of the Sublime and Beautiful.* London, 1757.

DU FRESNOY, CHARLES ALPHONSE. *The Art of Painting.* Translated by JOHN DRYDEN. London, 1695.

HOGARTH, WILLIAM. *The Analysis of Beauty.* London, 1753.
Edited by JOSEPH BURKE. Oxford: The Clarendon Press,
1955.

HUTCHESON, FRANCIS. *An Inquiry into the Original of Our Ideas of Beauty and Virtue.* London, 1725.

PILES, ROGER DE. *The Art of Painting and the Lives of the Painters.* London, 1751.

RICHARDSON, JONATHAN. *An Account of Some Statues, Bas-Reliefs, Drawings and Pictures in Italy.* London, 1722.

Works on Reynolds and His Time

BATE, WALTER JACKSON. *From Classic to Romantic: Premises of Taste in Eighteenth-Century England.* Cambridge, Mass.: Harvard University Press, 1946.

BURKE, JOSEPH. *Hogarth and Reynolds: A Contrast in English Art Theory.* London: Oxford University Press, 1943.

DRAPER, JOHN. *Eighteenth-Century English Aesthetics: A Bibliography.* Heidelberg: C. Winter, 1931.

HILLES, FREDERICK W. *The Literary Career of Sir Joshua Reynolds.* Cambridge, Eng.: Cambridge University Press, 1936.

HYAMS, EDWARD, and EDWIN SMITH. *The English Garden.* New York: Abrams, 1964.

LAMB, SIR WALTER RANGELEY MAITLAND. *The Royal Academy: A Short History of its Foundation and Development.* London: G. Bell & Sons, 1951.

LEE, RENSSELAER W. "Ut Pictura Poesis: The Humanistic Theory of Painting," *Art Bulletin,* XXII (1940), 197–269.

MACLEAN, KENNETH. *John Locke and English Literature of the 18th Century.* New Haven: Yale University Press, 1939.

MONK, SAMUEL H. *The Sublime: A Study of Critical Theories in Eighteenth-Century England.* New York: Modern Language Association of America, 1935.

NORTHCOTE, JAMES. *The Life of Sir Joshua Reynolds.* London, 1818.

WATERHOUSE, ELLIS KIRKHAM. *Reynolds.* London: Kegan Paul, 1941.

☜ A Note on the Text

This edition of Reynolds' *Discourses* is based on the 1797 text, the last edition in which Reynolds had any personal concern; presumably it reflects his own wishes. Since this is an eighteenth-century English text, original spellings have been retained so as to give some idea of the *Discourses* as Reynolds' first readers saw them; a few obvious misprints and typographical errors have been corrected, and the varieties of spellings, and the capitalization, regularized, but the body of the text remains in its original form. The editor's notes are distinguished by brackets; otherwise they are Reynolds' own glosses, and a part of the text.

Since the *Discourses* were given over a number of years, they can be found in a number of forms. Each discourse was printed individually, with the exception of *Discourses* Nine and Ten, which appeared together. In 1778, the first seven discourses were published in an octavo edition, followed by a Florentine edition, 1778; a German edition, 1781; a French edition, 1787; and a Venetian edition, 1787, which was simply a reprint of the Florentine edition. The first collected edition appeared in 1797 in Reynolds' *Works,* followed by the second collected edition in 1798. Both of these collected editions were edited by Edmond Malone, one of Reynolds' literary executors. Malone's few editorial notes are not distinguished in this edition from Reynolds'. A large number of other editions have since appeared, the best of which is that of Robert R. Wark, *Sir Joshua Reynolds: "Discourses on Art"* (San Marino, Calif.: Huntingdon Library, 1959), which gives the variant readings of earlier editions, and clarifies a number of potential obscurities. For fuller information on the literary background of the *Discourses* and Reynolds' use of various earlier works, the best source is F. W. Hilles, *The Literary Career of Sir Joshua Reynolds* (New York: Macmillan, 1936).

The illustrations were selected to show not only what Reynolds approved of, but also what he condemned, or found good in a limited way. Also, the plates illustrate representative work by those painters Reynolds cites most frequently, or those whose work throws some light on his own style.

In the notes by the present editor, quotations are identified as fully as possible, Latin tags are glossed, and Reynolds' more obscure allusions are explained. With a few exceptions, names are not glossed, since Reynolds is usually careful to explain their significance. There is also a representative selection of passages from *The Idler*, Reynolds' first published critical work. These show Reynolds ten years before the first discourse and illustrate the general uniformity of his critical position. They are, if you like, trials for the *Discourses;* in them some of Reynolds' most concise statements on art and critics can be found.

Special thanks are due the trustees of the Cronk fund, for their support in the preparation of this edition.

Discourses on Art

✒ To the King

[*1778*]

THE regular progress of cultivated life is from necessaries to accommodations, from accommodations to ornaments. By your illustrious predecessors were established marts for manufactures, and colleges for science; but for the arts of elegance, those arts by which manufactures are embellished, and science is refined, to found an Academy was reserved for Your Majesty.

Had such patronage been without effect, there had been reason to believe that nature had, by some insurmountable impediment, obstructed our proficiency; but the annual improvement of the Exhibitions which Your Majesty has been pleased to encourage, shews that only encouragement had been wanting.

To give advice to those who are contending for royal liberality, has been for some years the duty of my station in the Academy; and these discourses hope for Your Majesty's acceptance, as well-intended endeavours to incite that emulation which your notice has kindled, and direct those studies which your bounty has rewarded.

May it please Your Majesty,

Your Majesty's

Most dutiful servant,

and most faithful subject,

JOSHUA REYNOLDS

To The Members of
The Royal Academy

4

❧ Discourse 1

January 2, 1769

GENTLEMEN,

AN Academy, in which the polite arts may be regularly cultivated, is at last opened among us by Royal munificence. This must appear an event in the highest degree interesting, not only to the artists, but to the whole nation.

It is indeed difficult to give any other reason, why an empire like that of Britain, should so long have wanted an ornament so suitable to its greatness, than that slow progression of things, which naturally makes elegance and refinement the last effect of opulence and power.[1]

An institution like this has often been recommended upon considerations merely mercantile; but an Academy, founded upon such principles, can never effect even its own narrow purposes. If it has an origin no higher, no taste can ever be formed in manufactures; but if the higher arts of design flourish, these inferior ends will be answered of course.

We are happy in having a Prince, who has conceived the design of such an institution, according to its true dignity; and who promotes the arts, as the head of a great, a learned, a polite, and a commercial nation; and I can now congratulate you, gentlemen, on the accomplishment of your long and ardent wishes.

The numberless and ineffectual consultations which I have had with many in this assembly, to form plans and concert

[1] [The Italian Accademia Platonica was founded in 1442; the French Académie des Jeux Floraux in 1694.]

5

schemes for an Academy, afford a sufficient proof of the impossibility of succeeding but by the influence of Majesty. But there have, perhaps, been times, when even the influence of Majesty would have been ineffectual; and it is pleasing to reflect, that we are thus embodied, when every circumstance seems to concur from which honour and prosperity can probably arise.

There are, at this time, a greater number of excellent artists than were ever known before at one period in this nation; there is a general desire among our nobility to be distinguished as lovers and judges of the arts; there is a greater superfluity of wealth among the people to reward the professors; and, above all, we are patronized by a Monarch, who, knowing the value of science and of elegance, thinks every art worthy of his notice, that tends to soften and humanise the mind.

After so much has been done by His Majesty, it will be wholly our fault, if our progress is not in some degree correspondent to the wisdom and generosity of the institution: let us shew our gratitude in our diligence, that, though our merit may not answer his expectations, yet, at least, our industry may deserve his protection.

But whatever may be our proportion of success, of this we may be sure, that the present institution will at least contribute to advance our knowledge of the arts, and bring us nearer to that ideal excellence, which it is the lot of genius always to contemplate and never to attain.

The principal advantage of an Academy is, that, beside furnishing able men to direct the student, it will be a repository for the great examples of the art. These are the materials on which genius is to work, and without which the strongest intellect may be fruitlessly or deviously employed. By studying these authentick models, that idea of excellence which is the result of the accumulated experience of past ages, may be at once acquired; and the tardy and obstructed progress of our predecessors may teach us a shorter and easier way. The student receives, at one glance, the principles which many artists have spent their whole lives in ascertaining; and, satisfied with their effect, is spared the painful investigation by which they came to be known and fixed. How many men of great natural abilities have been lost to this nation, for want of these advantages! They never had an opportunity of seeing those masterly efforts of genius, which at once kindle the whole soul, and force it into sudden and irresistible approbation.

Raffaelle,[2] it is true, had not the advantage of studying in an Academy; but all Rome, and the works of Michael Angelo in particular, were to him an Academy. On the sight of the Capella Sistina, he immediately from a dry, Gothick,[3] and even insipid manner, which attends to the minute accidental discriminations of particular and individual objects, assumed that grand style of painting, which improves partial representation by the general and invariable ideas of nature.

Every seminary of learning may be said to be surrounded with an atmosphere of floating knowledge, where every mind may imbibe somewhat congenial to its own original conceptions. Knowledge, thus obtained, has always something more popular and useful than that which is forced upon the mind by private precepts, or solitary meditation. Besides, it is generally found, that a youth more easily receives instruction from the companions of his studies, whose minds are nearly on a level with his own, than from those who are much his superiors; and it is from his equals only that he catches the fire of emulation.

One advantage, I will venture to affirm, we shall have in our Academy, which no other nation can boast. We shall have nothing to unlearn. To this praise the present race of artists have a just claim. As far as they have yet proceeded, they are right. With us the exertions of genius will henceforward be directed to their proper objects. It will not be as it has been in other schools, where he that travelled fastest, only wandered farthest from the right way.

2 [That is, Raphael.]
3 [In this sense, uncivilized, crude.]

Impressed, as I am, therefore, with such a favourable opinion of my associates in this undertaking, it would ill become me to dictate to any of them. But as these institutions have so often failed in other nations; and as it is natural to think with regret, how much might have been done, I must take leave to offer a few hints, by which those errors may be rectified, and those defects supplied. These the professors and visitors may reject or adopt as they shall think proper.

I would chiefly recommend, that an implicit obedience to the *rules of art,* as established by the practice of the great Masters, should be exacted from the *young* students. That those models, which have passed through the approbation of ages, should be considered by them as perfect and infallible guides; as subjects for their imitation, not their criticism.

I am confident, that this is the only efficacious method of making a progress in the arts; and that he who sets out with doubting, will find life finished before he becomes master of the rudiments. For it may be laid down as a maxim, that he who begins by presuming on his own sense, has ended his studies as soon as he has commenced them. Every opportunity, therefore, should be taken to discountenance that false and vulgar opinion, that rules are the fetters of genius. They are fetters only to men of no genius; as that armour, which upon the strong is an ornament and a defence, upon the weak and mis-shapen becomes a load, and cripples the body which it was made to protect.

How much liberty may be taken to break through those rules, and, as the poet expresses it,

> "To snatch a grace beyond the reach of art," [4]

may be a subsequent consideration, when the pupils become masters themselves. It is then, when their genius has received its utmost improvement, that rules may possibly be dispensed with. But let us not destroy the scaffold, until we have raised the building.

---

[4] [Alexander Pope, "Essay on Criticism," 155: "And snatch a grace beyond the reach of Art."]

The Directors ought more particularly to watch over the genius of those students, who, being more advanced, are arrived at that critical period of study, on the nice management of which their future turn of taste [5] depends. At that age it is natural for them to be more captivated with what is brilliant than with what is solid, and to prefer splendid negligence to painful and humiliating exactness.

A facility in composing,—a lively, and what is called a masterly, handling of the chalk or pencil, are, it must be confessed, captivating qualities to young minds, and become of course the objects of their ambition. They endeavour to imitate those dazzling excellencies, which they will find no great labour in attaining. After much time spent in these frivolous pursuits, the difficulty will be to retreat; but it will be then too late; and there is scarce an instance of return to scrupulous labour, after the mind has been debauched and deceived by this fallacious mastery.

By this useless industry they are excluded from all power of advancing in real excellence. Whilst boys, they are arrived at their utmost perfection; they have taken the shadow for the substance; and make the mechanical felicity, the chief excellence of the art, which is only an ornament, and of the merit of which few but painters themselves are judges.

This seems to me to be one of the most dangerous sources of corruption; and I speak of it from experience, not as an error which may possibly happen, but which has actually infected all foreign Academies. The directors were probably pleased with this premature dexterity in their pupils, and praised their dispatch at the expence of their correctness.

But young men have not only this frivolous ambition of being thought masters of execution, inciting them on one hand, but also their natural sloth tempting them on the other. They are terrified at the prospect before them, of the toil required to attain exactness. The impetuosity of youth is disgusted at the slow approaches of a regular siege, and desires, from mere impatience of labour, to take the citadel by storm.

[5] [For the meaning of "taste," see Introduction, p. xxii.]

They wish to find some shorter path to excellence, and hope
to obtain the reward of eminence by other means, than those
which the indispensable rules of art have prescribed. They
must therefore be told again and again, that labour is the
only price of solid fame, and that whatever their force of
genius may be, there is no easy method of becoming a good
painter.

When we read the lives of the most eminent painters,
every page informs us, that no part of their time was spent in
dissipation. Even an increase of fame served only to aug-
ment their industry. To be convinced with what persevering
assiduity they pursued their studies, we need only reflect on
their method of proceeding in their most celebrated works.
When they conceived a subject, they first made a variety of
sketches; then a finished drawing of the whole; after that a
more correct drawing of every separate part,—heads, hands,
feet, and pieces of drapery; they then painted the picture, and
after all re-touched it from the life. The pictures, thus
wrought with such pains, now appear like the effect of en-
chantment, and as if some mighty genius had struck them
off at a blow.

But, whilst diligence is thus recommended to the students,
the visitors will take care that their diligence be effectual;
that it be well directed, and employed on the proper object.
A student is not always advancing because he is employed;
he must apply his strength to that part of the art where the
real difficulties lie; to that part which distinguishes it as a
liberal art; and not by mistaken industry lose his time in that
which is merely ornamental. The students, instead of vying
with each other which shall have the readiest hand, should be
taught to contend who shall have the purest and most correct
outline; instead of striving which shall produce the brightest
tint, or, curiously trifling, shall give the gloss of stuffs, so as
to appear real, let their ambition be directed to contend,
which shall dispose his drapery in the most graceful folds,
which shall give the most grace and dignity to the human
figure.

I must beg leave to submit one thing more to the consideration of the visitors, which appears to me a matter of very great consequence, and the omission of which I think a principal defect in the method of education pursued in all the Academies I have ever visited. The error I mean is, that the students never draw exactly from the living models which they have before them. It is not indeed their intention; nor are they directed to do it. Their drawings resemble the model only in the attitude. They change the form according to their vague and uncertain ideas of beauty, and make a drawing rather of what they think the figure ought to be, than of what it appears. I have thought this the obstacle, that has stopped the progress of many young men of real genius; and I very much doubt, whether a habit of drawing correctly what we see, will not give a proportionable power of drawing correctly what we imagine. He who endeavours to copy nicely the figure before him, not only acquires a habit of exactness and precision, but is continually advancing in his knowledge of the human figure; and though he seems to superficial observers to make a slower progress, he will be found at last capable of adding (without running into capricious wildness) that grace and beauty, which is necessary to be given to his more finished works, and which cannot be got by the moderns, as it was not acquired by the ancients, but by an attentive and well compared study of the human form.

What I think ought to enforce this method is, that it has been the practice (as may be seen by their drawings) of the great masters in the art. I will mention a drawing of Raffaelle, "The Dispute of the Sacrament," the print of which, by Count Cailus, is in every hand. It appears, that he made his sketch from one model; and the habit he had of drawing exactly from the form before him appears by his making all the figures with the same cap, such as his model then happened to wear; so servile a copyist was this great man, even at a time when he was allowed to be at his highest pitch of excellence.

I have seen also Academy figures by Annibale Caracci,

though he was often sufficiently licentious [6] in his finished works, drawn with all the peculiarities of an individual model.

This scrupulous exactness is so contrary to the practice of the Academies, that it is not without great deference, that I beg leave to recommend it to the consideration of the visitors; and submit to them, whether the neglect of this method is not one of the reasons why students so often disappoint expectation, and, being more than boys at sixteen, become less than men at thirty.

In short, the method I recommend can only be detrimental when there are but few living forms to copy; for then students, by always drawing from one alone, will by habit be taught to overlook defects, and mistake deformity for beauty. But of this there is no danger; since the Council has determined to supply the Academy with a variety of subjects; and indeed those laws which they have drawn up, and which the Secretary will presently read for your confirmation, have in some measure precluded me from saying more upon this occasion. Instead, therefore, of offering my advice, permit me to indulge my wishes, and express my hope, that this institution may answer the expectations of its Royal Founder; that the present age may vie in arts with that of Leo the Tenth; and that "the dignity of the dying art," (to make use of an expression of Pliny) may be revived under the Reign of George the Third.[7]

[6] ["Licentious" in this sense, "disregarding commonly accepted rules"; as used here, free in expression, not a slavish copy (after the *Oxford English Dictionary*).]

[7] ["Leo the Tenth" refers to the period during which Raphael and Michelangelo worked. The reference to Pliny is from *Historia naturalis* XXXV. 10.]

·⊷⊚ Discourse 2

December 11, 1769

GENTLEMEN,

I congratulate you on the honour which you have just received. I have the highest opinion of your merits, and could
wish to show my sense of them in something which possibly
may be more useful to you than barren praise. I could wish
to lead you into such a course of study as may render your
future progress answerable to your past improvement; and,
whilst I applaud you for what has been done, remind you
how much yet remains to attain perfection.

I flatter myself, that from the long experience I have had,
and the unceasing assiduity with which I have pursued those
studies, in which, like you, I have been engaged, I shall be
acquitted of vanity in offering some hints to your consideration. They are indeed in a great degree founded upon my
own mistakes in the same pursuit. But the history of errors,
properly managed, often shortens the road to truth. And
although no method of study that I can offer, will of itself
conduct to excellence, yet it may preserve industry from being
misapplied.

In speaking to you of the theory of the art, I shall only
consider it as it has a relation to the *method* of your studies.

Dividing the study of painting into three distinct periods,[1]

[1] [This and the subsequent five paragraphs are essential to an understanding of the first few discourses. Reynolds is explaining here his idea
of the progress of the painter through various levels to complete mastery.
If the distinctions made here are kept in mind, a number of seeming
contradictions will be resolved.]

I shall address you as having passed through the first of them, which is confined to the rudiments; including a facility of drawing any object that presents itself, a tolerable readiness in the management of colours, and an acquaintance with the most simple and obvious rules of composition.

This first degree of proficiency is, in painting, what grammar is in literature, a general preparation for whatever species of the art the student may afterwards choose for his more particular application. The power of drawing, modelling, and using colours, is very properly called the language of the art; and in this language, the honours you have just received, prove you to have made no inconsiderable progress.

When the artist is once enabled to express himself with some degree of correctness, he must then endeavour to collect subjects for expression; to amass a stock of ideas, to be combined and varied as occasion may require. He is now in the second period of study, in which his business is to learn all that has been known and done before his own time. Having hitherto received instructions from a particular master, he is now to consider the art itself as his master. He must extend his capacity to more sublime and general instructions. Those perfections which lie scattered among various masters, are now united in one general idea, which is henceforth to regulate his taste, and enlarge his imagination. With a variety of models thus before him, he will avoid that narrowness and poverty of conception which attends a bigotted admiration of a single master, and will cease to follow any favourite where he ceases to excel. This period is, however, still a time of subjection and discipline. Though the student will not resign himself blindly to any single authority, when he may have the advantage of consulting many, he must still be afraid of trusting his own judgment, and of deviating into any track where he cannot find the footsteps of some former master.

The third and last period emancipates the student from subjection to any authority, but what he shall himself judge to be supported by reason. Confiding now in his own judgment, he will consider and separate those different principles to which different modes of beauty owe their original. In the former period he sought only to know and combine excellence, wherever it was to be found, into one idea of perfection: in this, he learns, what requires the most attentive survey and the most subtle disquisition, to discriminate perfections that are incompatible with each other.

He is from this time to regard himself as holding the same rank with those masters whom he before obeyed as teachers; and as exercising a sort of sovereignty over those rules which have hitherto restrained him. Comparing now no longer the performances of art with each other, but examining the art itself by the standard of nature, he corrects what is erroneous, supplies what is scanty, and adds by his own observation what the industry of his predecessors may have yet left wanting to perfection. Having well established his judgment, and stored his memory, he may now without fear try the power of his imagination. The mind that has been thus disciplined, may be indulged in the warmest enthusiasm, and venture to play on the borders of the wildest extravagance. The habitual dignity which long converse with the greatest minds has imparted to him, will display itself in all his attempts; and he will stand among his instructors, not as an imitator, but a rival.

These are the different stages of the art. But as I now address myself particularly to those students who have been this day rewarded for their happy passage through the first period, I can with no propriety suppose they want any help in the initiatory studies. My present design is to direct your view to distant excellence, and to show you the readiest path that leads to it. Of this I shall speak with such latitude, as may leave the province of the professor uninvaded; and shall not anticipate those precepts, which it is his business to give, and your duty to understand.

It is indisputably evident that a great part of every man's life must be employed in collecting materials for the exercise of genius. Invention, strictly speaking, is little more than a new combination of those images which have been previously gathered and deposited in the memory: nothing can come of nothing: he who has laid up no materials, can produce no combinations.

A student unacquainted with the attempts of former adventurers, is always apt to over-rate his own abilities; to mistake the most trifling excursions for discoveries of moment, and every coast new to him, for a new-found country. If by chance he passes beyond his usual limits, he congratulates his own arrival at those regions which they who have steered a better course have long left behind them.

The productions of such minds are seldom distinguished by an air of originality: they are anticipated in their happiest efforts; and if they are found to differ in any thing from their predecessors, it is only in irregular sallies, and trifling conceits. The more extensive therefore your acquaintance is with the works of those who have excelled, the more extensive will be your powers of invention; and what may appear still more like a paradox, the more original will be your conceptions. But the difficulty on this occasion is to determine who ought to be proposed as models of excellence, and who ought to be considered as the properest guides.

To a young man just arrived in *Italy,* many of the present painters of that country are ready enough to obtrude their precepts, and to offer their own performances as examples of that perfection which they affect to recommend. The modern, however, who recommends *himself* as a standard, may justly be suspected as ignorant of the true end, and unacquainted with the proper object, of the art which he professes. To follow such a guide, will not only retard the student, but mislead him.

On whom then can he rely, or who shall show him the path that leads to excellence? the answer is obvious: those great masters who have travelled the same road with success, are the most likely to conduct others. The works of those who have stood the test of ages, have a claim to that respect and veneration to which no modern can pretend. The duration and stability of their fame, is sufficient to evince that it has not been suspended upon the slender thread of fashion and caprice, but bound to the human heart by every tie of sympathetick approbation.

There is no danger of studying too much the works of those great men; but how they may be studied to advantage is an enquiry of great importance.

Some who have never raised their minds to the consideration of the real dignity of the art, and who rate the works of an artist in proportion as they excel or are defective in the mechanical parts, look on theory as something that may enable them to talk but not to paint better; and confining themselves entirely to mechanical practice, very assiduously toil on in the drudgery of copying; and think they make a rapid progress while they faithfully exhibit the minutest part of a favourite picture. This appears to me a very tedious, and I think a very erroneous method of proceeding. Of every large composition, even of those which are most admired, a great part may be truly said to be *common-place*. This, though it takes up much time in copying, conduces little to improvement. I consider general copying as a delusive kind of industry; the student satisfies himself with the appearance of doing something; he falls into the dangerous habit of imitating without selecting, and of labouring without any determinate object; as it requires no effort of the mind, he sleeps over his work; and those powers of invention and composition which ought particularly to be called out, and put in action, lie torpid, and lose their energy for want of exercise.

How incapable those are of producing any thing of their own, who have spent much of their time in making finished copies, is well known to all who are conversant with our art.

To suppose that the complication of powers, and variety of ideas necessary to that mind which aspires to the first honours in the art of painting, can be obtained by the frigid contemplation of a few single models, is no less absurd, than it would be in him who wishes to be a poet, to imagine that by translating a tragedy he can acquire to himself sufficient knowledge of the appearances of nature, the operations of the passions, and the incidents of life.

The great use in copying, if it be at all useful, should seem to be in learning to colour; yet even colouring will never be perfectly attained by servilely copying the model before you. An eye critically nice can only be formed by observing well-coloured pictures with attention: and by close inspection, and minute examination, you will discover, at last, the manner of handling, the artifices of contrast, glazing, and other expedients, by which good colourists have raised the value of their tints, and by which nature has been so happily imitated.

I must inform you, however, that old pictures deservedly celebrated for their colouring, are often so changed by dirt and varnish, that we ought not to wonder if they do not appear equal to their reputation in the eyes of unexperienced painters, or young students. An artist whose judgment is matured by long observation, considers rather what the picture once was, than what it is at present. He has by habit acquired a power of seeing the brilliancy of tints through the cloud by which it is obscured. An exact imitation, therefore, of those pictures, is likely to fill the student's mind with false opinions; and to send him back a colourist of his own formation, with ideas equally remote from nature and from art, from the genuine practice of the masters, and the real appearances of things.

Following these rules, and using these precautions, when you have clearly and distinctly learned in what good colouring consists, you cannot do better than have recourse to nature herself, who is always at hand, and in comparison of whose true splendour the best coloured pictures are but faint and feeble.

However, as the practice of copying is not entirely to be excluded, since the mechanical practice of painting is learned in some measure by it, let those choice parts only be selected which have recommended the work to notice. If its excellence consists in its general effort, it would be proper to make slight sketches of the machinery and general management of the picture. Those sketches should be kept always by you for the regulation of your style. Instead of copying the touches of those great masters, copy only their conceptions. Instead of treading in their footsteps, endeavour only to keep the same road. Labour to invent on their general principles and way of thinking. Possess yourself with their spirit. Consider with yourself how a Michael Angelo or a Raffaelle would have treated this subject: and work yourself into a belief that your picture is to be seen and criticised by them when completed. Even an attempt of this kind will rouse your powers.

But as mere enthusiasm will carry you but a little way, let me recommend a practice that may be equivalent to and will perhaps more efficaciously contribute to your advancement, than even the verbal corrections of those masters themselves, could they be obtained. What I would propose is, that you should enter into a kind of competition, by painting a similar subject, and making a companion to any picture that you consider as a model. After you have finished your work, place it near the model, and compare them carefully together. You will then not only see, but feel your own deficiencies more sensibly than by precepts, or any other means of instruction. The true principles of painting will mingle with your thoughts. Ideas thus fixed by sensible objects, will be certain and definitive; and sinking deep into the mind, will not only be more just, but more lasting than those presented to you by precepts only; which will always be fleeting, variable, and undetermined.

This method of comparing your own efforts with those of some great master, is indeed a severe and mortifying task, to which none will submit, but such as have great views, with fortitude sufficient to forego the gratifications of present vanity for future honour. When the student has succeeded in some measure to his own satisfaction, and has felicitated himself on his success, to go voluntarily to a tribunal where he knows his vanity must be humbled, and all self-approbation must vanish, requires not only great resolution, but great humility. To him, however, who has the ambition to be a real master, the solid satisfaction which proceeds from a consciousness of his advancement, (of which seeing his own faults is the first step,) will very abundantly compensate for the mortification of present disappointment. There is, besides, this alleviating circumstance. Every discovery he makes, every acquisition of knowledge he attains, seems to proceed from his own sagacity; and thus he acquires a confidence in himself sufficient to keep up the resolution of perseverance.

We all must have experienced how lazily, and consequently how ineffectually, instruction is received when forced upon the mind by others. Few have been taught to any purpose who have not been their own teachers. We prefer those instructions which we have given ourselves, from our affection to the instructor; and they are more effectual, from being received into the mind at the very time when it is most open and eager to receive them.

With respect to the pictures that you are to choose for your models, I could wish that you would take the world's opinion rather than your own. In other words, I would have you choose those of established reputation, rather than follow your own fancy. If you should not admire them at first, you will, by endeavouring to imitate them, find that the world has not been mistaken.

It is not an easy task to point out those various excellencies for your imitation which lie distributed amongst the various schools. An endeavour to do this may perhaps be the subject of some future discourse. I will, therefore, at present only recommend a model for style in painting, which is a branch of the art more immediately necessary to the young student. Style in painting is the same as in writing, a power over materials, whether words or colours, by which conceptions or sentiments are conveyed. And in this Lodovico Carrache (I mean in his best works) appears to me to approach the nearest to perfection. His unaffected breadth of light and shadow, the simplicity of colouring, which holding its proper rank, does not draw aside the least part of the attention from the subject, and the solemn effect of that twilight which seems diffused over his pictures, appear to me to correspond with grave and dignified subjects, better than the more artificial brilliancy of sunshine which enlightens the pictures of Titian: though Tintoret thought that Titian's colouring was the model of perfection, and would correspond even with the sublime of Michael Angelo; and that if Angelo had coloured like Titian, or Titian designed like Angelo, the world would once have had a perfect painter.

It is our misfortune, however, that those works of Carrache which I would recommend to the student, are not often found out of *Bologna*. The "St. Francis in the Midst of His Friars," "The Transfiguration," "The Birth of St. John the Baptist," "The Calling of St. Matthew," "The St. Jerome," "The Fresco Paintings" in the Zampieri palace, are all worthy the attention of the student. And I think those who travel would do well to allot a much greater portion of their time to that city than it has been hitherto the custom to bestow.

In this art, as in others, there are many teachers who profess to shew the nearest way to excellence; and many expedients have been invented by which the toil of study might be saved. But let no man be seduced to idleness by specious promises. Excellence is never granted to man, but as the reward of labour. It argues indeed no small strength of mind to persevere in habits of industry, without the pleasure of perceiving those advances; which, like the hand of a clock, whilst they make hourly approaches to their point, yet proceed so slowly as to escape observation. A facility of drawing, like that of playing upon a musical instrument, cannot be acquired but by an infinite number of acts. I need not, therefore, enforce by many words the necessity of continual application; nor tell you that the porte-crayon [2] ought to be for ever in your hands. Various methods will occur to you by which this power may be acquired. I would particularly recommend, that after your return from the Academy (where I suppose your attendance to be constant) you would en-

2 [A device for holding a drawing crayon.]

deavour to draw the figure by memory. I will even venture
to add, that by perseverance in this custom, you will become
able to draw the human figure tolerably correct, with as
little effort of the mind as is required to trace with a pen
the letters of the alphabet.

That this facility is not unattainable, some members in this
Academy give a sufficient proof. And be assured, that if this
power is not acquired whilst you are young, there will be no
time for it afterwards: at least the attempt will be attended
with as much difficulty as those experience who learn to read
or write after they have arrived to the age of maturity.

But while I mention the porte-crayon as the student's constant companion, he must still remember, that the pencil [3] is
the instrument by which he must hope to obtain eminence.
What, therefore, I wish to impress upon you is, that whenever
an opportunity offers, you paint your studies instead of drawing them. This will give you such a facility in using colours,
that in time they will arrange themselves under the pencil,
even without the attention of the hand that conducts it. If one
act excluded the other, this advice could not with any propriety be given. But if painting comprises both drawing and
colouring, and if by a short struggle of resolute industry, the
same expedition is attainable in painting as in drawing on
paper, I cannot see what objection can justly be made to the
practice; or why that should be done by parts, which may be
done all together.

If we turn our eyes to the several schools of painting, and
consider their respective excellencies, we shall find that those
who excel most in colouring, pursued this method. The
Venetian and *Flemish* schools, which owe much of their fame
to colouring, have enriched the cabinets of the collectors of
drawings, with very few examples. Those of Titian, Paul
Veronese, Tintoret, and the Bassans,[4] are in general slight

---

3 ["Pencil" means paintbrush.]

4 [The Bassans, or Bassani, was a name applied to members of the Da-
Ponte family, who worked in northern Italy during the sixteenth and
seventeenth centuries.]

and undetermined. Their sketches on paper are as rude as their pictures are excellent in regard to harmony of colouring. Correggio and Barocci have left few, if any finished drawings behind them. And in the *Flemish* school, Rubens and Vandyck made their designs for the most part either in colours, or in chiaro oscuro. It is as common to find studies of the *Venetian* and *Flemish* painters on canvass, as of the schools of *Rome* and *Florence* on paper. Not but that many finished drawings are sold under the names of those masters. Those, however, are undoubtedly the productions either of engravers or of their scholars, who copied their works.

These instructions I have ventured to offer from my own experience; but as they deviate widely from received opinions, I offer them with diffidence; and when better are suggested, shall retract them without regret.

There is one precept, however, in which I shall only be opposed by the vain, the ignorant, and the idle. I am not afraid that I shall repeat it too often. You must have no dependence on your own genius. If you have great talents, industry will improve them; if you have but moderate abilities, industry will supply their deficiency. Nothing is denied to well directed labour: nothing is to be obtained without it. Not to enter into metaphysical discussions on the nature or essence of genius, I will venture to assert, that assiduity unabated by difficulty, and a disposition eagerly directed to the object of its pursuit, will produce effects similar to those which some call the result of *natural powers*.

Though a man cannot at all times, and in all places, paint or draw, yet the mind can prepare itself by laying in proper materials, at all times, and in all places. Both Livy and Plutarch, in describing Philopoemen, one of the ablest generals of antiquity, have given us a striking picture of a mind always intent on its profession, and by assiduity obtaining those excellencies which some all their lives vainly expect from nature. I shall quote the passage in Livy at length, as it runs parallel with the practice I would recommend to the painter, sculptor, and architect.

"Philopoemen was a man eminent for his sagacity and experience in choosing ground, and in leading armies; to which he formed his mind by perpetual meditation, in times of peace as well as war. When, in any occasional journey, he came to a strait difficult passage, if he was alone, he considered with himself, and if he was in company he asked his friends, what it would be best to do if in this place they had found an enemy, either in the front, or in the rear, on the one side, or on the other. 'It might happen,' says he, 'that the enemy to be opposed might come on drawn up in regular lines, or in a tumultuous body, formed only by the nature of the place.' He then considered a little what ground he should take; what number of soldiers he should use, and what arms he should give them; where he should lodge his carriages, his baggage, and the defenceless followers of his camp; how many guards, and of what kind, he should send to defend them; and whether it would be better to press forward along the pass, or recover by retreat his former station: he would consider likewise where his camp could most commodiously be formed; how much ground he should inclose within his trenches; where he should have the convenience of water, and where he might find plenty of wood and forage; and when he should break up his camp on the following day, through what road he could most safely pass, and in what form he should dispose his troops. With such thoughts and disquisitions he had from his early years so exercised his mind, that on these occasions nothing could happen which he had not been already accustomed to consider." [5]

I cannot help imagining that I see a promising young painter, equally vigilant, whether at home, or abroad, in the streets, or in the fields. Every object that presents itself, is to him a lesson. He regards all nature with a view to his profession; and combines her beauties, or corrects her defects. He examines the countenance of men under the influence of passion; and often catches the most pleasing hints from subjects of turbulence or deformity. Even bad pictures

5 [Livy, *Historiarum libri* XXXV. 28.]

themselves supply him with useful documents; and, as Leonardo da Vinci has observed, he improves upon the fanciful images that are sometimes seen in the fire, or are accidentally sketched upon a discoloured wall.[6]

The artist who has his mind thus filled with ideas, and his hand made expert by practice, works with ease and readiness; whilst he who would have you believe that he is waiting for the inspirations of genius, is in reality at a loss how to begin; and is at last delivered of his monsters, with difficulty and pain.

The well-grounded painter, on the contrary, has only maturely to consider his subject, and all the mechanical parts of his art follow without his exertion. Conscious of the difficulty of obtaining what he possesses, he makes no pretensions to secrets, except those of closer application. Without conceiving the smallest jealousy against others, he is contented that all shall be as great as himself, who have undergone the same fatigue; and as his pre-eminence depends not upon a trick, he is free from the painful suspicions of a juggler, who lives in perpetual fear lest his trick should be discovered.

---

[6] [Leonardo da Vinci, *Treatise on Painting*, trans. A. Philip McMahon (Princeton: Princeton University Press, 1956), I, 109.]

✥ Discourse 3

December 14, 1770

GENTLEMEN,

IT IS not easy to speak with propriety to so many students of different ages and different degrees of advancement. The mind requires nourishment adapted to its growth; and what may have promoted our earlier efforts, might retard us in our nearer approaches to perfection.

The first endeavours of a young painter, as I have remarked in a former discourse, must be employed in the attainment of mechanical dexterity, and confined to the mere imitation of the object before him. Those who have advanced beyond the rudiments, may, perhaps, find advantage in reflecting on the advice which I have likewise given them, when I recommended the diligent study of the works of our great predecessors; but I at the same time endeavoured to guard them against an implicit submission to the authority of any one master however excellent; or by a strict imitation of his manner, precluding themselves from the abundance and variety of nature.[1] I will now add that nature herself is not to be too closely copied. There are excellencies in the art of painting beyond what is commonly called the imitation of nature: and these excellencies I wish to point out. The students who, having passed through the initiatory exercises, are more advanced in the art, and who, sure of their hand, have leisure to exert their understanding, must now be told, that a

[1] [For the meaning of "nature," see Introduction, p. xxii.]

mere copier of nature can never produce any thing great; can never raise and enlarge the conceptions, or warm the heart of the spectator.

The wish of the genuine painter must be more extensive: instead of endeavouring to amuse mankind with the minute neatness of his imitations, he must endeavour to improve them by the grandeur of his ideas; instead of seeking praise, by deceiving the superficial sense of the spectator, he must strive for fame, by captivating the imagination.

The principle now laid down, that the perfection of this art does not consist in mere imitation, is far from being new or singular. It is, indeed, supported by the general opinion of the enlightened part of mankind. The poets, orators, and rhetoricians of antiquity, are continually enforcing this position; that all the arts receive their perfection from an ideal beauty, superior to what is to be found in individual nature. They are ever referring to the practice of the painters and sculptors of their times, particularly Phidias, (the favourite artist of antiquity,) to illustrate their assertions. As if they could not sufficiently express their admiration of his genius by what they knew, they have recourse to poetical enthusiasm. They call it inspiration; a gift from heaven. The artist is supposed to have ascended the celestial regions, to furnish his mind with this perfect idea of beauty. "He," says Proclus,[2] "who takes for his model such forms as nature produces, and confines himself to an exact imitation of them, will never attain to what is perfectly beautiful. For the works of nature are full of disproportion, and fall very short of the true standard of beauty. So that Phidias, when he formed his Jupiter, did not copy any object ever presented to his sight; but contemplated only that image which he had conceived in his mind from Homer's description." And thus Cicero, speaking of the same Phidias: "Neither did this artist," says he, "when he carved the image of Jupiter or Minerva, set before him any one human figure, as a pattern, which he was to copy; but having a more perfect idea of beauty

[2] Lib. 2, in Timaeum Platonis, as cited by Junius de Pictura Veterum.

fixed in his mind, this he steadily contemplated, and to the imitation of this all his skill and labour were directed."

The moderns are not less convinced than the ancients of this superior power existing in the art; nor less sensible of its effects. Every language has adopted terms expressive of this excellence. The *gusto grande* of the Italians, the *beau ideal* of the French, and the *great style, genius,* and *taste* among the English, are but different appellations of the same thing. It is this intellectual dignity, they say, that ennobles the painter's art; that lays the line between him and the mere mechanick; and produces those great effects in an instant, which eloquence and poetry, by slow and repeated efforts, are scarcely able to attain.

Such is the warmth with which both the ancients and moderns speak of this divine principle of the art; but, as I have formerly observed, enthusiastick admiration seldom promotes knowledge. Though a student by such praise may have his attention roused, and a desire excited, of running in this great career; yet it is possible that what has been said to excite, may only serve to deter him. He examines his own mind, and perceives there nothing of that divine inspiration, with which, he is told, so many others have been favoured. He never travelled to heaven to gather new ideas; and he finds himself possessed of no other qualifications than what mere common observation and a plain understanding can confer. Thus he becomes gloomy amidst the splendour of figurative declamation, and thinks it hopeless, to pursue an object which he supposes out of the reach of human industry.

But on this, as upon many other occasions, we ought to distinguish how much is to be given to enthusiasm, and how much to reason. We ought to allow for, and we ought to commend, that strength of vivid expression, which is necessary to convey, in its full force, the highest sense of the most complete effect of art; taking care at the same time, not to lose in terms of vague admiration, that solidity and truth of principle, upon which alone we can reason, and may be enabled to practise.

It is not easy to define in what this great style consists; nor to describe, by words, the proper means of acquiring it, if the mind of the student should be at all capable of such an acquisition. Could we teach taste or genius by rules, they would be no longer taste and genius. But though there neither are, nor can be, any precise invariable rules for the exercise, or the acquisition, of these great qualities, yet we may truly say that they always operate in proportion to our attention in observing the works of nature, to our skill in selecting, and to our care in digesting, methodizing, and comparing our observations. There are many beauties in our art, that seem, at first, to lie without the reach of precept, and yet may easily be reduced to practical principles. Experience is all in all; but it is not every one who profits by experience; and most people err, not so much from want of capacity to find their object, as from not knowing what object to pursue. This great ideal perfection and beauty are not to be sought in the heavens, but upon earth. They are about us, and upon every side of us. But the power of discovering what is deformed in nature, or in other words, what is particular and uncommon, can be acquired only by experience; and the whole beauty and grandeur of the art consists, in my opinion, in being able to get above all singular forms, local customs, particularities, and details of every kind.

All the objects which are exhibited to our view by nature, upon close examination will be found to have their blemishes and defects. The most beautiful forms have something about them like weakness, minuteness, or imperfection. But it is not every eye that perceives these blemishes. It must be an eye long used to the contemplation and comparison of these forms; and which, by a long habit of observing what any set of objects of the same kind have in common, has acquired the power of discerning what each wants in particular. This long laborious comparison should be the first study of the painter, who aims at the greatest style. By this means, he acquires a just idea of beautiful forms; he corrects nature by herself, her imperfect state by her more perfect. His eye

being enabled to distinguish the accidental deficiencies, ex-
crescences, and deformities of things, from their general
figures, he makes out an abstract idea of their forms more
perfect than any one original; and what may seem a paradox,
he learns to design naturally by drawing his figures unlike to
any one object. This idea of the perfect state of nature, which
the artist calls the ideal beauty, is the great leading principle,
by which works of genius are conducted. By this Phidias
acquired his fame. He wrought upon a sober principle, what
has so much excited the enthusiasm of the world; and by this
method you, who have courage to tread the same path, may
acquire equal reputation.

This is the idea which has acquired, and which seems to
have a right to the epithet of *divine;* as it may be said to preside, like a supreme judge, over all the productions of nature;
appearing to be possessed of the will and intention of the Crea-
tor, as far as they regard the external form of living beings.
When a man once possesses this idea in its perfection, there
is no danger, but that he will be sufficiently warmed by it himself, and be able to warm and ravish every one else.

Thus it is from a reiterated experience, and a close comparison of the objects in nature, that an artist becomes possessed of the idea of that central form, if I may so express it,
from which every deviation is deformity. But the investigation of this form, I grant, is painful, and I know but of one
method of shortening the road; this is, by a careful study of
the works of the ancient sculptors; who, being indefatigable
in the school of nature, have left models of that perfect form
behind them, which an artist would prefer as supremely
beautiful, who had spent his whole life in that single contemplation. But if industry carried them thus far, may not
you also hope for the same reward from the same labour?
We have the same school opened to us, that was opened to
them; for nature denies her instructions to none, who desire
to become her pupils.

This laborious investigation, I am aware, must appear
superfluous to those who think every thing is to be done by

felicity, and the powers of native genius. Even the great Bacon treats with ridicule the idea of confining proportion to rules, or of producing beauty by selection. "A man cannot tell," says he, "whether Apelles or Albert Durer were the more trifler: whereof the one would make a personage by geometrical proportions; the other, by taking the best parts out of divers faces, to make one excellent. . . . The painter, (he adds,) must do it by a kind of felicity, . . . and not by rule." [3]

It is not safe to question any opinion of so great a writer, and so profound a thinker, as undoubtedly Bacon was. But he studies brevity to excess; and therefore his meaning is sometimes doubtful. If he means that beauty has nothing to do with rule, he is mistaken. There is a rule, obtained out of general nature, to contradict which is to fall into deformity. Whenever any thing is done beyond this rule, it is in virtue of some other rule which is followed along with it, but which does not contradict it. Every thing which is wrought with certainty, is wrought upon some principle. If it is not, it cannot be repeated. If by felicity is meant any thing of chance or hazard, or something born with a man, and not earned, I cannot agree with this great philosopher. Every object which pleases must give us pleasure upon some certain principles; but as the objects of pleasure are almost infinite, so their principles vary without end, and every man finds them out, not by felicity or successful hazard, but by care and sagacity.

To the principle I have laid down, that the idea of beauty in each species of beings is an invariable one, it may be objected, that in every particular species there are various central forms, which are separate and distinct from each other, and yet are undeniably beautiful; that in the human figure, for instance, the beauty of "Hercules" is one, of the "Gladiator" another, of the "Apollo" another; which makes so many different ideas of beauty.

It is true, indeed, that these figures are each perfect in

---

[3] [Francis Bacon, "Of Beauty,"] *Essays*, p. 252, edit. 1625.

their kind, though of different characters and proportions; but still none of them is the representation of an individual, but of a class. And as there is one general form, which, as I have said, belongs to the human kind at large, so in each of these classes there is one common idea and central form, which is the abstract of the various individual forms belonging to that class. Thus, though the forms of childhood and age differ exceedingly, there is a common form in childhood, and a common form in age, which is the more perfect, as it is more remote from all peculiarities. But I must add further, that though the most perfect forms of each of the general divisions of the human figure are ideal, and superior to any individual form of that class; yet the highest perfection of the human figure is not to be found in any one of them. It is not in the "Hercules," nor in the "Gladiator," nor in the "Apollo"; but in that form which is taken from them all, and which partakes equally of the activity of the "Gladiator," of the delicacy of the "Apollo," and of the muscular strength of the "Hercules." For perfect beauty in any species must combine all the characters which are beautiful in that species. It cannot consist in any one to the exclusion of the rest: no one, therefore, must be predominant, that no one may be deficient.

The knowledge of these different characters, and the power of separating and distinguishing them, is undoubtedly necessary to the painter, who is to vary his compositions with figures of various forms and proportions, though he is never to lose sight of the general idea of perfection in each kind.

There is, likewise, a kind of symmetry, or proportion, which may properly be said to belong to deformity. A figure lean or corpulent, tall or short, though deviating from beauty, may still have a certain union of the various parts, which may contribute to make them on the whole not unpleasing.

When the artist has by diligent attention acquired a clear and distinct idea of beauty and symmetry; when he has reduced the variety of nature to the abstract idea; his next task will be to become acquainted with the genuine habits of nature, as distinguished from those of fashion. For in the same manner, and on the same principles, as he has acquired the knowledge of the real forms of nature, distinct from accidental deformity, he must endeavour to separate simple chaste nature, from those adventitious, those affected and forced airs or actions, with which she is loaded by modern education.

Perhaps I cannot better explain what I mean, than by reminding you of what was taught us by the professor of anatomy, in respect to the natural position and movement of the feet. He observed that the fashion of turning them outwards was contrary to the intent of nature, as might be seen from the structure of the bones, and from the weakness that proceeded from that manner of standing. To this we may add the erect position of the head, the projection of the chest, the walking with straight knees, and many such actions, which we know to be merely the result of fashion, and what nature never warranted, as we are sure that we have been taught them when children.

I have mentioned but a few of those instances, in which vanity or caprice have contrived to distort and disfigure the human form; your own recollection will add to these a thousand more of ill-understood methods, which have been practised to disguise nature, among our dancing-masters, hair-dressers, and tailors, in their various schools of deformity.[4]

However the mechanick and ornamental arts may sacrifice to fashion, she must be entirely excluded from the art of painting; the painter must never mistake this capricious changeling for the genuine offspring of nature; he must divest himself of all prejudices in favour of his age or country; he must disregard all local and temporary ornaments, and look only on those general habits which are every where and always the same. He addresses his works to the people of

4 ["Those," says Quintilian, "who are taken with the outward shew of things, think that there is more beauty in persons, who are trimmed, curled, and painted, than uncorrupt nature can give; as if beauty were merely the effect of the corruption of manners."]

every country and every age; he calls upon posterity to be his spectators, and says with Zeuxis, *in aeternitatem pingo.*[5]

The neglect of separating modern fashions from the habits of nature, leads to that ridiculous style which has been prac- tised by some painters, who have given to Grecian heroes the airs and graces practised in the court of Louis the Four- teenth; an absurdity almost as great as it would have been to have dressed them after the fashion of that court.

To avoid this error, however, and to retain the true sim- plicity of nature, is a task more difficult than at first sight it may appear. The prejudices in favour of the fashions and customs that we have been used to, and which are justly called a second nature, make it too often difficult to dis- tinguish that which is natural, from that which is the result of education; they frequently even give a predilection in favour of the artificial mode; and almost every one is apt to be guided by those local prejudices, who has not chastised his mind, and regulated the instability of his affections by the eternal invariable idea of nature.

Here then, as before, we must have recourse to the an- cients as instructors. It is from a careful study of their works that you will be enabled to attain to the real simplicity of nature; they will suggest many observations, which would probably escape you, if your study were confined to nature alone. And, indeed, I cannot help suspecting, that in this instance the ancients had an easier task than the moderns. They had, probably, little or nothing to unlearn, as their manners were nearly approaching to this desirable simplicity; while the modern artist, before he can see the truth of things, is obliged to remove a veil, with which the fashion of the times has thought proper to cover her.

Having gone thus far in our investigation of the great style in painting; if we now should suppose that the artist has formed the true idea of beauty, which enables him to give his

[5] ["I paint for eternity" (the phrase has been traced only as far back as the early eighteenth-century writer Richard Steele in the *Spectator*, No. 52).]

works a correct and perfect design; if we should suppose also, that he has acquired a knowledge of the unadulterated habits of nature, which gives him simplicity; the rest of his task is, perhaps, less than is generally imagined. Beauty and simplicity have so great a share in the composition of a great style, that he who has acquired them has little else to learn. It must not, indeed, be forgotten, that there is a nobleness of conception, which goes beyond any thing in the mere exhibition even of perfect form; there is an art of animating and dignifying the figures with intellectual grandeur, of impressing the appearance of philosophick wisdom, or heroick virtue. This can only be acquired by him that enlarges the sphere of his understanding by a variety of knowledge, and warms his imagination with the best productions of ancient and modern poetry.

A hand thus exercised, and a mind thus instructed, will bring the art to an higher degree of excellence than, perhaps, it has hitherto attained in this country. Such a student will disdain the humbler walks of painting, which, however profitable, can never assure him a permanent reputation. He will leave the meaner artist servilely to suppose that those are the best pictures, which are most likely to deceive the spectator. He will permit the lower painter, like the florist or collector of shells, to exhibit the minute discriminations, which distinguish one object of the same species from another; while he, like the philosopher, will consider nature in the abstract, and represent in every one of his figures the character of its species.

If deceiving the eye were the only business of the art, there is no doubt, indeed, but the minute painter would be more apt to succeed: but it is not the eye, it is the mind, which the painter of genius desires to address; nor will he waste a moment upon those smaller objects, which only serve to catch the sense, to divide the attention, and to counteract his great design of speaking to the heart.

This is the ambition which I wish to excite in your minds; and the object I have had in my view, throughout this discourse, is that one great idea, which gives to painting its true dignity, which entitles it to the name of a liberal art, and ranks it as a sister of poetry.

It may possibly have happened to many young students, whose application was sufficient to overcome all difficulties, and whose minds were capable of embracing the most extensive views, that they have, by a wrong direction originally given, spent their lives in the meaner walks of painting, without ever knowing there was a nobler to pursue. Albert Durer, as Vasari has justly remarked, would, probably, have been one of the first painters of his age, (and he lived in an era of great artists,) had he been initiated into those great principles of the art, which were so well understood and practised by his contemporaries in Italy. But unluckily having never seen or heard of any other manner, he, without doubt, considered his own as perfect.

As for the various departments of painting, which do not presume to make such high pretensions, they are many. None of them are without their merit, though none enter into competition with this universal presiding idea of the art. The painters who have applied themselves more particularly to low and vulgar characters, and who express with precision the various shades of passion, as they are exhibited by vulgar minds, (such as we see in the works of Hogarth,) deserve great praise; but as their genius has been employed on low and confined subjects, the praise which we give must be as limited as its object. The merry-making, or quarrelling, of the boors of Teniers; the same sort of productions of Brouwer, or Ostade, are excellent in their kind; and the excellence and its praise will be in proportion, as, in those limited subjects, and peculiar forms, they introduce more or less of the expression of those passions, as they appear in general and more enlarged nature. This principle may be applied to the battle-pieces of Bourgognone,[6] the French gallantries of Watteau,[7] and even beyond the exhibition of animal life, to the landscapes of Claude Lorrain, and the sea-views of

---

6 [Bourgognone, or Jacques Courtois le Bourguignon (fl. 1628–1679).]

7 [Jean Antoine Watteau (1684–1721).]

Vandervelde.[8] All these painters have, in general, the same right, in different degrees, to the name of a painter, which a satirist, an epigrammatist, a sonneteer, a writer of pastorals, or descriptive poetry, has to that of a poet.[9]

In the same rank, and perhaps of not so great merit, is the cold painter of portraits. But his correct and just imitation of his object has its merit. Even the painter of still life, whose highest ambition is to give a minute representation of every part of those low objects which he sets before him, deserves praise in proportion to his attainment; because no part of this excellent art, so much the ornament of polished life, is destitute of value and use. These, however, are by no means the views to which the mind of the student ought to be *primarily* directed. Having begun by aiming at better things, if from particular inclination, or from the taste of the time and place he lives in, or from necessity, or from failure in the highest attempts, he is obliged to descend lower, he will bring into the lower sphere of art a grandeur of composition and character, that will raise and ennoble his works far above their natural rank.

A man is not weak, though he may not be able to wield the club of Hercules; nor does a man always practise that which he esteems the best; but does that which he can best do. In moderate attempts, there are many walks open to the artist. But as the idea of beauty is of necessity but one, so there can be but one great mode of painting; the leading principle of which I have endeavoured to explain.

I should be sorry, if what is here recommended, should be at all understood to countenance a careless or indetermined manner of painting. For though the painter is to overlook the accidental discriminations of nature, he is to exhibit distinctly, and with precision, the general forms of things. A firm and determined outline is one of the characteristicks of the great style in painting; and let me add, that

8 [Probably Willem van der Velde II (1633–1707), a painter of seascapes.]
9 [Here Reynolds is introducing the topic of poetry, which he examines more fully in Discourse 8.]

he who possesses the knowledge of the exact form which every part of nature ought to have, will be fond of expressing that knowledge with correctness and precision in all his works.

To conclude; I have endeavoured to reduce the idea of beauty to general principles: and I had the pleasure to observe that the professor of painting [10] proceeded in the same method, when he shewed you that the artifice of contrast was founded but on one principle. I am convinced that this is the only means of advancing science, of clearing the mind from a confused heap of contradictory observations, that do but perplex and puzzle the student, when he compares them, or misguide him if he gives himself up to their authority: bringing them under one general head, can alone give rest and satisfaction to an inquisitive mind.

[10] [Edward Penny; the lectures referred to no longer exist in any published form.]

·⋙‖ Discourse 4

December 10, 1771

Gentlemen,

The value and rank of every art is in proportion to the
mental labour employed in it, or the mental pleasure produced
by it.[1] As this principle is observed or neglected, our profession becomes either a liberal art, or a mechanical trade. In
the hands of one man it makes the highest pretensions, as it
is addressed to the noblest faculties: in those of another it is
reduced to a mere matter of ornament; and the painter has
but the humble province of furnishing our apartments with
elegance.

This exertion of mind, which is the only circumstance that
truly ennobles our art, makes the great distinction between
the Roman and Venetian schools. I have formerly observed,
that perfect form is produced by leaving out particularities,
and retaining only general ideas: I shall now endeavour to
shew that this principle, which I have proved to be meta-
physically just, extends itself to every part of the art; that

---

1 [In this passage, and throughout the *Discourses*, Reynolds subscribes
to the idea that the arts may be given some sort of order. In this discourse, for example (p. 45), he apparently feels there is a national rank
or order to be assigned to painting, the Italians being the best and the
Dutch the weakest, with the French falling somewhere in between. Similar
ideas are to be found in Discourse 10 (p. 145), where sculpture is regarded
as subordinate to painting, and in Discourse 8 (p. 120), where painting is
said to be subordinate to poetry. This general idea, that the arts may be
ranked, accounts for many of Reynolds' most characteristic passages.]

it gives what is called the *grand style*,[2] to invention, to composition, to expression, and even to colouring and drapery.

Invention in painting does not imply the invention of the subject; for that is commonly supplied by the poet or historian. With respect to the choice, no subject can be proper that is not generally interesting. It ought to be either some eminent instance of heroick action, or heroick suffering. There must be something either in the action, or in the object, in which men are universally concerned, and which powerfully strikes upon the publick sympathy.

Strictly speaking, indeed, no subject can be of universal, hardly can it be of general, concern; but there are events and characters so popularly known in those countries where our art is in request, that they may be considered as sufficiently general for all our purposes. Such are the great events of Greek and Roman fable and history, which early education, and the usual course of reading, have made familiar and interesting to all Europe, without being degraded by the vulgarism of ordinary life in any country. Such too are the capital subjects of scripture history, which, besides their general notoriety, become venerable by their connection with our religion.

As it is required that the subject selected should be a general one, it is no less necessary that it should be kept unembarrassed with whatever may any way serve to divide the attention of the spectator. Whenever a story is related, every man forms a picture in his mind of the action and expression of the persons employed. The power of representing this mental picture on canvass is what we call invention in a painter. And as in the conception of this ideal picture, the mind does not enter into the minute peculiarities of the dress, furniture, or scene of action; so when the painter comes to represent it, he contrives those little necessary concomitant circumstances in such a manner, that they shall strike the spectator no more than they did himself in his first conception of the story.

2 [For "grand style," see Discourse 3, p. 28.]

I am very ready to allow that some circumstances of minuteness and particularity frequently tend to give an air of truth to a piece, and to interest the spectator in an extraordinary manner. Such circumstances therefore cannot wholly be rejected: but if there be any thing in the art which requires peculiar nicety of discernment, it is the disposition of these minute circumstantial parts; which, according to the judgment employed in the choice, become so useful to truth, or so injurious to grandeur.

However, the usual and most dangerous error is on the side of minuteness; and therefore I think caution most necessary where most have failed. The general idea constitutes real excellence. All smaller things, however perfect in their way, are to be sacrificed without mercy to the greater. The painter will not enquire what things may be admitted without much censure: he will not think it enough to shew that they may be there; he will shew that they must be there; that their absence would render his picture maimed and defective.

Thus, though to the principal group a second or third be added, and a second and third mass of light, care must be yet taken that these subordinate actions and lights, neither each in particular, nor all together, come into any degree of competition with the principal; they should merely make a part of that whole which would be imperfect without them. To every kind of painting this rule may be applied. Even in portraits, the grace, and, we may add, the likeness, consists more in taking the general air, than in observing the exact similitude of every feature.

Thus figures must have a ground whereon to stand; they must be cloathed; there must be a background; there must be light and shadow: but none of these ought to appear to have taken up any part of the artist's attention They should be so managed as not even to catch that of the spectator. We know well enough, when we analyze a piece, the difficulty and the subtilty with which an artist adjusts the background, drapery, and masses of light; we know that a considerable part of the grace and effect of his picture depends upon them; but this art is so much concealed, even to a judicious eye, that no remains of any of these subordinate parts occur to the memory when the picture is not present.

The great end of the art is to strike the imagination. The painter is therefore to make no ostentation of the means by which this is done; the spectator is only to feel the result in his bosom. An inferior artist is unwilling that any part of his industry should be lost upon the spectator. He takes as much pains to discover, as the greater artist does to conceal, the marks of his subordinate assiduity. In works of the lower kind, every thing appears studied, and encumbered; it is all boastful art, and open affectation. The ignorant often part from such pictures with wonder in their mouths, and indifference in their hearts.

But it is not enough in invention that the artist should restrain and keep under all the inferior parts of his subject; he must sometimes deviate from vulgar and strict historical truth, in pursuing the grandeur of his design.

How much the great style exacts from its professors to conceive and represent their subjects in a poetical manner, not confined to mere matter of fact, may be seen in the cartoons [3] of Raffaelle. In all the pictures in which the painter has represented the apostles, he has drawn them with great nobleness; he has given them as much dignity as the human figure is capable of receiving; yet we are expressly told in scripture they had no such respectable appearance; and of St. Paul in particular, we are told by himself, that his *bodily* presence was *mean*.[4] Alexander is said to have been of a low stature: a painter ought not so to represent him. Agesilaus was low, lame, and of a mean appearance: none of these defects ought to appear in a piece of which he is the hero. In conformity to custom, I call this part of the art history painting; it ought to be called poetical, as in reality it is.

All this is not falsifying any fact; it is taking an allowed

3 ["Cartoons," here preliminary drawings.]

4 [II Corinthians 10:9–10: ". . . his bodily presence is weak, and his speech contemptible."]

poetical licence. A painter of portraits retains the individual likeness; a painter of history shews the man by shewing his actions. A painter must compensate the natural deficiencies of his art. He has but one sentence to utter, but one moment to exhibit. He cannot, like the poet or historian, expatiate, and impress the mind with great veneration for the character of the hero or saint he represents, though he lets us know at the same time, that the saint was deformed, or the hero lame. The painter has no other means of giving an idea of the dignity of the mind, but by that external appearance which grandeur of thought does generally, though not always, impress on the countenance; and by that correspondence of figure to senti- ment and situation, which all men wish, but cannot command. The painter, who may in this one particular attain with ease what others desire in vain, ought to give all that he possibly can, since there are so many circumstances of true greatness that he cannot give at all. He cannot make his hero talk like a great man; he must make him look like one. For which reason, he ought to be well studied in the analysis of those circumstances, which constitute dignity of appearance in real life.[5]

As in invention, so likewise in expression, care must be taken not to run into particularities. Those expressions alone should be given to the figures which their respective situations generally produce. Nor is this enough; each person should also have that expression which men of his rank generally exhibit. The joy, or the grief of a character of dignity, is not to be expressed in the same manner as a similar passion in a vulgar face. Upon this principle, Bernini, perhaps, may be subject to censure. This sculptor, in many respects admirable, has given a very mean expression to his statue of David, who is repre- sented as just going to throw the stone from the sling; and in order to give it the expression of energy, he has made him biting his under-lip. This expression is far from being general, and still farther from being dignified. He might have seen it in an instance or two; and he mistook accident for generality.

[5] [See illustrations, Raphael's "Portrait of a Cardinal" (detail).]

With respect to colouring, though it may appear at first a part of painting merely mechanical, yet it still has its rules, and those grounded upon that presiding principle which regulates both the great and the little in the study of a painter. By this, the first effect of the picture is produced; and as this is performed, the spectator as he walks the gallery, will stop, or pass along. To give a general air of grandeur at first view, all trifling or artful play of little lights, or an attention to a variety of tints is to be avoided; a quietness and simplicity must reign over the whole work; to which a breadth of uniform, and simple colour, will very much contribute. Grandeur of effect is produced by two different ways, which seem entirely opposed to each other. One is, by reducing the colours to little more than chiaro oscuro, which was often the practice of the Bolognian schools; and the other, by making the colours very distinct and forcible, such as we see in those of Rome and Florence; but still, the presiding principle of both those manners is simplicity. Certainly, nothing can be more simple than monotony; and the distinct blue, red, and yellow colours which are seen in the draperies of the Roman and Florentine schools, though they have not that kind of harmony which is produced by a variety of broken and transparent colours, have that effect of grandeur which was intended. Perhaps these distinct colours strike the mind more forcibly, from there not being any great union between them; as martial musick, which is intended to rouse the nobler passions, has its effect from the sudden and strongly marked transitions from one note to another, which that style of musick requires; whilst in that which is intended to move the softer passions, the notes imperceptibly melt into one another.

In the same manner as the historical painter never enters into the detail of colours, so neither does he debase his conceptions with minute attention to the discriminations of drapery. It is the inferior style that marks the variety of stuffs. With him, the cloathing is neither woollen, nor linen, nor silk, satin, or velvet: it is drapery; it is nothing more. The art of disposing the foldings of the drapery make a very consider-

able part of the painter's study. To make it merely natural is
a mechanical operation, to which neither genius or taste are
required; whereas, it requires the nicest judgment to dispose
the drapery, so that the folds shall have an easy communica-
tion, and gracefully follow each other, with such natural negligence as to look like the effect of chance, and at the same
time shew the figure under it to the utmost advantage.

Carlo Maratti was of opinion, that the disposition of
drapery was a more difficult art than even that of drawing the
human figure; that a student might be more easily taught the
latter than the former; as the rules of drapery, he said, could
not be so well ascertained as those for delineating a correct
form. This, perhaps, is a proof how willingly we favour our
own peculiar excellence. Carlo Maratti is said to have valued
himself particularly upon his skill in this part of his art; yet in
him, the disposition appears so ostentatiously artificial, that he
is inferior to Raffaelle, even in that which gave him his best
claim to reputation.

Such is the great principle by which we must be directed in
the nobler branches of our art. Upon this principle, the Roman, the Florentine, the Bolognese schools, have formed their
practice; and by this they have deservedly obtained the highest
praise. These are the three great schools of the world in
the epick style. The best of the French school, Poussin, Le
Sueur, and Le Brun, have formed themselves upon these
models, and consequently may be said, though Frenchmen, to
be a colony from the Roman school. Next to these, but in a
very different style of excellence, we may rank the Venetian,
together with the Flemish and the Dutch schools; all professing
to depart from the great purposes of painting, and catching at
applause by inferior qualities.

I am not ignorant that some will censure me for placing the
Venetians in this inferior class, and many of the warmest admirers of painting will think them unjustly degraded; but I
wish not to be misunderstood. Though I can by no means
allow them to hold any rank with the nobler schools of painting, they accomplished perfectly the thing they attempted. But

as mere elegance is their principal object, as they seem more
willing to dazzle than to affect, it can be no injury to them to
suppose that their practice is useful only to its proper end.
But what may heighten the elegant may degrade the sublime.[6]
There is simplicity, and I may add, severity, in the great manner, which is, I am afraid, almost incompatible with this comparatively sensual style.

Tintoret, Paul Veronese, and others of the Venetian
school, seem to have painted with no other purpose than to be
admired for their skill and expertness in the mechanism of
painting, and to make a parade of that art, which as I before
observed, the higher style requires its followers to conceal.

In a conference of the French Academy, at which were
present Le Brun, Sebastian Bourdon, and all the eminent art-
tists of that age, one of the academicians desired to have their
opinion on the conduct of Paul Veronese, who, though a
painter of great consideration, had, contrary to the strict rules
of art, in his picture of Perseus and Andromeda, represented
the principal figure in shade. To this question no satisfactory
answer was then given. But I will venture to say, that if they
had considered the class of the artist, and ranked him as an
ornamental painter, there would have been no difficulty in
answering—"It was unreasonable to expect what was never
intended. His intention was solely to produce an effect of
light and shadow; every thing was to be sacrificed to that
intent, and the capricious composition of that picture suited
very well with the style which he professed."

Young minds are indeed too apt to be captivated by this
splendour of style; and that of the Venetians is particularly
pleasing; for by them, all those parts of the art that gave
pleasure to the eye or sense, have been cultivated with care,
and carried to the degree nearest to perfection. The powers
exerted in the mechanical part of the art have been called *the
language of painters;* but we may say, that it is but poor eloquence which only shews that the orator can talk. Words

6 [For "the elegant" and "the sublime," see Introduction, p. xxii.]

should be employed as the means, not as the end: language is the instrument, conviction is the work.

The language of painting must indeed be allowed these masters; but even in that, they have shewn more copiousness than choice, and more luxuriancy than judgment. If we consider the uninteresting subjects of their invention, or at least the uninteresting manner in which they are treated; if we attend to their capricious composition, their violent and affected contrasts, whether of figures or of light and shadow, the richness of their drapery, and at the same time, the mean effect which the discrimination of stuffs gives to their pictures; if to these we add their total inattention to expression; and then reflect on the conceptions and the learning of Michael Angelo, or the simplicity of Raffaelle, we can no longer dwell on the comparison. Even in colouring, if we compare the quietness and chastity of the Bolognese pencil to the bustle and tumult that fills every part of a Venetian picture, without the least attempt to interest the passions, their boasted art will appear a mere struggle without effect; "a tale told by an ideot, full of sound and fury, signifying nothing." [7]

Such as suppose that the great style might happily be blended with the ornamental, that the simple, grave and majestick dignity of Raffaelle could unite with the glow and bustle of a Paul,[8] or Tintoret, are totally mistaken. The principles by which each are attained are so contrary to each other, that they seem, in my opinion, incompatible, and as impossible to exist together, as that in the mind the most sublime ideas and the lowest sensuality should at the same time be united.

The subjects of the Venetian painters are mostly such as give them an opportunity of introducing a great number of figures; such as feasts, marriages, and processions, publick martyrdoms, or miracles. I can easily conceive that Paul

[7] [*Macbeth*, V.v.26.]
[8] ["Paul" is Paul Veronese.]

Veronese, if he were asked, would say, that no subject was proper for an historical picture, but such as admitted at least forty figures; for in a less number, he would assert, there could be no opportunity of the painter's shewing his art in composition, his dexterity of managing and disposing the masses of light and groups of figures, and of introducing a variety of Eastern dresses and characters in their rich stuffs.

But the thing is very different with a pupil of the greater schools. Annibal Carrache thought twelve figures sufficient for any story: he conceived that more would contribute to no end but to fill space; that they would be but cold spectators of the general action, or, to use his own expression, that they would be "figures to be let." Besides, it is impossible for a picture composed of so many parts to have that effect so indispensably necessary to grandeur, that of one complete whole. However contradictory it may be in geometry, it is true in taste, that many little things will not make a great one. The sublime impresses the mind at once with one great idea; it is a single blow: the elegant indeed may be produced by repetition; by an accumulation of many minute circumstances.

However great the difference is between the composition of the Venetian, and the rest of the Italian schools, there is full as great a disparity in the effect of their pictures as produced by colours. And though in this respect the Venetians must be allowed extraordinary skill, yet even that skill, as they have employed it, will but ill correspond with the great style. Their colouring is not only too brilliant, but, I will venture to say, too harmonious, to produce that solidity, steadiness, and simplicity of effect, which heroick subjects require, and which simple or grave colours only can give to a work. That they are to be cautiously studied by those who are ambitious of treading the great walk of history, is confirmed, if it wants confirmation, by the greatest of all authorities, Michael Angelo. This wonderful man, after having seen a picture by Titian, told Vasari, who accompanied him,[9] "that he liked much his

9 Dicendo, che molto gli piaceva il colorito suo, e la maniera; mà che era un peccato, che a Venezia non s'imparasse da principio, a disegnare

colouring and manner"; but then he added, that "it was a pity
the Venetian painters did not learn to draw correctly in their
early youth, and adopt a better *manner of study.*"

By this it appears, that the principal attention of the Venetian painters, in the opinion of Michael Angelo, seemed to be
engrossed by the study of colours, to the neglect of the *ideal
beauty of form,* or propriety of expression. But if general
censure was given to that school from the sight of a picture of
Titian, how much more heavily, and more justly, would the
censure fall on Paul Veronese, and more especially on Tintoret? And here I cannot avoid citing Vasari's opinion of the
style and manner of Tintoret. "Of all the extraordinary
geniuses," says he, "that have ever practised the art of
painting, for wild, capricious, extravagant and fantastical inventions, for furious impetuosity and boldness in the execution of his work, there is none like Tintoret; his strange
whimsies are even beyond extravagance, and his works seem
to be produced rather by chance, than in consequence of any
previous design, as if he wanted to convince the world that
the art was a trifle, and of the most easy attainment." [10]

For my own part, when I speak of the Venetian painters, I
wish to be understood to mean Paul Veronese and Tintoret,
to the exclusion of Titian; for though his style is not so pure
as that of many other of the Italian schools, yet there is a sort

---

bene, e che non havessano que' pittori miglior modo nello studio. Vas.
tom. iii. p. 226. Vita di Tiziano. [Giorgio Vasari's *Lives of Seventy of the
Most Eminent Painters, Sculptors, and Architects* can be found in an
English translation by E. H. and E. W. Blashfield and A. A. Hopkins,
4 vols. (New York: Charles Scribner's Sons, 1907).]

[10] Nelle cose della pittura, stravagante, capriccioso, presto, e resoluto,
et il più terribile cervello, che habbia havuto mai la pittura, come si
può vedere in tutte le sue opere; e ne' componimenti delle storie, fan-
tastiche, e fatte da lui diversamente, e fuori dell' uso degli altri pittori:
anzi hà superato la stravaganza, con le nuove, e capricciose inventioni, e
strani ghiribizzi del suo intelleto, che ha lavorato a caso, e senza disegno,
quasi monstrando che quest' arte è una baia. [The full English quotation
can be found in Vasari, "The Life of Battista Franco," *Lives of the Most
Eminent Painters, Sculptors, and Architects,* trans. Mrs. Jonathan Foster
(London, 1878–1881), V, 50.]

of senatorial dignity about him, which, however awkward in his imitators, seems to become him exceedingly. His portraits alone, from the nobleness and simplicity of character which he always gave them, will entitle him to the greatest respect, as he undoubtedly stands in the first rank in this branch of the art.[11]

It is not with Titian, but with the seducing qualities of the two former, that I could wish to caution you against being too much captivated. These are the persons who may be said to have exhausted all the powers of florid eloquence, to debauch the young and unexperienced, and have, without doubt, been the cause of turning off the attention of the connoisseur and of the patron of art, as well as that of the painter, from those higher excellencies of which the art is capable, and which ought to be required in every considerable production. By them, and their imitators, a style merely ornamental has been disseminated throughout all Europe. Rubens carried it to Flanders; Vouet, to France; and Luca Giordano, to Spain and Naples.

The Venetian is indeed the most splendid of the schools of elegance; and it is not without reason, that the best performances in this lower school are valued higher than the second rate performances of those above them: for every picture has value when it has a decided character, and is excellent in its kind. But the student must take care not to be so much dazzled with this splendour, as to be tempted to imitate what must ultimately lead from perfection. Poussin, whose eye was always steadily fixed on the sublime, has been often heard to say, "That a particular attention to colouring was an obstacle to the student, in his progress to the great end and design of the art; and that he who attaches himself to this principal end, will acquire by practice a reasonable good method of colouring." [12]

11 [See illustrations, Titian's "Self-Portrait."]

12 Que cette application singuliere n'etoit qu'un obstacle pour empêcher de parvenir au veritable but de la peinture, & celui qui s'attache au principal, acquiert par la pratique une assez belle maniere de peindre. Conference de l'Acad. Franc.

Though it be allowed that elaborate harmony of colouring, a brilliancy of tints, a soft and gradual transition from one to another, present to the eye, what an harmonious concert of musick does to the ear, it must be remembered, that painting is not merely a gratification of the sight. Such excellence, though properly cultivated, where nothing higher than elegance is intended, is weak and unworthy of regard, when the work aspires to grandeur and sublimity.

The same reasons that have been urged to shew that a mixture of the Venetian style cannot improve the great style, will hold good in regard to the Flemish and Dutch schools. Indeed, the Flemish school, of which Rubens is the head, was formed upon that of the Venetian; like them, he took his figures too much from the people before him. But it must be allowed in favour of the Venetians, that he was more gross than they, and carried all their mistaken methods to a far greater excess. In the Venetian school itself, where they all err from the same cause, there is a difference in the effect. The difference between Paul and Bassano seems to be only, that one introduced Venetian gentlemen into his pictures, and the other boors of the district of Bassano, and called them patriarchs and prophets.

The painters of the Dutch school have still more locality.[13] With them, a history-piece is properly a portrait of themselves; whether they describe the inside or outside of their houses, we have their own people engaged in their own peculiar occupations; working, or drinking, playing, or fighting. The circumstances that enter into a picture of this kind, are so far from giving a general view of human life, that they exhibit all the minute particularities of a nation differing in several respects from the rest of mankind. Yet, let them have their share of more humble praise. The painters of this school are excellent in their own way; they are only ridiculous when they attempt

13 [Reynolds is here invoking his rule that general subjects require general figures and general treatment. For further discussion, see Introduction, p. xxii.]

general history on their own narrow principles, and debase
great events by the meanness of their characters.

Some inferior dexterity, some extraordinary mechanical
power is apparently that from which they seek distinction.
Thus, we see, that school alone has the custom of representing
candle-light, not as it really appears to us by night, but red, as
it would illuminate objects to a spectator by day. Such tricks,
however pardonable in the little style, where petty effects are
the sole end, are inexcusable in the greater, where the attention should never be drawn aside by trifles, but should be entirely occupied by the subject itself.

The same local principles which characterize the Dutch
school extend even to their landscape painters; and Rubens
himself, who has painted many landscapes, has sometimes
transgressed in this particular. Their pieces in this way are, I
think, always a representation of an individual spot, and each
in its kind a very faithful but very confined portrait.

Claude Lorrain, on the contrary, was convinced, that
taking nature as he found it seldom produced beauty. His
pictures are a composition of the various draughts which he
had previously made from various beautiful scenes and prospects. However, Rubens in some measure has made amends
for the deficiency with which he is charged; he has contrived
to raise and animate his otherwise uninteresting views, by introducing a rainbow, storm, or some particular accidental
effect of light. That the practice of Claude Lorrain, in respect
to his choice, is to be adopted by landscape painters, in opposition to that of the Flemish and Dutch schools, there can be
no doubt, as its truth is founded upon the same principle as
that by which the historical painter acquires perfect form.
But whether landscape painting has a right to aspire so far
as to reject what the painters call accidents of nature, is not
easy to determine. It is certain Claude Lorrain seldom, if
ever, availed himself of those accidents; either he thought that
such peculiarities were contrary to that style of general nature
which he professed, or that it would catch the attention too
strongly, and destroy that quietness and repose which he
thought necessary to that kind of painting.

A portrait painter likewise, when he attempts history, unless he is upon his guard, is likely to enter too much into the detail. He too frequently makes his historical heads look like portraits; and this was once the custom amongst those old painters, who revived the art before general ideas were practised or understood. An history-painter paints man in general; a portrait-painter, a particular man, and consequently a defective model.

Thus an habitual practice in the lower exercises of the art will prevent many from attaining the greater. But such of us who move in these humbler walks of the profession, are not ignorant that, as the natural dignity of the subject is less, the more all the little ornamental helps are necessary to its embellishment. It would be ridiculous for a painter of domestick scenes, of portraits, landscapes, animals, or of still life, to say that he despised those qualities which has made the subordinate schools so famous. The art of colouring, and the skillful management of light and shadow, are essential requisites in his confined labours. If we descend still lower, what is the painter of fruit and flowers without the utmost art in colouring, and what the painters call handling; that is, a lightness of pencil that implies great practice, and gives the appearance of being done with ease? Some here, I believe, must remember a flower-painter[14] whose boast it was, that he scorned to paint for the *million:* no, he professed to paint in the true Italian taste; and despising the crowd, called strenuously upon the *few* to admire him. His idea of the Italian taste was to paint as black and dirty as he could, and to leave all clearness and brilliancy of colouring to those who were fonder of money than of immortality. The consequence was such as might be expected. For these petty excellencies are here essential beauties; and without this merit the artist's work will be more short-lived than the object of his imitation.

From what has been advanced, we must now be convinced that there are two distinct styles in history-painting: the grand, and the splendid or ornamental.

[14] [Perhaps Joseph Cooper (1682–1743); the identification is not certain.]

The great style stands alone, and does not require, perhaps
does not so well admit, any addition from inferior beauties.
The ornamental style also possesses its own peculiar merit.
However, though the union of the two may make a sort of
composite style, yet that style is likely to be more imperfect
than either of those which go to its composition. Both kinds
have merit, and may be excellent though in different ranks, if
uniformity be preserved, and the general and particular ideas
of nature be not mixed. Even the meanest of them is difficult
enough to attain; and the first place being already occupied
by the great artists in each department, some of those who
followed thought there was less room for them, and feeling
the impulse of ambition and the desire of novelty, and being
at the same time perhaps willing to take the shortest way,
endeavoured to make for themselves a place between both.
This they have effected by forming an union of the different
orders. But as the grave and majestick style would suffer by
an union with the florid and gay, so also has the Venetian ornament in some respect been injured by attempting an alliance
with simplicity.

It may be asserted, that the great style is always more or
less contaminated by any meaner mixture. But it happens in
a few instances, that the lower may be improved by borrowing
from the grand. Thus if a portrait-painter is desirous to raise
and improve his subject, he has no other means than by approaching it to a general idea. He leaves out all the minute
breaks and peculiarities in the face, and changes the dress
from a temporary fashion to one more permanent, which has
annexed to it no ideas of meanness from its being familiar to
us. But if an exact resemblance of an individual be considered as the sole object to be aimed at, the portrait-painter
will be apt to lose more than he gains by the acquired dignity
taken from general nature. It is very difficult to ennoble the
character of a countenance but at the expense of the likeness,
which is what is most generally required by such as sit to the
painter.

Of those who have practised the composite style, and have

succeeded in this perilous attempt, perhaps the foremost is Correggio.[15] His style is founded upon modern grace and elegance, to which is superadded something of the simplicity of the grand style. A breadth of light and colour, the general ideas of the drapery, an uninterrupted flow of outline, all conspire to this effect. Next to him (perhaps equal to him) Parmegiano [16] has dignified the genteelness of modern effeminacy, by uniting it with the simplicity of the ancients and the grandeur and severity of Michael Angelo. It must be confessed however that these two extraordinary men, by endeavouring to give the utmost degree of grace, have sometimes perhaps exceeded its boundaries, and have fallen into the most hateful of all hateful qualities, affectation. Indeed, it is the peculiar characteristick of men of genius to be afraid of coldness and insipidity, from which they think they never can be too far removed. It particularly happens to these great masters of grace and elegance. They often boldly drive on to the very verge of ridicule; the spectator is alarmed, but at the same time admires their vigour and intrepidity:

"Strange graces still, and stranger flights they had,

. . . .

Yet ne'er so sure our passion to create,
As when they touch'd the brink of all we hate." [17]

The errors of genius, however, are pardonable, and none even of the more exalted painters are wholly free from them; but they have taught us, by the rectitude of their general practice, to correct their own affected or accidental deviation. The very first have not been always upon their guard, and perhaps

15 [Antonio Allegri da Correggio, born 1494 at Correggio, near Modena, Italy; died 1534.]

16 [Parmegiano (Francesco Maria Mazzuola), born 1504 at Parma, Italy; died 1540.]

17 [Alexander Pope, *Moral Essays*, Epistle II ("To a Lady"), 49–52:
    Strange graces still, and stranger flights she had,
    Was just not ugly, and was just not mad;
    Yet ne'er so sure our passion to create,
    As when she touch'd the brink of all we hate.]

there is not a fault, but what may take shelter under the most venerable authorities; yet that style only is perfect, in which the noblest principles are uniformly pursued; and those masters only are entitled to the first rank in our estimation, who have enlarged the boundaries of their art, and have raised it to its highest dignity, by exhibiting the general ideas of nature.

On the whole, it seems to me that there is but one presiding principle which regulates, and gives stability to every art. The works, whether of poets, painters, moralists, or historians, which are built upon general nature, live for ever; while those which depend for their existence on particular customs and habits, a partial view of nature, or the fluctuation of fashion, can only be coeval with that which first raised them from obscurity. Present time and future may be considered as rivals, and he who solicits the one must expect to be discountenanced by the other.

◆ Discourse 5

December 10, 1772

GENTLEMEN,

I PURPOSE to carry on in this discourse the subject which I began in my last. It was my wish upon that occasion to incite you to pursue the higher excellencies of the art. But I fear that in this particular I have been misunderstood. Some are ready to imagine, when any of their favourite acquirements in the art are properly classed, that they are utterly disgraced. This is a very great mistake: nothing has its proper lustre but in its proper place. That which is most worthy of esteem in its allotted sphere, becomes an object, not of respect, but of derision, when it is forced into a higher, to which it is not suited; and there it becomes doubly a source of disorder, by occupying a situation which is not natural to it, and by putting down from the first place what is in reality of too much magnitude to become with grace and proportion that subordinate station, to which something of less value would be much better suited.

My advice in a word is this: keep your principal attention fixed upon the higher excellencies. If you compass them and compass nothing more, you are still in the first class. We may regret the innumerable beauties which you may want; you may be very imperfect; but still, you are an imperfect artist of the highest order.

If, when you have got thus far, you can add any, or all, of the subordinate qualifications, it is my wish and advice that you should not neglect them. But this is as much a matter of circumspection and caution at least, as of eagerness and pursuit.

The mind is apt to be distracted by a multiplicity of objects; and that scale of perfection, which I wish always to be preserved, is in the greatest danger of being totally disordered, and even inverted.

Some excellencies bear to be united, and are improved by union; others are of a discordant nature, and the attempt to join them, only produces a harsh jarring of incongruent principles. The attempt to unite contrary excellencies (of form, for instance,) in a single figure, can never escape degenerating into the monstrous, but by sinking into the insipid; by taking away its marked character, and weakening its expression.

This remark is true to a certain degree with regard to the passions. If you mean to preserve the most perfect beauty *in its most perfect state,* you cannot express the passions, all of which produce distortion and deformity, more or less, in the most beautiful faces.

Guido, from want of choice in adapting his subject to his ideas and his powers, or from attempting to preserve beauty where it could not be preserved, has in this respect succeeded very ill. His figures are often engaged in subjects that required great expression: yet his "Judith and Holofernes," the "Daughter of Herodias with the Baptist's Head," the "Andromeda," and some even of the "Mothers of the Innocents," have little more expression than his "Venus Attired by the Graces."

Obvious as these remarks appear, there are many writers on our art, who, not being of the profession, and consequently not knowing what can or cannot be done, have been very liberal of absurd praises in their descriptions of favourite works. They always find in them what they are resolved to find. They praise excellencies that can hardly exist together; and above all things are fond of describing with great exactness the expression of a mixed passion, which more particularly appears to me out of the reach of our art.

Such are many disquisitions which I have read on some of the cartoons and other pictures of Raffaelle, where the criticks have described their own imaginations; or indeed where

Hudson, "Sir John and Lady Pole"

Sir John Carew Pole, Bart., Antony House, Devon

Reynolds, "Commodore Keppel"
By Courtesy of the Trustees of the National Maritime Museum, Greenwich, London

Raphael, "Portrait of a Cardinal" (detail)
Prado, Madrid

Titian, "Self-Portrait"
Prado, Madrid

Raphael, "Vision of a Knight"
National Gallery, London

Rubens, "The Kermesse" (detail)
Louvre, Paris

Poussin, "The Triumph of Neptune and Amphitrite"
Philadelphia Museum of Art: George W. Elkins Collection

Steen, "Merry Company"
Collection Mauritshuis, The Hague

Tintoretto, "The Way to Golgotha"
Scuola di S. Rocco, Venice

Antoine Coypel, "Le Père éternel promettant le Messie
à la terre" (detail)
Ceiling of the Chapelle de Versailles, Paris

Veronese, "Marriage at Cana"
Louvre, Paris

Michelangelo, "Study of the Nude for a Dead Christ"
Louvre, Paris

Gainsborough, "Portrait of Mrs. David Garrick"
National Portrait Gallery, London

Gainsborough, "Gainsborough's Forest"
National Gallery, London

Michelangelo, "The Delphic Sibyl"
Sistine Chapel, Vatican Palace, Rome

the excellent master himself may have attempted this expression of passions above the powers of the art; and has therefore, by an indistinct and imperfect marking, left room for every imagination, with equal probability to find a passion of his own. What has been, and what can be done in the art, is sufficiently difficult; we need not be mortified or discouraged at not being able to execute the conceptions of a romantick [1] imagination. Art has its boundaries, though imagination [2] has none. We can easily, like the Ancients, suppose a Jupiter to be possessed of all those powers and perfections which the subordinate deities were endowed with separately. Yet, when they employed their art to represent him, they confined his character to majesty alone. Pliny, therefore, though we are under great obligations to him for the information he has given us in relation to the works of the ancient artists, is very frequently wrong when he speaks of them, which he does very often in the style of many of our modern connoisseurs. He observes, that in a statue of Paris, by Euphranor, you might discover at the same time three different characters; the dignity of a judge of the goddesses, the lover of Helen, and the conqueror of Achilles.[3] A statue in which you endeavour to unite stately dignity, youthful elegance, and stern valour, must surely possess none of these to any eminent degree.

From hence it appears, that there is much difficulty as well as danger, in an endeavour to concentrate in a single subject those various powers, which, rising from different points, naturally move in different directions.

The summit of excellence seems to be an assemblage of contrary qualities, but mixed, in such proportions, that no one part is found to counteract the other. How hard this is to be attained in every art, those only know, who have made the greatest progress in their respective professions.

To conclude what I have to say on this part of the subject,

---

[1] ["Romantick," as used here, "boundless, beyond what is practical" (after entry 3, *Oxford English Dictionary*).]

[2] ["Imagination," in this sense, mental activity.]

[3] [Pliny, *Historia naturalis* XXXIV. 19, 77.]

which I think of great importance, I wish you to understand, that I do not discourage the younger students from the noble attempt of uniting all the excellencies of art; but suggest to them, that, beside the difficulties which attend every arduous attempt, there is a peculiar difficulty in the choice of the excellencies which ought to be united. I wish you to attend to this, that you may try yourselves, whenever you are capable of that trial, what you can, and what you cannot do; and that, instead of dissipating your natural facilities over the immense field of possible excellence, you may choose some particular walk in which you may exercise all your powers; in order that each of you may become the first in his way. If any man shall be master of such a transcendent, commanding, and ductile genius, as to enable him to rise to the highest, and to stoop to the lowest, flights of art, and to sweep over all of them unobstructed and secure, he is fitter to give example than to receive instruction.

Having said thus much on the *union* of excellencies, I will next say something of the subordination in which various excellencies ought to be kept.

I am of opinion, that the ornamental style, which in my discourse of last year I cautioned you against, considering it as *principal,* may not be wholly unworthy the attention even of those who aim at the grand style, when it is properly placed and properly reduced.

But this study will be used with far better effect, if its principles are employed in softning the harshness and mitigating the rigour of the great style, than if it attempt to stand forward with any pretensions of its own to positive and original excellence. It was thus Lodovico Carracci, whose example I formerly recommended to you, employed it. He was acquainted with the works both of Correggio and the Venetian painters, and knew the principles by which they produced those pleasing effects which at the first glance prepossess us so much in their favour; but he took only as much from each as would embellish, but not over-power, that manly strength and energy of style, which is his peculiar character.

Since I have already expatiated so largely in my former discourse, and in my present, upon the *styles* and *characters* of painting, it will not be at all unsuitable to my subject if I mention to you some particulars relative to the leading principles, and capital works of those who excelled in the *great style;* that I may bring you from abstraction nearer to practice, and by exemplifying the positions which I have laid down, enable you to understand more clearly what I would enforce.

The principal words of modern art are in *fresco;* a mode of painting which excludes attention to minute elegancies: yet these works in fresco, are the productions on which the fame of the greatest masters depend: such are the pictures of Michael Angelo and Raffaelle in the Vatican; to which we may add the cartoons; which, though not strictly to be called fresco, yet may be put under that denomination; and such are the works of Giulio Romano at Mantua. If these performances were destroyed, with them would be lost the best part of the reputation of those illustrious painters; for these are justly considered as the greatest efforts of our art which the world can boast. To these, therefore, we should principally direct our attention for higher excellencies. As for the lower arts, as they have been once discovered, they may be easily attained by those possessed of the former.

Raffaelle, who stands in general foremost of the first painters, owes his reputation, as I have observed, to his excellence in the higher parts of the art: his works in *fresco,* therefore, ought to be the first object of our study and attention.[4] His *easel*-works stand in a lower degree of estimation; for though he continually, to the day of his death, embellished his performances more and more with the addition of those lower ornaments, which entirely make the merit of some painters, yet he never arrived at such perfection as to make him an object of imitation. He never was able to conquer perfectly that dryness, or even littleness of manner, which he inherited from his master. He never acquired that nicety of taste in colours, that breadth of light and shadow, that art and man-

4 [See illustrations, Raphael's "Vision of a Knight."]

agement of uniting light to light, and shadow to shadow, so as
to make the object rise out of the ground with that plenitude
of effect so much admired in the works of Correggio. When he
painted in oil, his hand seemed to be so cramped and confined, that he not only lost that facility and spirit, but I think
even that correctness of form, which is so perfect and admirable in his *fresco*-works. I do not recollect any pictures of
his of this kind, except perhaps the "Transfiguration," in which
there are not some parts that appear to be even feebly drawn.
That this is not a necessary attendant on oil-painting, we
have abundant instances in more modern painters. Lodovico
Carracci, for instance, preserved in his works in oil the same
spirit, vigour, and correctness, which he had in *fresco*. I have
no desire to degrade Raffaelle from the high rank which he
deservedly holds; but by comparing him with himself, he does
not appear to me to be the same man in oil as in fresco.

From those who have ambition to tread in this great walk
of the art, Michael Angelo claims the next attention. He did
not possess so many excellencies as Raffaelle, but those which
he had were of the highest kind. He considered the art as consisting of little more than what may be attained by sculpture;
correctness of form, and energy of character. We ought not
to expect more than an artist intends in his work. He never
attempted those lesser elegancies and graces in the art. Vasari
says, he never painted but one picture in oil, and resolved
never to paint another, saying, it was an employment only fit
for women and children.

If any man had a right to look down upon the lower accomplishments as beneath his attention, it was certainly Michael Angelo, nor can it be thought strange, that such a mind
should have slighted or have been withheld from paying due
attention to all those graces and embellishments of art, which
have diffused such lustre over the works of other painters.

It must be acknowledged, however, that together with these,
which we wish he had more attended to, he has rejected all
the false, though specious ornaments, which disgrace the
works even of the most esteemed artists; and I will venture to

say, that when those higher excellencies are more known and cultivated by the artists and the patrons of arts, his fame and credit will encrease with our encreasing knowledge. His name will then be held in the same veneration as it was in the enlightened age of Leo the Tenth: and it is remarkable that the reputation of this truly great man has been continually declining as the art itself has declined. For I must remark to you, that it has long been much on the decline, and that our only hope of its revival will consist in your being thoroughly sensible of its depravation and decay. It is to Michael Angelo, that we owe even the existence of Raffaelle: it is to him Raffaelle owes the grandeur of his style. He was taught by him to elevate his thoughts, and to conceive his subjects with dignity. His genius, however formed to blaze and to shine, might, like fire in combustible matter, for ever have lain dormant, if it had not caught a spark by its contact with Michael Angelo: and though it never burst out with *his* extraordinary heat and vehemence, yet it must be acknowledged to be a more pure, regular, and chaste flame. Though our judgment must upon the whole decide in favour of Raffaelle, yet he never takes such a firm hold and entire possession of the mind as to make us desire nothing else, and to feel nothing wanting. The effect of the capital works of Michael Angelo perfectly corresponds to what Bouchardon said he felt from reading Homer; his whole frame appeared to himself to be enlarged, and all nature which surrounded him, diminished to atoms.

If we put these great artists in a light of comparison with each other, Raffaelle had more taste and fancy, Michael Angelo more genius and imagination. The one excelled in beauty, the other in energy. Michael Angelo has more of the poetical inspiration; his ideas are vast and sublime; his people are a superior order of beings; there is nothing about them, nothing in the air of their actions or their attitudes, or the style and cast of their limbs or features, that reminds us of their belonging to our own species. Raffaelle's imagination is not so elevated; his figures are not so much disjoined from our own diminutive race of beings, though his ideas are chaste, noble, and of great conformity to their subjects. Michael Angelo's works have a strong, peculiar, and marked character: they seem to proceed from his own mind entirely, and that mind so rich and abundant, that he never needed, or seemed to disdain, to look abroad for foreign help. Raffaelle's materials are generally borrowed, though the noble structure is his own. The excellency of this extraordinary man lay in the propriety, beauty, and majesty of his characters, the judicious contrivance of his composition, his correctness of drawing, purity of taste, and skilful accommodation of other men's conceptions to his own purpose. Nobody excelled him in that judgment, with which he united to his own observation on nature, the energy of Michael Angelo, and the beauty and simplicity of the antique. To the question therefore, which ought to hold the first rank, Raffaelle or Michael Angelo, it must be answered, that if it is to be given to him who possessed a greater combination of the higher qualities of the art than any other man, there is no doubt but Raffaelle is the first. But if, as Longinus thinks, the sublime, being the highest excellence that human composition can attain to, abundantly compensates the absence of every other beauty, and atones for all other deficiencies, then Michael Angelo demands the preference.

These two extraordinary men carried some of the higher excellencies of the art to a greater degree of perfection than probably they ever arrived at before. They certainly have not been excelled, nor equalled since. Many of their successors were induced to leave this great road as a beaten path, endeavouring to surprise and please by something uncommon or new. When this desire of novelty has proceeded from mere idleness or caprice, it is not worth the trouble of criticism; but when it has been the result of a busy mind of a peculiar complexion, it is always striking and interesting, never insipid.

Such is the great style, as it appears in those who possessed it at its height: in this, search after novelty, in conception or in treating the subject, has no place.

But there is another style, which, though inferior to the former, has still great merit, because it shews that those who cultivated it were men of lively and vigorous imagination. This, which may be called the original or characteristical style, being less referred to any true archetype existing either in general or particular nature, must be supported by the painter's consistency in the principles which he has assumed, and in the union and harmony of his whole design. The excellency of every style, but of the subordinate styles more especially, will very much depend on preserving that union and harmony between all the component parts, that they may appear to hang well together, as if the whole proceeded from one mind. It is in the works of art, as in the characters of men. The faults or defects of some men seem to become them, when they appear to be the natural growth, and of a piece with the rest of their character. A faithful picture of a mind, though it be not of the most elevated kind, though it be irregular, wild, and incorrect, yet if it be marked with that spirit and firmness which characterises works of genius, will claim attention, and be more striking than a combination of excellencies that do not seem to unite well together; or we may say, than a work that possesses even all excellencies, but those in a moderate degree.

One of the strongest-marked characters of this kind, which must be allowed to be subordinate to the great style, is that of Salvator Rosa.[5] He gives us a peculiar cast of nature, which, though void of all grace, elegance, and simplicity, though it has nothing of that elevation and dignity which belongs to the grand style, yet, has that sort of dignity which belongs to savage and uncultivated nature: but what is most to be admired in him, is, the perfect correspondence which he observed between the subjects which he chose and his manner of treating them. Every thing is of a piece: his rocks, trees, sky, even to his handling, have the same rude and wild character which animates his figures.

With him we may contrast the character of Carlo Maratti,

5 [Salvator Rosa, born 1615 near Naples, Italy; died 1673.]

who, in my opinion, had no great vigour of mind or strength of original genius. He rarely seizes the imagination by exhibiting the higher excellencies, nor does he captivate us by that originality which attends the painter who thinks for himself. He knew and practised all the rules of art, and from a composition of Raffaelle, Carracci, and Guido, made up a style, of which the only fault was, that it had no manifest defects and no striking beauties; and that the principles of his composition are never blended together, so as to form one uniform body, original in its kind, or excellent in any view.

I will mention two other painters, who, though entirely dissimilar, yet by being each consistent with himself and possessing a manner entirely his own, have both gained reputation, though for very opposite accomplishments. The painters I mean, are Rubens and Poussin. Rubens I mention in this place, as I think him a remarkable instance of the same mind being seen in all the various parts of the art. The whole is so much of a piece, that one can scarce be brought to believe but that if any one of the qualities he possessed had been more correct and perfect, his works would not have been so complete as they now appear. If we should allow him a greater purity and correctness of drawing, his want of simplicity in composition, colouring, and drapery, would appear more gross.

In his composition his art is too apparent. His figures have expression, and act with energy, but without simplicity or dignity. His colouring, in which he is eminently skilled, is notwithstanding too much of what we call tinted. Throughout the whole of his works, there is a proportionable want of that nicety of distinction and elegance of mind, which is required in the higher walks of painting; and to this want it may be in some degree ascribed, that those qualities which make the excellency of this subordinate style, appear in him with their greatest lustre. Indeed the facility with which he invented, the richness of his composition, the luxuriant harmony and brilliancy of his colouring, so dazzle the eye, that whilst his works continue before us, we cannot help thinking that all his deficiencies are fully supplied.[6]

Opposed to this florid, careless, loose, and inaccurate style, that of the simple, careful, pure, and correct style of Poussin seems to be a complete contrast. Yet however opposite their characters, in one thing they agreed; both of them always preserving a perfect correspondence between all the parts of their respective manners: insomuch that it may be doubted whether any alteration of what is considered as defective in either, would not destroy the effect of the whole.

Poussin lived and conversed with the ancient statues so long, that he may be said to have been better acquainted with them, than with the people who were about him. I have often thought that he carried his veneration for them so far as to wish to give his works the air of ancient paintings. It is certain he copied some of the antique paintings, particularly the Marriage in the Aldobrandini-Palace at Rome, which I believe to be the best relique of those remote ages that has yet been found.

No works of any modern has so much of the air of antique painting as those of Poussin. His best performances have a remarkable dryness of manner, which though by no means to be recommended for imitation, yet seems perfectly correspondent to that ancient simplicity which distinguishes his style. Like Polidoro[7] he studied the ancients so much, that he acquired a habit of thinking in their way, and seemed to know perfectly the actions and gestures they would use on every occasion.

Poussin in the latter part of his life changed from his dry manner to one much softer and richer, where there is a greater union between the figures and the ground; as in the "Seven Sacraments" in the Duke of Orleans's collection; but neither these, nor any of his other pictures in this manner, are at all comparable to many in his dry manner which we have in England.

6 [See illustrations, Rubens' "The Kermesse" (detail).]
7 [Polidoro da Caravaggio (ca. 1495–1543).]

The favourite subjects of Poussin were ancient fables; and no painter was ever better qualified to paint such subjects, not only from his being eminently skilled in the knowledge of the ceremonies, customs and habits of the ancients, but from his being so well acquainted with the different characters which those who invented them gave to their allegorical figures. Though Rubens has shewn great fancy in his satyrs, Silenuses, and fauns, yet they are not that distinct separate class of beings, which is carefully exhibited by the ancients, and by Poussin. Certainly when such subjects of antiquity are represented, nothing in the picture ought to remind us of modern times. The mind is thrown back into antiquity, and nothing ought to be introduced that may tend to awaken it from the illusion.

Poussin seemed to think that the style and the language in which such stories are told, is not the worse for preserving some relish of the old way of painting, which seemed to give a general uniformity to the whole, so that the mind was thrown back into antiquity not only by the subject, but the execution.[8]

If Poussin in imitation of the ancients represents Apollo driving his chariot out of the sea by way of representing the sun rising, if he personifies lakes and rivers, it is nowise offensive in him; but seems perfectly of a piece with the general air of the picture. On the contrary, if the figures which people his pictures had a modern air or countenance, if they appeared like our countrymen, if the draperies were like cloth or silk of our manufacture, if the landscape had the appearance of a modern view, how ridiculous would Apollo appear instead of the sun; an old man, or a nymph with an urn, to represent a river or a lake?

I cannot avoid mentioning here a circumstance in portrait-painting, which may help to confirm what has been said. When a portrait is painted in the historical style, as it is neither an exact minute representation of an individual, nor

[8] [See illustrations, Poussin's "The Triumph of Neptune and Amphitrite."]

completely ideal, every circumstance ought to correspond to
this mixture. The simplicity of the antique air and attitude,
however much to be admired, is ridiculous when joined to a
figure in a modern dress. It is not to my purpose to enter into
the question at present, whether this mixed style ought to be
adopted or not; yet if it is chosen, 'tis necessary it should be
complete and all of a piece: the difference of stuffs, for instance, which make the cloathing, should be distinguished in
the same degree as the head deviates from a general idea.
Without this union, which I have so often recommended, a
work can have no marked and determined character, which
is the peculiar and constant evidence of genius. But when
this is accomplished to a high degree, it becomes in some sort
a rival to that style which we have fixed as the highest.

Thus I have given a sketch of the characters of Rubens
and Salvator Rosa, as they appear to me to have the greatest
uniformity of mind throughout their whole work. But we may
add to these, all those artists who are at the head of a class,
and have had a school of imitators from Michael Angelo
down to Watteau. Upon the whole it appears, that setting
aside the ornamental style, there are two different modes,
either of which a student may adopt without degrading the
dignity of his art. The object of the first is, to combine the
higher excellencies and embellish them to the greatest advantage; of the other, to carry one of these excellencies to the
highest degree. But those who possess neither must be classed
with them, who, as Shakspeare says, are "men of no mark or
likelihood." [9]

I inculcate as frequently as I can your forming yourselves
upon great principles and great models. Your time will be
much misspent in every other pursuit. Small excellencies
should be viewed, not studied; they ought to be viewed, because nothing ought to escape a painter's observation; but for
no other reason.

There is another caution which I wish to give you. Be as
select in those whom you endeavour to please, as in those

[9] [*I Henry IV*, III.ii.45.]

whom you endeavour to imitate. Without the love of fame
you can never do any thing excellent; but by an excessive and
undistinguishing thirst after it, you will come to have vulgar
views; you will degrade your style; and your taste will be
entirely corrupted. It is certain that the lowest style will be
the most popular, as it falls within the compass of ignorance
itself; and the vulgar will always be pleased with what is
natural, in the confined and misunderstood sense of the word.

One would wish that such depravation of taste should be
counteracted with that manly pride which actuated Euripides
when he said to the Athenians who criticised his works, "I do
not compose my works in order to be corrected by you,
but to instruct you." [10] It is true, to have a right to speak thus,
a man must be an Euripides. However, thus much may be
allowed, that when an artist is sure that he is upon firm
ground, supported by the authority and practice of his predecessors of the greatest reputation, he may then assume the
boldness and intrepidity of genius; at any rate he must not
be tempted out of the right path by any allurement of popularity, which always accompanies the lower styles of painting.

I mention this, because our Exhibitions, while they produce such admirable effects by nourishing emulation and calling out genius, have also a mischievous tendency, by seducing
the painter to an ambition of pleasing indiscriminately the
mixed multitude of people who resort to them.

10 [Valerius Maximus, III. 7.]

⟡ Discourse 6

December 10, 1774

GENTLEMEN,

WHEN I have taken the liberty of addressing you on the course and order of your studies, I never proposed to enter into a minute detail of the art. This I have always left to the several professors, who pursue the end of our institution with the highest honour to themselves, and with the greatest advantage to the students.

My purpose in the discourses I have held in the Academy has been, to lay down certain general positions, which seem to me proper for the formation of a sound taste: principles, necessary to guard the pupils against those errors, into which the sanguine temper common to their time of life has a tendency to lead them; and which have rendered abortive the hopes of so many successions of promising young men in all parts of Europe. I wished also, to intercept and suppress those prejudices which particularly prevail when the mechanism of painting is come to its perfection; and which, when they do prevail, are certain utterly to destroy the higher and more valuable parts of this literate and liberal profession.

These two have been my principal purposes; they are still as much my concern, as ever; and if I repeat my own notions on the subject, you who know how fast mistake and prejudice, when neglected, gain ground upon truth and reason, will easily excuse me. I only attempt to set the same thing in the greatest variety of lights.

The subject of this discourse will be *imitation*, as far as a painter is concerned in it. By imitation I do not mean imitation in its largest sense,[1] but simply the following of other masters, and the advantage to be drawn from the study of their works.

Those who have undertaken to write on our art, and have represented it as a kind of *inspiration*,[2] as a *gift* bestowed upon peculiar favourites at their birth, seem to insure a much more favourable disposition from their readers, and have a much more captivating and liberal air, than he who attempts to examine, coldly, whether there are any means by which this art may be acquired; how the mind may be strengthened and expanded, and what guides will shew the way to eminence.

It is very natural for those who are unacquainted with the *cause* of any thing extraordinary, to be astonished at the *effect*, and to consider it as a kind of magick. They, who have never observed the gradation by which art is acquired; who see only what is the full result of long labour and application of an infinite number and infinite variety of acts, are apt to conclude from their entire inability to do the same at once, that it is not only inaccessible to themselves, but can be done by those only, who have some gift of the nature of inspiration bestowed upon them.

The travellers into the East tell us, that when the ignorant inhabitants of those countries are asked concerning the ruins of stately edifices yet remaining amongst them, the melancholy monuments of their former grandeur and long-lost science, they always answer, that they were built by magicians. The untaught mind finds a vast gulph between its own powers, and those works of complicated art, which it is utterly unable to

---

[1] [The "largest sense" would be imitation of an idea or ideal, rather than some specific trait.]

[2] [Reynolds is referring to the ancient dispute between those who claimed that art was a product of inspiration from outside the artist (e.g., a Muse) and those who claimed that art could be achieved by following a series of more or less mechanical procedures (that therefore could be taught.) Reynolds again speaks of these ideas in Discourse 7, p. 92.]

fathom; and it supposes that such a void can be passed only by supernatural powers.

And, as for artists themselves, it is by no means their interest to undeceive such judges, however conscious they may be of the very natural means by which their extraordinary powers were acquired; though our art, being intrinsically imitative, rejects this idea of inspiration, more perhaps than any other.

It is to avoid this plain confession of truth, as it should seem, that this imitation of masters, indeed almost all imitation, which implies a more regular and progressive method of attaining the ends of painting, has ever been particularly inveighed against with great keenness, both by ancient and modern writers.

To derive all from native power, to owe nothing to another, is the praise which men, who do not much think on what they are saying, bestow sometimes upon others, and sometimes on themselves; and their imaginary dignity is naturally heightened by a supercilious censure of the low, the barren, the groveling, the servile imitator. It would be no wonder if a student, frightened by these terrifick and disgraceful epithets, with which the poor imitators are so often loaded, should let fall his pencil in mere despair; (conscious as he must be, how much he has been indebted to the labours of others, how little, how very little of his art was born with him;) and, consider it as hopeless, to set about acquiring by the imitation of any human master, what he is taught to suppose is matter of inspiration from heaven.

Some allowance must be made for what is said in the gaiety or ambition of rhetorick. We cannot suppose that any one can really mean to exclude all imitation of others. A position so wild would scarce deserve a serious answer; for it is apparent, if we were forbid to make use of the advantages which our predecessors afford us, the art would be always to begin, and consequently remain always in its infant state; and it is a common observation, that no art was ever invented and carried to perfection at the same time.

But to bring us entirely to reason and sobriety, let it be observed, that a painter must not only be of necessity an imitator of the works of nature, which alone is sufficient to dispel this phantom of inspiration, but he must be as necessarily an imitator of the works of other painters: this appears more humiliating, but is equally true; and no man can be an artist, whatever he may suppose, upon any other terms.

However, those who appear more moderate and reasonable, allow, that our study is to begin by imitation; but maintain that we should no longer use the thoughts of our predecessors, when we are become able to think for ourselves. They hold that imitation is as hurtful to the more advanced student, as it was advantageous to the beginner.

For my own part, I confess, I am not only very much disposed to maintain the absolute necessity of imitation in the first stages of the art; but am of opinion, that the study of other masters, which I here call imitation, may be extended throughout our whole lives, without any danger of the inconveniences with which it is charged, of enfeebling the mind, or preventing us from giving that original air which every work undoubtedly ought always to have.

I am on the contrary persuaded, that by imitation only, variety, and even originality of invention, is produced. I will go further; even genius, at least what generally is so called, is the child of imitation. But as this appears to be contrary to the general opinion, I must explain my position before I enforce it.[3]

Genius is supposed to be a power of producing excellencies, which are out of the reach of the rules of art; a power which no precepts can teach, and which no industry can acquire.

This opinion of the impossibility of acquiring those beauties, which stamp the work with the character of genius, supposes, that it is something more fixed than in reality it is; and that we always do, and ever did agree in opinion, with respect to

3 [For the meaning of "genius," see Introduction, p. xxii.]

what should be considered as the characteristick of genius. But the truth is, that the *degree* of excellence which proclaims *genius* is different, in different times and different places; and what shews it to be so is, that mankind have often changed their opinion upon this matter.

When the arts were in their infancy, the power of merely drawing the likeness of any object, was considered as one of its greatest efforts. The common people, ignorant of the principles of art, talk the same language, even to this day. But when it was found that every man could be taught to do this, and a great deal more, merely by the observance of certain precepts; the name of genius then shifted its application, and was given only to him who added the peculiar character of the object he represented; to him who had invention, expression, grace, or dignity; in short, those qualities, or excellencies, the power of producing which, could not *then* be taught by any known and promulgated rules.

We are very sure that the beauty of form, the expression of the passions, the art of composition, even the power of giving a general air of grandeur to a work, is at present very much under the dominion of rules. These excellencies were, heretofore, considered merely as the effects of genius; and justly, if genius is not taken for inspiration, but as the effect of close observation and experience.[4]

He who first made any of these observations, and digested them, so as to form an invariable principle for himself to work by, had that merit, but probably no one went very far at once; and generally, the first who gave the hint, did not know how to pursue it steadily, and methodically; at least not in the beginning. He himself worked on it, and improved it; others worked more, and improved further; until the secret was discovered, and the practice made as general, as refined practice can be made. How many more principles may be fixed and ascertained, we cannot tell; but as criticism is likely to go hand

[4] [The psychology that Reynolds uses and assumes throughout is that of John Locke.]

in hand with the art which is its subject, we may venture to say, that as that art shall advance, its powers will be still more and more fixed by rules.

But by whatever strides criticism may gain ground, we need be under no apprehension, that invention will ever be annihilated, or subdued; or intellectual energy be brought entirely within the restraint of written law. Genius will still have room enough to expatiate, and keep always at the same distance from narrow comprehension and mechanical performance.

What we now call genius, begins, not where rules, abstractedly taken, end; but where known vulgar and trite rules have no longer any place. It must of necessity be, that even works of genius, like every other effect, as they must have their cause, must likewise have their rules; it cannot be by chance, that excellencies are produced with any constancy or any certainty, for this is not the nature of chance; but the rules by which men of extraordinary parts, and such as are called men of genius work, are either such as they discover by their own peculiar observations, or of such a nice texture as not easily to admit being expressed in words; especially as artists are not very frequently skilful in that mode of communicating ideas. Unsubstantial, however, as these rules may seem, and difficult as it may be to convey them in writing, they are still seen and felt in the mind of the artist; and he works from them with as much certainty, as if they were embodied, as I may say, upon paper. It is true, these refined principles cannot be always made palpable, like the more gross rules of art; yet it does not follow, but that the mind may be put in such a train, that it shall perceive, by a kind of scientifick sense, that propriety, which words, particularly words of unpractised writers, such as we are, can but very feebly suggest.

Invention is one of the great marks of genius; but if we consult experience, we shall find, that it is by being conversant with the inventions of others, that we learn to invent; as by reading the thoughts of others we learn to think.

Whoever has so far formed his taste, as to be able to relish

and feel the beauties of the great masters, has gone a great
way in his study; for, merely from a consciousness of this
relish of the right, the mind swells with an inward pride, and
is almost as powerfully affected, as if it had itself produced
what it admires. Our hearts frequently warmed in this manner
by the contact of those whom we wish to resemble, will undoubtedly catch something of their way of thinking; and we
shall receive in our own bosoms some radiation at least of
their fire and splendour. That disposition, which is so strong
in children, still continues with us, of catching involuntarily
the general air and manner of those with whom we are most
conversant; with this difference only, that a young mind is
naturally pliable and imitative; but in a more advanced state
it grows rigid, and must be warmed and softened, before it
will receive a deep impression.

From these considerations, which a little of your own reflection will carry a great way further, it appears, of what great
consequence it is, that our minds should be habituated to the
contemplation of excellence; and that, far from being contented to make such habits the discipline of our youth only,
we should, to the last moment of our lives, continue a settled
intercourse with all the true examples of grandeur. Their inventions are not only the food of our infancy, but the substance which supplies the fullest maturity of our vigour.

The mind is but a barren soil; a soil which is soon exhausted, and will produce no crop, or only one, unless it be
continually fertilized and enriched with foreign matter.

When we have had continually before us the great works
of art to impregnate our minds with kindred ideas, we are
then, and not till then, fit to produce something of the same
species. We behold all about us with the eyes of those penetrating observers whose works we contemplate; and our minds
accustomed to think the thoughts of the noblest and brightest
intellects, are prepared for the discovery and selection of all
that is great and noble in nature. The greatest natural genius
cannot subsist on its own stock: he who resolves never to
ransack any mind but his own, will be soon reduced, from

mere barrenness, to the poorest of all imitations; he will be obliged to imitate himself, and to repeat what he has before often repeated. When we know the subject designed by such men, it will never be difficult to guess what kind of work is to be produced.

It is vain for painters or poets to endeavour to invent without materials on which the mind may work, and from which invention must originate. Nothing can come of nothing.

Homer is supposed to be possessed of all the learning of his time: and we are certain that Michael Angelo, and Raffaelle, were equally possessed of all the knowledge in the art which had been discovered in the works of their predecessors.

A mind enriched by an assemblage of all the treasures of ancient and modern art, will be more elevated and fruitful in resources in proportion to the number of ideas which have been carefully collected and thoroughly digested. There can be no doubt but that he who has the most materials has the greatest means of invention; and if he has not the power of using them, it must proceed from a feebleness of intellect; or from the confused manner in which those collections have been laid up in his mind.

The addition of other men's judgment is so far from weakening our own, as is the opinion of many, that it will fashion and consolidate those ideas of excellence which lay in embryo, feeble, ill-shaped, and confused, but which are finished and put in order by the authority and practice of those, whose works may be said to have been consecrated by having stood the test of ages.

The mind, or genius, has been compared to a spark of fire, which is smothered by a heap of fuel, and prevented from blazing into a flame: This simile, which is made use of by the younger Pliny,[5] may be easily mistaken for argument or proof. But there is no danger of the mind's being over-burdened with knowledge, or the genius extinguished by any addition of images; on the contrary, these acquisitions may as well, perhaps better, be compared, if comparisons signified any thing

5 [Reynolds' attribution to Pliny is in error.]

in reasoning, to the supply of living embers, which will contribute to strengthen the spark, that without the association of more fuel would have died away. The truth is, he whose feebleness is such, as to make other men's thoughts an incumbrance to him, can have no very great strength of mind or genius of his own to be destroyed; so that not much harm will be done at worst.

We may oppose to Pliny the greatest authority of Cicero, who is continually enforcing the necessity of this method of study. In his dialogue on oratory, he makes Crassus say, that one of the first and most important precepts is, to choose a proper model for our imitation. *Hoc sit primum in praeceptis meis ut demonstremus quem imitemur.*[6]

When I speak of the habitual imitation and continued study of masters, it is not to be understood, that I advise any endeavour to copy the exact peculiar colour and complexion of another man's mind; the success of such an attempt must always be like his, who imitates exactly the air, manner, and gestures, of him whom he admires. His model may be excellent, but the copy will be ridiculous; this ridicule does not arise from his having imitated, but from his not having chosen the right mode of imitation.

It is a necessary and warrantable pride to disdain to walk servilely behind any individual, however elevated his rank. The true and liberal ground of imitation is an open field; where, though he who precedes has had the advantage of starting before you, you may always propose to overtake him: it is enough however to pursue his course; you need not tread in his footsteps; and you certainly have a right to outstrip him if you can.

Nor whilst I recommend studying the art from artists, can I be supposed to mean, that nature is to be neglected: I take this study in aid, and not in exclusion, of the other. Nature is, and must be the fountain which alone is inexhaustible; and from which all excellencies must originally flow.

---

[6] ["This, then, is my first advice, that we show the students whom to follow" (Cicero, *De oratore* II. 22. 90).]

The great use of studying our predecessors is, to open the mind, to shorten our labour, and to give us the result of the selection made by those great minds of what is grand or beautiful in nature: her rich stores are all spread out before us; but it is an art and no easy art, to know how or what to choose, and how to attain and secure the object of our choice period. Thus the highest beauty of form must be taken from nature; but it is an art of long deduction, and great experience, to know how to find it. We must not content ourselves with merely admiring and relishing; we must enter into the principles on which the work is wrought: these do not swim on the superficies, and consequently are not open to superficial observers.

Art in its perfection is not ostentatious; it lies hid, and works its effect, itself unseen. It is the proper study and labour of an artist to uncover and find out the latent cause of conspicuous beauties, and from thence form principles for his own conduct: such an examination is a continual exertion of the mind; as great, perhaps, as that of the artist whose works he is thus studying.

The sagacious imitator does not content himself with merely remarking what distinguishes the different manner or genius of each master; he enters into the contrivance in the composition, how the masses of lights are disposed, the means by which the effect is produced, how artfully some parts are lost in the ground, others boldly relieved, and how all these are mutually altered and interchanged according to the reason and scheme of the work. He admires not the harmony of colouring alone, but examines by what artifice one colour is a foil to its neighbour. He looks close into the tints, examines of what colours they are composed, till he has formed clear and distinct ideas, and has learnt to see in what harmony and good colouring consists. What is learned in this manner from the works of others becomes really our own, sinks deep, and is never forgotten, nay, it is by seizing on this clue that we proceed forward, and, get further and further in enlarging the principles and improving the practice of our art.

There can be no doubt, but the art is better learnt from the works themselves than from the precepts which are formed upon those works; but if it is difficult to choose proper models for imitation, it requires no less circumspection to separate and distinguish what in those models we ought to imitate.

I cannot avoid mentioning here, though it is not my intention at present to enter into the art and method of study, an error which students are too apt to fall into. He that is forming himself, must look with great caution and wariness on those peculiarities, or prominent parts, which at first force themselves upon view; and are the marks, or what is commonly called the manner, by which that individual artist is distinguished.

Peculiar marks, I hold to be, generally, if not always, defects; however difficult it may be wholly to escape them.

Peculiarities in the works of art, are like those in the human figure; it is by them that we are cognizable and distinguished one from another, but they are always so many blemishes; which, however, both in real life and in painting, cease to appear deformities, to those who have them continually before their eyes. In the works of art, even the most enlightened mind, when warmed by beauties of the highest kind, will by degrees find a repugnance within him to acknowledge any defects; nay, his enthusiasm will carry him so far, as to transform them into beauties, and objects of imitation.

It must be acknowledged, that a peculiarity of style, either from its novelty, or by seeming to proceed from a peculiar turn of mind, often escapes blame; on the contrary, it is sometimes striking and pleasing; but this it is a vain labour to endeavour to imitate; because novelty and peculiarity being its only merit, when it ceases to be new, it ceases to have value.

A manner therefore being a defect, and every painter, however excellent, having a manner, it seems to follow, that all kinds of faults, as well as beauties, may be learned under the sanction of the greatest authorities. Even the great name of Michael Angelo may be used, to keep in countenance a deficiency or rather neglect of colouring, and every other ornamental part of the art. If the young student is dry and hard, Poussin is the same. If his work has a careless and unfinished air, he has most of the Venetian school to support him. If he makes no selection of objects, but takes individual nature just as he finds it, he is like Rembrandt. If he is incorrect in the proportions of his figures, Correggio was likewise incorrect. If his colours are not blended and united, Rubens was equally crude. In short, there is no defect that may not be excused, if it is a sufficient excuse that it can be imputed to considerable artists; but it must be remembered, that is was not by these defects they acquired their reputation; they have a right to our pardon, but not to our admiration.

However, to imitate peculiarities or mistake defects for beauties, that man will be most liable, who confines his imitation to one favourite master; and even though he chooses the best, and is capable of distinguishing the real excellencies of his model, it is not by such narrow practice, that a genius or mastery in the art is acquired. A man is as little likely to form a true idea of the perfection of the art, by studying a single artist, as he would be to produce a perfectly beautiful figure, by an exact imitation of any individual living model. And as the painter, by bringing together in one piece, those beauties which are dispersed among a great variety of individuals, produces a figure more beautiful than can be found in nature, so that artist who can unite in himself the excellencies of the various great painters, will approach nearer to perfection than any one of his masters. He, who confines himself to the imitation of an individual, as he never proposes to surpass, so he is not likely to equal, the object of his imitation. He professes only to follow; and he that follows must necessarily be behind.

We should imitate the conduct of the great artists in the course of their studies, as well as the works which they produced, when they were perfectly formed. Raffaelle began by imitating implicitly the manner of Pietro Perugino,[7] under

7 [Perugino (Pietro Vanucci), born at Città della Pieve, Italy, 1446; died 1524.]

whom he studied; hence his first works are scarce to be distinguished from his master's; but soon forming higher and more extensive views, he imitated the grand outline of Michael Angelo; he learned the manner of using colours from the works of Leonardo da Vinci, and Frate Bartolomeo: [8] to all this he added the contemplation of all the remains of antiquity that were within his reach; and employed others to draw for him what was in Greece and distant places. And it is from his having taken so many models, that he became himself a model for all succeeding painters; always imitating, and always original.

If your ambition, therefore, be to equal Raffaelle, you must do as Raffaelle did; take many models, and not even *him* for your guide alone to the exclusion of others.[9] And yet the number is infinite of those who seem, if one may judge by their style, to have seen no other works but those of their master, or of some favourite, whose *manner* is their first wish, and their last.

I will mention a few that occur to me of this narrow, confined, illiberal, unscientifick, and servile kind of imitators. Guido was thus meanly copied by Elizabetta Sirani, and Simone Cantarini; Poussin, by Verdier, and Cheron; Parmegiano, by Jeronimo Mazzuoli, Paul Veronese, and Iacomo Bassano, had for their imitators their brothers and sons. Pietro de Cortona was followed by Ciro Ferri, and Romanelli; Rubens, by Jacques Jordans, and Diepenbeck; Guercino, by his own family, the Gennari. Carlo Maratti was imitated by Giuseppe Chiari, and Pietro da Pietri; and Rembrandt, by Bramer, Eckhout, and Flink. All these, to whom may be added a much longer list of painters whose works among the ignorant pass for those of their masters, are justly to be censured for barrenness and servility.

To oppose to this list a few that have adopted a more liberal

---

8 [Fra Bartolommeo (Baccio della Porta), born at Savignano, Italy, 1475; died 1517.]

9 Sed non qui maxime imitandus, etiam solus imitandus est. Quintilian [*Institutio oratoria*, X. 2. 24].

style of imitation;—Pelegrino Tibaldi, Rosso, and Primaticcio, did not coldly imitate, but caught something of the fire that animates the works of Michael Angelo. The Caraccis formed their style from Pelegrino Tibaldi, Correggio, and the Venetian school. Domenichino, Guido, Lanfranco, Albano, Guercino, Cavidone, Schidone, Tiarini, though it is sufficiently apparent that they came from the school of the Caraccis, have yet the appearance of men who extended their views beyond the model that lay before them, and have shewn that they had opinions of their own, and thought for themselves, after they had made themselves masters of the general principles of their schools.

Le Sueur's first manner resembles very much that of his master Vouet: but as he soon excelled him, so he differed from him in every part of the art. Carlo Maratti succeeded better than those I have first named, and I think owes his superiority to the extension of his views; beside his master Andrea Sacchi, he imitated Raffaelle, Guido, and the Caraccis. It is true, there is nothing very captivating in Carlo Maratti; but this proceeded from a want which cannot be completely supplied; that is, want of strength of parts. In this certainly men are not equal; and a man can bring home wares only in proportion to the capital with which he goes to market. Carlo, by diligence, made the most of what he had; but there was undoubtedly a heaviness about him, which extended itself, uniformly, to his invention, expression, his drawing, colouring, and the general effect of his pictures. The truth is, he never equalled any of his patterns in any one thing, and he added little of his own.

But we must not rest contented even in this general study of the moderns; we must trace back the art to its fountainhead; to that source from whence they drew their principal excellencies, the monuments of pure antiquity. All the inventions and thoughts of the ancients, whether conveyed to us in statues, bas-relievos, intaglios, cameos, or coins, are to be sought after and carefully studied: the genius that hovers over these venerable reliques, may be called the father of modern art.

From the remains of the works of the ancients the modern arts were revived, and it is by their means that they must be restored a second time. However it may mortify our vanity, we must be forced to allow them our masters; and we may venture to prophecy, that when they shall cease to be studied, arts will no longer flourish, and we shall again relapse into barbarism.

The fire of the artist's own genius operating upon these materials which have been thus diligently collected, will enable him to make new combinations, perhaps, superior to what had ever before been in the possession of the art: as in the mixture of the variety of metals, which are said to have been melted and run together at the burning of Corinth, a new and till then unknown metal was produced, equal in value to any of those that had contributed to its composition. And though a curious refiner should come with his crucibles, analyse and separate its various component parts, yet Corinthian brass would still hold its rank amongst the most beautiful and valuable of metals.

We have hitherto considered the advantages of imitation as it tends to form the taste, and as a practice by which a spark of that genius may be caught, which illumines those noble works that ought always to be present to our thoughts.

We come now to speak of another kind of imitation; the borrowing a particular thought, an action, attitude, or figure, and transplanting it into your own work: this will either come under the charge of plagiarism, or be warrantable, and deserve commendation, according to the address with which it is performed. There is some difference likewise, whether it is upon the ancients or the moderns that these depredations are made. It is generally allowed, that no man need be ashamed of copying the ancients: their works are considered as a magazine of common property, always open to the publick, whence every man has a right to take what materials he pleases; and if he has the art of using them, they are supposed to become to all intents and purposes his own property. The collection of the thoughts of the ancients, which Raffaelle made with so much trouble, is a proof of his opinion on this subject. Such collections may be made with much more ease, by means of an art scarce known in his time; I mean that of engraving; by which, at an easy rate, every man may now avail himself of the inventions of antiquity.

It must be acknowledged that the works of the moderns are more the property of their authors; he, who borrows an idea from an ancient, or even from a modern artist not his contemporary, and so accommodates it to his own work, that it makes a part of it, with no seam or joining appearing, can hardly be charged with plagiarism: poets practise this kind of borrowing, without reserve. But an artist should not be contented with this only; he should enter into a competition with his original, and endeavour to improve what he is appropriating to his own work. Such imitation is so far from having any thing in it of the servility of plagiarism, that it is a perpetual exercise of the mind, a continual invention. Borrowing or stealing with such art and caution, will have a right to the same lenity as was used by the Lacedemonians; who did not punish theft, but the want of artifice to conceal it.

In order to encourage you to imitation, to the utmost extent, let me add, that very finished artists in the inferior branches of the art, will contribute to furnish the mind and give hints, of which a skilful painter, who is sensible of what he wants, and is in no danger of being infected by the contact of vicious models, will know how to avail himself. He will pick up from dunghills what by a nice chymistry, passing through his own mind, shall be converted into pure gold; and, under the rudeness of Gothick essays, he will find original, rational, and even sublime inventions.

The works of Albert Durer, Lucas Van Leyden, the numerous inventions of Tobias Stimer, and Jost Ammon, afford a rich mass of genuine materials, which wrought up and polished to elegance, will add copiousness to what, perhaps, without such aid, could have aspired only to justness and propriety. In the luxuriant style of Paul Veronese, in the capricious compositions of Tintoret, he will find something, that will assist his invention, and give points, from which his own imagination shall rise and take flight, when the subject which he treats will with propriety admit of splendid effects.

In every school, whether Venetian, French, or Dutch, he will find, either ingenious compositions, extraordinary effects, some peculiar expressions, or some mechanical excellence, well worthy of his attention, and, in some measure, of his imitation. Even in the lower class of the French painters great beauties are often found united with great defects. Though Coypel wanted a simplicity of taste, and mistook a presumptuous and assuming air for what is grand and majestick; yet he frequently has good sense and judgment in his manner of telling his stories, great skill in his compositions, and is not without a considerable power of expressing the passions. The modern affectation of grace in his works, as well as in those of Boucher and Watteau, may be said to be separated, by a very thin partition, from the more simple and pure grace of Correggio and Parmegiano.

Among the Dutch painters, the correct, firm, and determined pencil, which was employed by Bamboccio[10] and Jean Miel, on vulgar and mean subjects, might, without any change, be employed on the highest; to which, indeed, it seems more properly to belong. The greatest style, if that style is confined to small figures, such as Poussin generally painted, would receive an additional grace by the elegance and precision of pencil so admirable in the works of Teniers; and though the school to which he belonged more particularly excelled in the mechanism of painting, yet it produced many, who have shewn great abilities in expressing what must be ranked above mechanical excellencies. In the works of Frank Halls,[11] the portrait-painter may observe the composition of a face, the

10 [Bamboccio, or Pieter van Laer.]
11 [Frank Halls, that is, Frans Hals.]

features well put together, as the painters express it; from whence proceeds that strong-marked character of individual nature, which is so remarkable in his portraits, and is not found in an equal degree in any other painter. If he had joined to this most difficult part of the art, a patience in finishing what he had so correctly planned, he might justly have claimed the place which Vandyck, all things considered, so justly holds as the first of portrait-painters.

Others of the same school have shewn great power in expressing the character and passions of those vulgar people, which were the subjects of their study and attention. Among those Jean Stein seems to be one of the most diligent and accurate observers of what passed in those scenes which he frequented, and which were to him an academy. I can easily imagine, that if this extraordinary man had had the good fortune to have been born in Italy, instead of Holland, had he lived in Rome instead of Leyden, and been blessed with Michael Angelo and Raffaelle for his masters, instead of Brower and Van Gowen; the same sagacity and penetration which distinguished so accurately the different characters and expression in his vulgar figures, would, when exerted in the selection and imitation of what was great and elevated in nature, have been equally successful; and he now would have ranged with the great pillars and supporters of our art.[12]

Men who although thus bound down by the almost invincible powers of early habits, have still exerted extraordinary abilities within their narrow and confined circle; and have, from the natural vigour of their mind, given a very interesting expression, and great force and energy to their works; though they cannot be recommended to be exactly imitated, may yet invite an artist to endeavour to transfer, by a kind of parody, their excellencies to his own performances. Whoever has acquired the power of making this use of the Flemish, Venetian, and French schools, is a real genius, and has sources of knowledge open to him which were wanting to the great artists who lived in the great age of painting.

12 [See illustrations, Jan Steen's "Merry Company."]

To find excellencies, however dispersed, to discover beauties, however concealed by the multitude of defects with which they are surrounded, can be the work only of him, who having a mind always alive to his art, has extended his views to all ages and to all schools; and has acquired from that comprehensive mass which he has thus gathered to himself, a well-digested and perfect idea of his art, to which every thing is referred. Like a sovereign judge and arbiter of art, he is possessed of that presiding power which separates and attracts every excellence from every school; selects both from what is great, and what is little; brings home knowledge from the East and from the West; making the universe tributary towards furnishing his mind and enriching his works with originality, and variety of inventions.

Thus I have ventured to give my opinion of what appears to me the true and only method by which an artist makes himself master of his profession; which I hold ought to be one continued course of imitation that is not to cease but with his life.

Those, who either from their own engagements and hurry of business, or from indolence, or from conceit and vanity, have neglected looking out of themselves, as far as my experience and observation reaches, have from that time, not only ceased to advance, and improve in their performances, but have gone backward. They may be compared to men who have lived upon their principal till they are reduced to beggary, and left without resources.

I can recommend nothing better, therefore, than that you endeavour to infuse into your works what you learn from the contemplation of the works of others. To recommend this has the appearance of needless and superfluous advice; but it has fallen within my own knowledge, that artists, though they were not wanting in a sincere love for their art, though they had great pleasure in seeing good pictures, and were well skilled to distinguish what was excellent or defective in them, yet have gone on in their own manner, without any endeavour to give a little of those beauties, which they admired in others, to their own works. It is difficult to conceive how the present Italian painters, who live in the midst of the treasures of art, should be contented with their own style. They proceed in their common-place inventions, and never think it worth while to visit the works of those great artists with which they are surrounded.

I remember, several years ago, to have conversed at Rome with an artist of great fame throughout Europe; he was not without a considerable degree of abilities, but those abilities were by no means equal to his own opinion of them. From the reputation he had acquired, he too fondly concluded that he stood in the same rank, when compared with his predecessors, as he held with regard to his miserable contemporary rivals. In conversation about some particulars of the works of Raffaelle, he seemed to have, or to affect to have, a very obscure memory of them. He told me that he had not set his foot in the Vatican for fifteen years together; that indeed he had been in treaty to copy a capital picture of Raffaelle, but that the business had gone off; however, if the agreement had held, his copy would have greatly exceeded the original. The merit of this artist, however great we may suppose it, I am sure would have been far greater, and his presumption would have been far less, if he had visited the Vatican, as in reason he ought to have done, at least once every month of his life.

I address myself, gentlemen, to you who have made some progress in the art, and are to be, for the future, under the guidance of your own judgment and discretion. I consider you as arrived to that period, when you have a right to think for yourselves, and to presume that every man is fallible; to study the masters with a suspicion, that great men are not always exempt from great faults; to criticise, compare, and rank their works in your own estimation, as they approach to, or recede from, that standard of perfection which you have formed in your own minds, but which those masters themselves, it must be remembered, have taught you to make; and which you will cease to make with correctness, when you cease to study them. It is their excellencies which have taught you their defects.

I would wish you to forget where you are, and who it is that speaks to you. I only direct you to higher models and better advisers. We can teach you here but very little; you are henceforth to be your own teachers. Do this justice, however, to the English Academy; to bear in mind, that in this place you contracted no narrow habits, no false ideas, nothing that could lead you to the imitation of any living master, who may be the fashionable darling of the day. As you have not been taught to flatter us, do not learn to flatter yourselves. We have endeavoured to lead you to the admiration of nothing but what is truly admirable. If you choose inferior patterns, or if you make your own *former* works your patterns for your *latter,* it is your own fault.

The purport of this discourse, and, indeed, of most of my other discourses, is to caution you against the false opinion, but too prevalent among artists, of the imaginary power of native genius, and its sufficiency in great works. This opinion, according to the temper of mind it meets with, almost always produces, either a vain confidence, or a sluggish despair, both equally fatal to all proficiency.

Study therefore the great works of the great masters, for ever. Study as nearly as you can, in the order, in the manner, and on the principles, on which they studied. Study nature attentively, but always with those masters in your company; consider them as models which you are to imitate, and at the same time as rivals with whom you are to contend.

·❦· Discourse 7

December 10, 1776

GENTLEMEN,

IT HAS been my uniform endeavour, since I first addressed you from this place, to impress you strongly with one ruling idea. I wished you to be persuaded, that success in your art depends almost entirely on your own industry; but the industry which I principally recommended, is not the industry of the *hands,* but of the *mind.*

As our art is not a divine *gift,* so neither is it a mechanical *trade.* Its foundations are laid in solid science: and practice, though essential to perfection, can never attain that to which it aims, unless it works under the direction of principle.

Some writers upon art carry this point too far, and suppose that such body of universal and profound learning is requisite, that the very enumeration of its kinds is enough to frighten a beginner. Vitruvius, after going through the many accomplishments of nature, and the many acquirements of learning, necessary to an architect, proceeds with great gravity to assert, that he ought to be well skilled in the civil law; that he may not be cheated in the title of the ground he builds on.[1]

But without such exaggeration, we may go so far as to assert, that a painter stands in need of more knowledge than is to be picked off his pallet, or collected by looking on his model,

---

[1] [Pollio Marcus Vitruvius, born at Verona, a famous Roman architect and engineer. His book, *De architectura,* was basic to much Renaissance architectural theory. The reference is to *De architectura* I. 1. 10.]

whether it be in life or in picture. He can never be a great
artist, who is grossly illiterate.

Every man whose business is description, ought to be tolerably conversant with the poets, in some language or other;
that he may imbibe a poetical spirit, and enlarge his stock of
ideas. He ought to acquire an habit of comparing and digesting his notions. He ought not to be wholly unacquainted with
that part of philosophy which gives an insight into human
nature, and relates to the manners, characters, passions, and
affections. He ought to know *something* concerning the mind,
as well as *a great deal* concerning the body of man. For this
purpose, it is not necessary that he should go into such a compass of reading, as must, by distracting his attention, disqualify
him for the practical part of his profession, and make him
sink the performer in the critick. Reading, if it can be made
the favourite recreation of his leisure hours, will improve and
enlarge his mind, without retarding his actual industry. What
such partial and desultory reading cannot afford, may be
supplied by the conversation of learned and ingenious men,
which is the best of all substitutes for those who have not the
means or opportunities of deep study. There are many such
men in this age; and they will be pleased with communicating
their ideas to artists, when they see them curious and docile,
if they are treated with that respect and deference which is
so justly their due. Into such society, young artists, if they make
it the point of their ambition, will by degrees be admitted.
There, without formal teaching, they will insensibly come to
feel and reason like those they live with, and find a rational
and systematick taste imperceptibly formed in their minds,
which they will know how to reduce to a standard, by applying general truth to their own purposes, better perhaps than
those to whom they owed the original sentiment.

Of these studies, and this conversation, the desired and
legitimate offspring is a power of distinguishing right from
wrong; which power applied to works of art, is denominated
taste. Let me then, without further introduction, enter upon
an examination, whether taste be so far beyond our reach, as

to be unattainable by care; or be so very vague and capricious, that no care ought to be employed about it.

It has been the fate of arts to be enveloped in mysterious and incomprehensible language, as if it was thought necessary that even the terms should correspond to the idea entertained of the instability and uncertainty of the rules which they expressed.

To speak of genius and taste, as in any way connected with reason or common sense,[2] would be, in the opinion of some towering talkers, to speak like a man who possessed neither; who had never felt that enthusiasm, or, to use their own in-flated language, was never warmed by that Promethean fire, which animates the canvas and vivifies the marble.

If, in order to be intelligible, I appear to degrade art by bringing her down from her visionary situation in the clouds, it is only to give her a more solid mansion upon the earth. It is necessary that at some time or other we should see things as they really are, and not impose on ourselves by that false magnitude with which objects appear when viewed indistinctly as through a mist.

We will allow a poet to express his meaning, when his meaning is not well known to himself, with a certain degree of obscurity, as it is one source of the sublime. But when, in plain prose, we gravely talk of courting the muse in shady bowers; waiting the call and inspiration of genius, finding out where he inhabits, and where he is to be invoked with the greatest success; of attending to times and seasons when the imagination shoots with the greatest vigour, whether at the summer solstice or the vernal equinox; sagaciously observing how much the wild freedom and liberty of imagination is cramped by attention to established rules; and how this same imagination begins to grow dim in advanced age, smothered and deadened by too much judgment; when we talk such language, or entertain such sentiments as these, we generally rest contented with mere words or at best entertain notions not only groundless, but pernicious.

2 [For discussion of these terms, see Introduction, p. xxii.]

If all this means, what it is very possible was originally intended only to be meant, that in order to cultivate an art, a man secludes himself from the commerce of the world, and retires into the country at particular seasons; or that at one time of the year his body is in better health, and consequently his mind fitter for the business of hard thinking than at another time; or that the mind may be fatigued and grow confused by long and unremitted application; this I can understand. I can likewise believe, that a man eminent when young for possessing poetical imagination, may, from having taken another road, so neglect its cultivation, as to shew less of its powers in his latter life. But I am persuaded, that scarce a poet is to be found, from Homer down to Dryden, who preserved a sound mind in a sound body, and continued practising his profession to the very last, whose latter works are not as replete with the fire of imagination, as those which were produced in his more youthful days.

To understand literally these metaphors or ideas expressed in poetical language, seems to be equally absurd as to conclude, that because painters sometimes represent poets writing from the dictates of a little winged boy or genius, that this same genius did really inform him in a whisper what he was to write; and that he is himself but a mere machine, unconscious of the operations of his own mind.

Opinions generally received and floating in the world, whether true or false, we naturally adopt and make our own; they may be considered as a kind of inheritance to which we succeed and are tenants for life, and which we leave to our posterity very nearly in the condition in which we received it; it not being much in any one man's power either to impair or improve it. The greatest part of these opinions, like current coin in its circulation, we are used to take without weighing or examining; but by this inevitable inattention many adulterated pieces are received, which, when we seriously estimate our wealth, we must throw away. So the collector of popular opinions, when he embodies his knowledge, and forms a system, must separate those which are true from those which are only plausible. But it becomes more peculiarly a duty to the professors of art not to let any opinions relating to *that* art pass unexamined. The caution and circumspection required in such examination we shall presently have an opportunity of explaining.

Genius and taste, in their common acceptation, appear to be very nearly related; the difference lies only in this, that genius has super-added to it a habit of power of execution: or we may say, that taste, when this power is added, changes its name, and is called genius. They both, in the popular opinion, pretend to an entire exemption from the restraint of rules. It is supposed that their powers are intuitive; that under the name of genius great works are produced, and under the name of taste an exact judgment is given, without our knowing why, and without our being under the least obligation to reason, precept, or experience.

One can scarce state these opinions without exposing their absurdity; yet they are constantly in the mouths of men, and particularly of artists. They who have thought seriously on this subject, do not carry the point so far; yet I am persuaded, that even among those few who may be called thinkers, the prevalent opinion allows less than it ought to the powers of reason; and considers the principles of taste, which give all their authority to the rules of art, as more fluctuating, and as having less solid foundations, than we shall find, upon examination, they really have.

The common saying, that "tastes are not to be disputed," owes its influence, and its general reception, to the same error which leads us to imagine this faculty of too high an original to submit to the authority of an earthly tribunal. It likewise corresponds with the notions of those who consider it as a mere phantom of the imagination, so devoid of substance as to elude all criticism.

We often appear to differ in sentiments from each other, merely from the inaccuracy of terms, as we are not obliged to speak always with critical exactness. Something of this too may arise from want of words in the language in which we speak, to express the more nice discriminations which a deep investigation discovers. A great deal however of this difference vanishes, when each opinion is tolerably explained and understood by constancy and precision in the use of terms.

We apply the term *taste* to that act of the mind by which we like or dislike, whatever be the subject. Our judgment upon an airy nothing, a fancy which has no foundation, is called by the same name which we give to our determination concerning those truths which refer to the most general and most unalterable principles of human nature; to the works which are only to be produced by the greatest efforts of the human understanding, However inconvenient this may be, we are obliged to take words as we find them; all we can do is to distinguish the *things* to which they are applied.

We may let pass those things which are at once subjects of taste and sense, and which having as much certainty as the senses themselves, give no occasion to enquiry or dispute. The natural appetite or taste of the human mind is for *truth;* whether that truth results from the real agreement or equality of original ideas among themselves; from the agreement of the representation of any object with the thing represented; or from the correspondence of the several parts of any arrangement with each other. It is the very same taste which relishes a demonstration in geometry, that is pleased with the resemblance of a picture to an original, and touched with the harmony of musick.

All these have unalterable and fixed foundations in nature, and are therefore equally investigated by reason, and known by study; some with more, some with less clearness, but all exactly in the same way. A picture that is unlike, is false. Disproportionate ordonnance of parts is not right; because it cannot be true, until it ceases to be a contradiction to assert, that the parts have no relation to the whole. Colouring is true when it is naturally adapted to the eye, from brightness, from softness, from harmony, from resemblance; because these agree with their object, *nature,* and therefore are true; as true as mathematical demonstration; but known to be true only to those who study these things.

But beside *real,* there is also *apparent* truth, or opinion, or prejudice. With regard to real truth, when it is known, the taste which conforms to it, is, and must be, uniform. With regard to the second sort of truth, which may be called truth upon sufferance, or truth by courtesy, it is not fixed, but variable. However, whilst these opinions and prejudices, on which it is founded, continue, they operate as truth; and the art, whose office it is to please the mind, as well as instruct it, must direct itself according to *opinion,* or it will not attain its end.

In proportion as these prejudices are known to be generally diffused, or long received, the taste which conforms to them approaches nearer to certainty, and to a sort of resemblance to real science, even where opinions are found to be no better than prejudices. And since they deserve, on account of their duration and extent, to be considered as really true, they become capable of no small degree of stability and determination by their permanent and uniform nature.

As these prejudices become more narrow, more local, more transitory, this secondary taste becomes more and more fantastical; recedes from real science; is less to be approved by reason, and less followed in practice; though in no case perhaps to be wholly neglected, where it does not stand, as it sometimes does, in direct defiance of the most respectable opinions received amongst mankind.

Having laid down these positions, I shall proceed with less method, because less will serve, to explain and apply them.

We will take it for granted, that reason is something invariable and fixed in the nature of things; and without endeavouring to go back to an account of first principles, which for ever will elude our search, we will conclude, that whatever goes under the name of taste, which we can fairly bring under the dominion of reason, must be considered as equally exempt from change. If therefore, in the course of this enquiry, we can shew that there are rules for the conduct of the artist which are fixed and invariable, it follows of course, that the art of the connoisseur, or, in other words, taste, has likewise invariable principles.

Of the judgment which we make on the works of art, and the preference that we give to one class of art over another, if a reason be demanded, the question is perhaps evaded by answering, I judge from my taste; but it does not follow that a better answer cannot be given, though, for common gazers, this may be sufficient. Every man is not obliged to investigate the causes of his approbation or dislike.

The arts would lie open for ever to caprice and casualty, if those who are to judge of their excellencies had no settled principles by which they are to regulate their decisions, and the merit or defect of performances were to be determined by unguided fancy. And indeed we may venture to assert, that whatever speculative knowledge is necessary to the artist, is equally and indispensably necessary to the connoisseur.

The first idea that occurs in the consideration of what is fixed in art, or in taste, is that presiding principle of which I have so frequently spoken in former discourses,—the general idea of nature. The beginning, the middle, and the end of every thing that is valuable in taste, is comprised in the knowledge of what is truly nature; for whatever notions are not comformable to those of nature, or universal opinion, must be considered as more or less capricious.

My notion of nature comprehends not only the forms which nature produces, but also the nature and internal fabrick and organization, as I may call it, of the human mind and imagination. The terms beauty, or nature, which are general ideas, are but different modes of expressing the same thing, whether we apply these terms to statues, poetry, or picture. Deformity is not nature, but an accidental deviation from her accustomed practice. This general idea therefore ought to be called nature, and nothing else, correctly speaking, has a right to that name. But we are so far from speaking, in common conversation, with any such accuracy, that, on the contrary, when we criticise Rembrandt and other Dutch painters, who introduced into their historical pictures exact representations of individual objects with all their imperfections, we say,—though it is not in good taste, yet it is nature.

This misapplication of terms must be very often perplexing to the young student. Is not art, he may say, an imitation of nature? Must he not therefore who imitates her with the greatest fidelity, be the best artist? By this mode of reasoning Rembrandt has a higher place than Raffaelle. But a very little reflection will serve to shew us that these particularities cannot be nature: for how can that be the nature of man, in which no two individuals are the same?

It plainly appears, that as a work is conducted under the influence of general ideas, or partial, it is principally to be considered as the effect of a good or a bad taste.

As beauty therefore does not consist in taking what lies immediately before you, so neither, in our pursuit of taste, are those opinions which we first received and adopted, the best choice, or the most natural to the mind and imagination. In the infancy of our knowledge we seize with greediness the good that is within our reach; it is by after-consideration, and in consequence of discipline, that we refuse the present for a greater good at a distance. The nobility or elevation of all arts, like the excellency of virtue itself, consists in adopting this enlarged and comprehensive idea; and all criticism built upon the more confined view of what is natural, may properly be called *shallow* criticism, rather than false: its defect is, that the truth is not sufficiently extensive.

It has sometimes happened, that some of the greatest men in our art have been betrayed into errors by this confined mode of reasoning. Poussin, who, upon the whole, may be produced as an artist strictly attentive to the most enlarged and extensive ideas of nature, from not having settled principles on this point, has in one instance at least, I think, deserted truth for prejudice. He is said to have vindicated the conduct of Giulio Romano for his inattention to the masses of light and shade, or grouping the figures in "The Battle of Constantine," as if designedly neglected, the better to correspond with the hurry and confusion of a battle. Poussin's own conduct in many of his pictures, makes us more easily give credit to this report. That it was too much his own practice, "The Sacrifice to Silenus," and "The Triumph of Bacchus and Ariadne," [3] may be produced as instances; but this principle is still more apparent, and may be said to be even more ostentatiously displayed in his "Perseus" and "Medusa's Head." [4]

This is undoubtedly a subject of great bustle and tumult, and that the first effect of the picture may correspond to the subject, every principle of composition is violated; there is no principal figure, no principal light, no groups; every thing is dispersed, and in such a state of confusion that the eye finds no repose any where. In consequence of the forbidding appearance, I remember turning from it with disgust, and should not have looked a second time, if I had not been called back to a closer inspection. I then indeed found, what we may expect always to find in the works of Poussin, correct drawing, forcible expression, and just character; in short all the excellencies which so much distinguish the works of this learned painter.

This conduct of Poussin I hold to be entirely improper to imitate. A picture should please at first sight, and appear to invite the spectator's attention: if on the contrary the general effect offends the eye, a second view is not always sought, whatever more substantial and intrinsick merit it may possess.

Perhaps no apology ought to be received for offences committed against the vehicle (whether it be the organ of seeing, or of hearing,) by which our pleasures are conveyed to the mind. We must take care that the eye be not perplexed and distracted by a confusion of equal parts, or equal lights, or offended by an unharmonious mixture of colours, as we should guard against offending the ear by unharmonious sounds. We may venture to be more confident of the truth of this observation, since we find that Shakspeare, on a parallel

3 In the Cabinet of the Earl of Ashburnham.
4 In the Cabinet of Sir Peter Burrel.

occasion, has made Hamlet recommend to the players a precept of the same kind,—never to offend the ear by harsh sounds:
"In the very torrent, tempest, and whirlwind of your passion,"
says he, "you must acquire and beget a temperance that may
give it smoothness." And yet, at the same time, he very justly
observes, "The end of playing, both at the first, and now, was
and is, to hold, as 'twere, the mirrour up to nature." [5] No one
can deny, that violent passions will naturally emit harsh and
disagreeable tones: yet this great poet and critick thought that
this imitation of nature would cost too much, if purchased at
the expence of disagreeable sensations, or, as he expresses it,
of "splitting the ear." The poet and actor, as well as the painter
of genius who is well acquainted with all the variety and
sources of pleasure in the mind and imagination, has little
regard or attention to common nature, or creeping after common sense. By overleaping those narrow bounds, he more
effectually seizes the whole mind, and more powerfully accomplishes his purpose. This success is ignorantly imagined to
proceed from inattention to all rules, and a defiance of reason
and judgment; whereas it is in truth acting according to the
best rules and the justest reason.

He who thinks nature, in the narrow sense of the word, is
alone to be followed, will produce but a scanty entertainment
for the imagination: every thing is to be done with which it is
natural for the mind to be pleased, whether it proceeds from
simplicity or variety, uniformity or irregularity; whether the
scenes are familiar or exotick; rude and wild, or enriched and
cultivated; for it is natural for the mind to be pleased with all
these in their turn. In short, whatever pleases has in it what
is analogous to the mind, and is therefore, in the highest and
best sense of the word, natural.

It is the sense of nature or truth which ought more particularly to be cultivated by the professors of art; and it may be
observed, that many wise and learned men, who have accustomed their minds to admit nothing for truth but what can be
proved by mathematical demonstration, have seldom any

5 [*Hamlet*, III.ii.5–8, 22–24.]

relish for those arts which address themselves to the fancy, the rectitude and truth of which is known by another kind of proof: and we may add, that the acquisition of this knowledge requires as much circumspection and sagacity, as is necessary to attain those truths which are more capable of demonstration. Reason must ultimately determine our choice on every occasion; but this reason may still be exerted ineffectually by applying to taste principles which, though right as far as they go, yet do not reach the object. No man, for instance, can deny, that it seems at first view very reasonable, that a statue which is to carry down to posterity the resemblance of an individual, should be dressed in the fashion of the times, in the dress which he himself wore: this would certainly be true, if the dress were part of the man; but after a time, the dress is only an amusement for an antiquarian; and if it obstructs the general design of the piece, it is to be disregarded by the artist. Common sense must here give way to a higher sense. In the naked form, and in the disposition of the drapery, the difference between one artist and another is principally seen. But if he is compelled to exhibit the modern dress, the naked form is entirely hid, and the drapery is already disposed by the skill of the tailor. Were a Phidias to obey such absurd commands, he would please no more than an ordinary sculptor; since in the inferior parts of every art, the learned and the ignorant are nearly upon a level.

These were probably among the reasons that induced the sculptor of that wonderful figure of Laocoon to exhibit him naked, notwithstanding he was surprised in the act of sacrificing to Apollo, and consequently ought to have been shewn in his sacerdotal habits, if those greater reasons had not preponderated. Art is not yet in so high estimation with us, as to obtain so great a sacrifice as the ancients made, especially the Grecians; who suffered themselves to be represented naked, whether they were generals, lawgivers, or kings.

Under this head of balancing and choosing the greater reason, or of two evils taking the least, we may consider the conduct of Rubens in the Luxembourg gallery, where he has mixed allegorical figures with representations of real personages, which must be acknowledged to be a fault; yet, if the artist considered himself as engaged to furnish this gallery with a rich, various, and splendid ornament, this could not be done, at least in an equal degree, without peopling the air and water with these allegorical figures: he therefore accomplished all that he purposed. In this case all lesser considerations, which tend to obstruct the great end of the work, must yield and give way.

The variety which portraits and modern dresses, mixed with allegorical figures, produce, is not to be slightly given up upon a punctilio of reason, when that reason deprives the art in a manner of its very existence. It must always be remembered that the business of a great painter, is to produce a great picture, he must therefore take especial care not to be cajoled by specious arguments out of his materials.

What has been so often said to the disadvantage of allegorical poetry,—that it is tedious, and uninteresting,—cannot with the same propriety be applied to painting, where the interest is of a different kind. If allegorical painting produces a greater variety of ideal beauty, a richer, a more various and delightful composition, and gives to the artist a greater opportunity of exhibiting his skill, all the interest he wishes for is accomplished: such a picture not only attracts, but fixes the attention.

If it be objected that Rubens judged ill at first in thinking it necessary to make his work so very ornamental, this puts the question upon new ground. It was his peculiar style; he could paint in no other; and he was selected for that work, probably, because it was his style. Nobody will dispute but some of the best of the Roman and Bolognian schools would have produced a more learned and more noble work.

This leads us to another important province of taste, that of weighing the value of the different classes of the art, and of estimating them accordingly.

All arts have means within them of applying themselves with success both to the intellectual and sensitive part of our natures. It cannot be disputed, supposing both these means put in practice with equal abilities, to which we ought to give the preference; to him who represents the heroick arts and more dignified passions of man, or to him who, by the help of meretricious ornaments, however elegant and graceful, captivates the sensuality, as it may be called, of our taste. Thus the Roman and Bolognian schools are reasonably preferred to the Venetian, Flemish, or Dutch schools, as they address themselves to our best and noblest faculties.

Well-turned periods in eloquence, or harmony of numbers in poetry, which are in those arts what colouring is in painting, however highly we may esteem them, can never be considered as of equal importance with the art of unfolding truths that are useful to mankind, and which make us better or wiser. Nor can those works which remind us of the poverty and meanness of our nature, be considered as of equal rank with what excites ideas of grandeur, or raises and dignifies humanity; or, in the words of a late poet, which makes the beholder "learn to venerate himself as man." [6]

It is reason and good sense therefore which ranks and estimates every art, and every part of that art, according to its importance, from the painter of animated, down to inanimated nature. We will not allow a man, who shall prefer the inferior style, to say it is his taste; taste here has nothing, or at least ought to have nothing to do with the question. He wants not taste, but sense, and soundness of judgment.

Indeed perfection in an inferior style may be reasonably preferred to mediocrity in the highest walks of art. A landscape of Claude Lorrain may be preferred to a history by Luca Giordano; but hence appears the necessity of the connoisseur's knowing in what consists the excellency of each class, in order to judge how near it approaches perfection.

Even in works of the same kind, as in history-painting, which is composed of various parts, excellence of an inferior species, carried to a very high degree, will make a work very valuable, and in some measure compensate for the absence of the higher kinds of merit. It is the duty of the connois-

---

[6] Dr. Goldsmith ["The Traveller," 334].

seur to know and esteem, as much as it may deserve, every
part of painting: he will not then think even Bassano unworthy of his notice; who, though totally devoid of expression, sense, grace, or elegance, may be esteemed on account
of his admirable taste of colours, which, in his best works,
are little inferior to those of Titian.

Since I have mentioned Bassano, we must do him likewise
the justice to acknowledge, that though he did not aspire to
the dignity of expressing the characters and passions of men,
yet, with respect to facility and truth in his manner of
touching animals of all kinds, and giving them what painters
call *their character*, few have ever excelled him.

To Bassano we may add Paul Veronese and Tintoret,[7] for
their entire inattention to what is justly thought the most
essential part of our art, the expression of the passions.
Notwithstanding these glaring deficiencies, we justly esteem
their works; but it must be remembered, that they do not
please from those defects, but from their great excellencies
of another kind, and in spite of such transgressions. These
excellencies too, as far as they go, are founded in the truth
of *general* nature: they tell the *truth,* though not *the whole
truth.*

By these considerations, which can never be too frequently impressed, may be obviated two errors which I observed to have been, formerly at least, the most prevalent,
and to be most injurious to artists; that of thinking taste and
genius to have nothing to do with reason, and that of taking
particular living objects for nature.

I shall now say something on that part of *taste,* which, as
I have hinted to you before, does not belong so much to the
external form of things, but is addressed to the mind, and depends on its original frame, or, to use the expression, the
organization of the soul; I mean the imagination and the passions. The principles of these are as invariable as the former, and are to be known and reasoned upon in the same
manner, by an appeal to common sense deciding upon the

---

[7] [See illustrations, Tintoretto's "The Way to Golgotha."]

common feelings of mankind. This sense, and these feelings, appear to me of equal authority, and equally conclusive. Now this appeal implies a general uniformity and agreement in the minds of men. It would be else an idle and vain endeavour to establish rules of art; it would be pursuing a phantom to attempt to move affections with which we were entirely unacquainted. We have no reason to suspect there is a greater difference between our minds than between our forms; of which, though there are no two alike, yet there is a general similitude that goes through the whole race of mankind; and those who have cultivated their taste can distinguish what is beautiful or deformed, or, in other words, what agrees with or deviates from the general idea of nature, in one case, as well as in the other.

The internal fabrick of our minds, as well as the external form of our bodies, being nearly uniform; it seems then to follow of course, that as the imagination is incapable of producing any thing originally of itself, and can only vary and combine those ideas with which it is furnished by means of the senses,[8] there will be necessarily an agreement in the imaginations as in the senses of men. There being this agreement, it follows, that in all cases, in our lightest amusements, as well as in our most serious actions and engagements of life, we must regulate our affections of every kind by that of others. The well-disciplined mind acknowledges this authority, and submits its own opinion to the publick voice. It is from knowing what are the general feelings and passions of mankind, that we acquire a true idea of what imagination is; though it appears as if we had nothing to do but to consult our own particular sensations, and these were sufficient to ensure us from all error and mistake.

A knowledge of the disposition and character of the human mind can be acquired only by experience: a great deal will be learned, I admit, by a habit of examining what passes

[8] [Reynolds' psychology here is that of John Locke, who postulated that all mental activity depends upon sense impression and memory of sense impression.]

in our bosoms, what are our own motives of action, and of what kind of sentiments we are conscious on any occasion. We may suppose an uniformity, and conclude that the same effect will be produced by the same cause in the minds of others. This examination will contribute to suggest to us matters of enquiry; but we can never be sure that our own sensations are true and right, till they are confirmed by more extensive observation. One man opposing another determines nothing; but a general union of minds, like a general combination of the forces of all mankind, makes a strength that is irresistible. In fact, as he who does not know himself does not know others, so it may be said with equal truth, that he who does not know others, knows himself but very imperfectly.

A man who thinks he is guarding himself against prejudices by resisting the authority of others, leaves open every avenue to singularity, vanity, self-conceit, obstinacy, and many other vices, all tending to warp the judgment, and prevent the natural operation of his faculties. This submission to others is a deference which we owe, and indeed are forced involuntarily to pay. In fact, we never are satisfied with our opinions, whatever we may pretend, till they are ratified and confirmed by the suffrages of the rest of mankind. We dispute and wrangle for ever; we endeavour to get men to come to us, when we do not go to them.

He therefore who is acquainted with the works which have pleased different ages and different countries, and has formed his opinion on them, has more materials, and more means of knowing what is analogous to the mind of man, than he who is conversant only with the works of his own age or country. What has pleased, and continues to please, is likely to please again: hence are derived the rules of art, and on this immovable foundation they must ever stand.

This search and study of the history of the mind ought not to be confined to one art only. It is by the analogy that one art bears to another, that many things are ascertained, which either were but faintly seen, or, perhaps, would not have been discovered at all, if the inventor had not received the first hints from the practices of a sister art on a similar occasion.[9] The frequent allusions which every man who treats of any art is obliged to make to others in order to illustrate and confirm his principles, sufficiently shew their near connexion and inseparable relation.

All arts having the same general end, which is to please; and addressing themselves to the same faculties through the medium of the senses; it follows that their rules and principles must have as great affinity as the different materials and the different organs or vehicles by which they pass to the mind, will permit them to retain.[10]

We may therefore conclude, that the real substance, as it may be called, of what goes under the name of taste, is fixed and established in the nature of things; that there are certain and regular causes by which the imagination and passions of men are affected; and that the knowledge of these causes is acquired by a laborious and diligent investigation of nature, and by the same slow progress as wisdom or knowledge of every kind, however instantaneous its operations may appear, when thus acquired.

It has been often observed, that the good and virtuous man alone can acquire this true or just relish even of works of art. This opinion will not appear entirely without foundation, when we consider that the same habit of mind which is acquired by our search after truth in the more serious duties of life, is only transferred to the pursuit of lighter amusements. The same disposition, the same desire to find something steady, substantial, and durable, on which the mind can lean as it were, and rest with safety, actuates us in both cases. The

[9] Nulla ars, non alterius artis, aut mater, aut propinqua est. Tertull, as cited by Junius.

[10] Omnes artes quae ad humanitaten pertinent, habent quoddam commune vinculum, et quasi cognatione inter se continentur. Cicero.

subject only is changed. We pursue the same method in our search after the idea of beauty and perfection in each; of virtue, by looking forwards beyond ourselves to society, and to the whole; of arts, by extending our views in the same manner to all ages and all times.

Every art, like our own, has in its composition fluctuating as well as fixed principles. It is an attentive enquiry into their difference that will enable us to determine how far we are influenced by custom and habit, and what is fixed in the nature of things.

To distinguish how much has solid foundation, we may have recourse to the same proof by which some hold that wit ought to be tried; whether it preserves itself when translated. That wit is false, which can subsist only in one language; and that picture which pleases only one age or one nation, owes its reception to some local or accidental association of ideas.

We may apply this to every custom and habit of life. Thus the general principles of urbanity, politeness, or civility, have been ever the same in all nations; but the mode in which they are dressed, is continually varying. The general idea of shewing respect is by making yourself less; but the manner, whether by bowing the body, kneeling, prostration, pulling off the upper part of our dress, or taking away the lower,[11] is a matter of custom.

Thus in regard to ornaments, it would be unjust to conclude that because they were at first arbitrarily contrived, they are therefore undeserving of our attention; on the contrary, he who neglects the cultivation of those ornaments, acts contrary to nature and reason. As life would be imperfect without its highest ornaments, the arts, so these arts themselves would be imperfect without *their* ornaments. Though we by no means ought to rank these with positive and substantial beauties, yet it must be allowed that a knowledge of both is essentially requisite towards forming a complete, whole, and perfect taste. It is in reality from the ornaments that arts receive their

11 Put off thy shoes from off thy feet; for the place whereon thou standest is holy ground. Exodus, iii. 5.

peculiar character and complexion; we may add, that in them we find the characteristical mark of a national taste; as by throwing up a feather in the air, we know which way the wind blows, better than by a more heavy matter.

The striking distinction between the works of the Roman, Bolognian, and Venetian schools, consists more in that general effect which is produced by colours, than in the more profound excellencies of the art; at least it is from thence that each is distinguished and known at first sight. Thus it is the ornaments, rather than the proportions of architecture, which at the first glance distinguish the different orders from each other; the Dorick is known by its triglyphs, the Ionick by its volutes, and the Corinthian by its acanthus.

What distinguishes oratory from a cold narration, is a more liberal, though chaste, use of those ornaments which go under the name of figurative and metaphorical expressions; and poetry distinguishes itself from oratory by words and expressions still more ardent and glowing. What separates and distinguishes poetry, is more particularly the ornament of *verse:* it is this which gives it its character, and is an essential without which it cannot exist. Custom has appropriated different metre to different kinds of composition, in which the world is not perfectly agreed. In England the dispute is not yet settled, which is to be preferred, rhyme or blank verse. But however we disagree about what these metrical ornaments shall be, that some metre is essentially necessary, is universally acknowledged.

In poetry or eloquence, to determine how far figurative or metaphorical language may proceed, and when it begins to be affectation or beside the truth, must be determined by taste; though this taste, we must never forget, is regulated and formed by the presiding feelings of mankind, by those works which have approved themselves to all times and all persons. Thus, though eloquence has undoubtedly an essential and intrinsick excellence, and immoveable principles common to all languages, founded in the nature of our passions and affections; yet it has its ornaments and modes of address, which are merely arbitrary. What is approved in the eastern nations as grand and majestick, would be considered by the Greeks and Romans as turgid and inflated; and they, in return, would be thought by the Orientals to express themselves in a cold and insipid manner.[12]

We may add likewise to the credit of ornaments, that it is by their means that art itself accomplishes its purpose. Fresnoy calls colouring, which is one of the chief ornaments of painting, *lena sororis*,[13] that which procures lovers and admirers to the more valuable excellencies of the art.

It appears to be the same right turn of mind which enables a man to acquire the *truth,* or the just idea of what is right, in the ornaments, as in the more stable principles of art. It has still the same centre of perfection, though it is the centre of a smaller circle.

To illustrate this by the fashion of dress, in which there is allowed to be a good or bad taste. The component parts of dress are continually changing from great to little, from short to long; but the general form still remains: it is still the same general dress which is comparatively fixed, though on a very slender foundation; but it is on this which fashion must rest. He who invents with the most success, or dresses in the best taste, would probably, from the same sagacity employed to greater purposes, have discovered equal skill, or have formed the same correct taste, in the highest labours of art.

I have mentioned taste in dress, which is certainly one of the lowest subjects to which this word is applied; yet, as I have before observed, there is a right even here, however narrow its foundation respecting the fashion of any particular nation. But we have still more slender means of determining, to which of the different customs of different ages or countries

12 [In these two paragraphs, Reynolds is indulging his taste for literary parallels or examples (cf. Discourse 13, p. 197). The best statement contemporary with Reynolds on poetry and allied subjects is Pope's *Essay on Criticism*.]

13 ["Seductive sister" (Charles Alphonse du Fresnoy, *De Arte Graphica* [London, 1695], 1, 263).]

we ought to give the preference, since they seem to be all equally removed from nature. If an European, when he has cut off his beard, and put false hair on his head, or bound up his own natural hair in regular hard knots, as unlike nature as he can possibly make it; and after having rendered them immoveable by the help of the fat of hogs, has covered the whole with flour, laid on by a machine with the utmost regularity; if, when thus attired he issues forth, and meets a Cherokee Indian, who has bestowed as much time at his toilet, and laid on with equal care and attention his yellow and red oker on particular parts of his forehead or cheeks; as he judges most becoming; whoever of these two despises the other for this attention to the fashion of his country, which ever first feels himself provoked to laugh, is the barbarian.

All these fashions are very innocent; neither worth disquisition, nor any endeavour to alter them; as the change would, in all probability, be equally distant from nature. The only circumstances against which indignation may reasonably be moved, is where the operation is painful or destructive of health, such as some of the practices at Otaheite, and the straight lacing of the English ladies; of the last of which practices, how destructive it must be to health and long life, the professor of anatomy took an opportunity of proving a few days since in this Academy.

It is in dress as in things of greater consequence. Fashions originate from those only who have the high and powerful advantages of rank, birth, and fortune. Many of the ornaments of art, those at least for which no reason can be given, are transmitted to us, are adopted, and acquire their consequence from the company in which we have been used to see them. As Greece and Rome are the fountains from whence have flowed all kinds of excellence, to that veneration which they have a right to claim for the pleasure and knowledge which they have afforded us, we voluntarily add our approbation of every ornament and every custom that belonged to them, even to the fashion of their dress. For it may be observed that, not satisfied with them in their own place, we make no difficulty of dressing statues of modern heroes or senators in the fashion of the Roman armour or peaceful robe; we go so far as hardly to bear a statue in any other drapery.

The figures of the great men of those nations have come down to us in sculpture. In sculpture remain almost all the excellent specimens of ancient art. We have so far associated personal dignity to the persons thus represented, and the truth of art to their manner of representation, that it is not in our power any longer to separate them. This is not so in painting; because having no excellent ancient portraits, that connexion was never formed. Indeed we could no more venture to paint a general officer in a Roman military habit, than we could make a statue in the present uniform. But since we have no ancient portraits,—to shew how ready we are to adopt those kind of prejudices, we make the best authority among the moderns serve the same purpose. The great variety of excellent portraits with which Vandyck has enriched this nation, we are not content to admire for their real excellence, but extend our approbation even to the dress which happened to be the fashion of that age. We all very well remember how common it was a few years ago for portraits to be drawn in this fantastick dress, and this custom is not yet entirely laid aside. By this means it must be acknowledged very ordinary pictures acquired something of the air and effect of the works of Vandyck, and appeared therefore at first sight to be better pictures than they really were; they appeared so, however, to those only who had the means of making this association; and when made, it was irresistible. But this association is nature, and refers to that secondary truth that comes from conformity to general prejudice and opinion; it is therefore not merely fantastical. Besides the prejudice which we have in favour of ancient dresses, there may be likewise other reasons for the effect which they produce; among which we may justly rank the simplicity of them, consisting of little more than one single piece of drapery, without those whimsical capricious forms by which all other dresses are embarrassed.

Thus, though it is from the prejudice we have in favour of the ancients, who have taught us architecture, that we have adopted likewise their ornaments; and though we are satisfied that neither nature nor reason are the foundation of those beauties which we imagine we see in that art, yet if any one, persuaded of this truth, should therefore invent new orders of equal beauty, which we will suppose to be possible, they would not please; nor ought he to complain, since the old has that great advantage of having custom and prejudice on its side. In this case we leave what has every prejudice in its favour, to take that which will have no advantage over what we have left, but novelty; which soon destroys itself, and at any rate is but a weak antagonist against custom.

Ancient ornaments, having the right of possession, ought not to be removed, unless to make room for that which not only has higher pretensions, but such pretensions as will balance the evil and confusion which innovation always brings with it.

To this we may add, that even the durability of the materials will often contribute to give a superiority to one object over another. Ornaments in buildings, with which taste is principally concerned, are composed of materials which last longer than those of which dress is composed; the former therefore make higher pretensions to our favour and prejudice.

Some attention is surely due to what we can no more get rid of than we can go out of ourselves. We are creatures of prejudice; we neither can nor ought to eradicate it; we must only regulate it by reason; which kind of regulation is indeed little more than obliging the lesser, the local and temporary prejudices, to give way to those which are more durable and lasting.

He therefore who in his practice of portrait-painting wishes to dignify his subject, which we will suppose to be a lady, will not paint her in the modern dress, the familiarity of which alone is sufficient to destroy all dignity. He takes care that his work shall correspond to those ideas and that imagination which he knows will regulate the judgment of others; and therefore dresses his figure something with the general air of the antique for the sake of dignity, and preserves something of the modern for the sake of likeness. By this conduct his works correspond with those prejudices which we have in favour of what we continually see; and the relish of the antique simplicity corresponds with what we may call the more learned and scientifick prejudice.

There was a statue made not long since of Voltaire, which the sculptor, not having that respect for the prejudices of mankind which he ought to have had, made entirely naked, and as meagre and emaciated as the original is said to be. The consequence was what might have been expected; it remained in the sculptor's shop, though it was intended as a publick ornament and a publick honour to Voltaire, for it was procured at the expence of his contemporary wits and admirers.

Whoever would reform a nation, supposing a bad taste to prevail in it, will not accomplish his purpose by going directly against the stream of their prejudices. Men's minds must be prepared to receive what is new to them. Reformation is a work of time. A national taste, however wrong it may be, cannot be totally changed at once; we must yield a little to the prepossession which has taken hold on the mind, and we may then bring people to adopt what would offend them, if endeavoured to be introduced by violence. When Battista Franco was employed, in conjunction with Titian, Paul Veronese and Tintoret, to adorn the library of St. Mark, his work, Vasari says,[14] gave less satisfaction than any of the others: the dry manner of the Roman school was very ill calculated to please eyes that had been accustomed to the luxuriancy, splendour, and richness of Venetian colouring. Had the Romans been the judges of this work, probably the determination would have been just contrary; for in the more noble parts of the art, Battista Franco was perhaps not inferior to any of his rivals.

GENTLEMEN,

It has been the main scope and principal end of this discourse to demonstrate the reality of a standard in taste, as well as in

14 [This passage can be found in Volume V, p. 48, of Mrs. Foster's translation of Vasari: see note 10, p. 49.]

corporeal beauty; that a false or depraved taste is a thing as well known, as easily discovered, as any thing that is deformed, mis-shapen, or wrong, in our form and outward make; and that this knowledge is derived from the uniformity of sentiments among mankind, from whence proceeds the knowledge of what are the general habits of nature; the result of which is an idea of perfect beauty.

If what has been advanced be true, that beside this beauty or truth, which is formed on the uniform, eternal and immutable laws of nature, and which of necessity can be but *one;* that beside this one immutable verity there are likewise what we have called apparent or secondary truths, proceeding from local and temporary prejudices, fancies, fashions, or accidental connexion of ideas; if it appears that these last have still their foundation, however slender, in the original fabrick of our minds; it follows that all these truths or beauties deserve and require the attention of this artist, in proportion to their stability or duration, or as their influence is more or less extensive. And let me add, that as they ought not to pass their just bounds, so neither do they, in a well-regulated taste, at all prevent or weaken the influence of those general principles, which alone can give to art its true and permanent dignity.

To form this just taste is undoubtedly in your own power, but it is to reason and philosophy that you must have recourse; from them you must borrow the balance by which is to be weighed and estimated the value of every pretension that intrudes itself on your notice.

The general objection which is made to the introduction of philosophy into the regions of taste, is, that it checks and restrains the flights of the imagination, and gives that timidity which an over-carefulness not to err or act contrary to reason is likely to produce. It is not so. Fear is neither reason nor philosophy. The true spirit of philosophy, by giving knowledge, gives a manly confidence, and substitutes rational firmness in the place of vain presumption. A man of real taste is always a man of judgment in other respects; and those inventions which either disdain or shrink from reason, are gen-

erally, I fear, more like the dreams of a distempered brain
than the exalted enthusiasm of a sound and true genius. In
the midst of the highest flights of fancy or imagination, reason
ought to preside from first to last, though I admit her more
powerful operation is upon reflection.

Let me add, that some of the greatest names of antiquity,
and those who have most distinguished themselves in works of
genius and imagination, were equally eminent for their critical
skill. Plato, Aristotle, Cicero, and Horace; and among the
moderns, Boileau, Corneille, Pope, and Dryden, are at least
instances of genius not being destroyed by attention or subjection to rules and science. I should hope therefore, that the
natural consequence of what has been said, would be, to excite in you a desire of knowing the principles and conduct of
the great masters of our art, and respect and veneration for
them when known.

~❦ Discourse 8

December 10, 1778

GENTLEMEN,

I HAVE recommended, in former discourses,[1] that artists should learn their profession by endeavouring to form an idea of perfection from the different excellencies which lie dispersed in the various schools of painting. Some difficulty will still occur, to know what is beauty, and where it may be found: one would wish not to be obliged to take it entirely on the credit of fame; though to this, I acknowledge, the younger students must unavoidably submit. Any suspicion in them of the chance of their being deceived, will have more tendency to obstruct their advancement, than even an enthusiastick confidence in the perfection of their models. But to the more advanced in the art, who wish to stand on more stable and firmer ground, and to establish principles on a stronger foundation than authority, however venerable or powerful, it may be safely told, that there is still a higher tribunal, to which those great masters themselves must submit, and to which indeed every excellence in art must be ultimately referred. He who is ambitious to enlarge the boundaries of his art, must extend his views, beyond the precepts which are found in books or may be drawn from the practice of his predecessors, to a knowledge of those precepts in the mind, those operations of intellectual nature,—to which every thing that aspires to please, must be proportioned and accommodated.

[1] Discourses 2 and 6.

119

ₒetry having a more extensive power than our art,[2] exerts
s influence over almost all the passions; among those may be
reckoned one of our most prevalent dispositions, anxiety for
the future. Poetry operates by raising our curiosity, engaging
the mind by degrees to take an interest in the event, keeping
that event suspended, and surprising at last with an unexpected catastrophe.

The painter's art is more confined, and has nothing that
corresponds with, or perhaps is equivalent to, this power and
advantage of leading the mind on, till attention is totally engaged. What is done by painting, must be done at one blow;
curiosity has received at once all the satisfaction it can ever
have. There are, however, other intellectual qualities and
dispositions which the painter can satisfy and affect as powerfully as the poet; among those we may reckon our love of
novelty, variety, and contrast; these qualities, on examination,
will be found to refer to a certain activity and restlessness,
which has a pleasure and delight in being exercised and put in
motion: Art therefore only administers to those wants and
desires of the mind.

It requires no long disquisition to shew, that the dispositions which I have stated actually subsist in the human mind.
Variety reanimates the attention, which is apt to languish
under a continual sameness. Novelty makes a more forcible
impression on the mind, than can be made by the representation of what we have often seen before; and contrasts rouse
the power of comparison by opposition. All this is obvious;
but, on the other hand, it must be remembered, that the mind,
though an active principle,[3] has likewise a disposition to indolence; and though it loves exercise, loves it only to a cer-

2 [For a discussion of the comparisons between poetry and painting
which occurred in the eighteenth century, see Introduction, p. xxii.]

3 ["Active principle": this is a continuation of Reynolds' use of Locke's
psychology in which the mind is an active agent in the creation of new
ideas, using sensory impressions as initial data. A portion of this activity
is dependent on the "association of ideas," a term first coined by Locke.]

tain degree, beyond which it is very unwilling to be led, or driven; the pursuit therefore of novelty and variety may be carried to excess. When variety entirely destroys the pleasure proceeding from uniformity and repetition, and when novelty counteracts and shuts out the pleasure arising from old habits and customs, they oppose too much the indolence of our disposition: the mind therefore can bear with pleasure but a small portion of novelty at a time. The main part of the work must be in the mode to which we have been used. An affection to old habits and customs I take to be the predominant disposition of the mind, and novelty comes as an exception: where all is novelty, the attention, the exercise of the mind is too violent. Contrast, in the same manner, when it exceeds certain limits, is as disagreeable as a violent and perpetual opposition; it gives to the senses, in their progress, a more sudden change than they can bear with pleasure.

It is then apparent, that those qualities, however they contribute to the perfection of art, when kept within certain bounds, if they are carried to excess, become defects, and require correction: a work consequently will not proceed better and better as it is more varied; variety can never be the groundwork and principle of the performance, it must be only employed to recreate and relieve.

To apply these general observations which belong equally to all arts, to ours in particular. In a composition, when the objects are scattered and divided into many equal parts, the eye is perplexed and fatigued, from not knowing where to rest, where to find the principal action, or which is the principal figure; for where all are making equal pretensions to notice, all are in equal danger of neglect.

The expression which is used very often on these occasions is, the piece wants *repose;* a word which perfectly expresses a relief of the mind from that state of hurry and anxiety which it suffers, when looking at a work of this character.

On the other hand, absolute unity, that is, a large work, consisting of one group or mass of light only, would be as de-

fective as an heroick poem without episode, or any collateral
incidents to recreate the mind with that variety which it always
requires.

An instance occurs to me of two painters, (Rembrandt and
Poussin,) of characters totally opposite to each other in every
respect, but in nothing more than in their mode of composition, and management of light and shadow. Rembrandt's
manner is absolute unity; he often has but one group, and
exhibits little more than one spot of light in the midst of a
large quantity of shadow; if he has a second mass, that
second bears no proportion to the principal. Poussin, on the
contrary, has scarce any principal mass of light at all, and his
figures are often too much dispersed, without sufficient attention to place them in groups.

The conduct of these two painters is entirely the reverse of
what might be expected from their general style and character; the works of Poussin being as much distinguished for
simplicity, as those of Rembrandt for combination. Even this
conduct of Poussin might proceed from too great an affection
to simplicity of *another kind;* to great a desire to avoid that
ostentation of art, with regard to light and shadow, on which
Rembrandt so much wished to draw the attention: however,
each of them ran into contrary extremes, and it is difficult to
determine which is the most reprehensible, both being equally
distant from the demands of nature, and the purposes of art.

The same just moderation must be observed in regard to
ornaments; nothing will contribute more to destroy repose
than profusion, of whatever kind, whether it consists in the
multiplicity of objects, or the variety and brightness of colours.
On the other hand, a work without ornament, instead of simplicity, to which it makes pretensions, has rather the appearance of poverty. The degree to which ornaments are
admissible, must be regulated by the professed style of the
work; but we may be sure of this truth,—that the most ornamental style requires repose to set off even its ornaments to
advantage. I cannot avoid mentioning here an instance of repose in that faithful and accurate painter of nature, Shak-

speare; the short dialogue between Duncan and Banquo, whilst they are approaching the gates of Macbeth's castle. Their conversation very naturally turns upon the beauty of its situation, and the pleasantness of the air; and Banquo observing the martlets' nests in every recess of the cornice, remarks, that where those birds most breed and haunt, the air is delicate.[4] The subject of this quiet and easy conversation gives that repose so necessary to the mind, after the tumultuous bustle of the preceding scenes, and perfectly contrasts the scene of horrour that immediately succeeds. It seems as if Shakspeare asked himself, What is a Prince likely to say to his attendants on such an occasion? The modern writers seem, on the contrary, to be always searching for new thoughts, such as never could occur to men in the situation represented. This is also frequently the practice of Homer, who, from the midst of battles and horrours, relieves and refreshes the mind of the reader, by introducing some quiet rural image, or picture of familiar domestick life. The writers of every age and country, where taste has begun to decline, paint and adorn every object they touch; are always on the stretch; never deviate or sink a moment from the pompous and the brilliant. Lucan, Statius, and Claudian, (as a learned critick [5] has observed,) are examples of this bad taste and want of judgment; they never soften their tones, or condescend to be natural: all is exaggeration and perpetual splendour, without affording repose of any kind.

As we are speaking of excesses, it will not be remote from our purpose to say a few words upon simplicity; which, in one of the senses in which it is used, is considered as the general corrector of excess. We shall at present forbear to consider it as implying that exact conduct which proceeds from an intimate knowledge of simple unadulterated nature, as it is then only another word for perfection, which neither stops short of, nor oversteps, reality and truth.

In our enquiry after simplicity, as in many other enquiries

4 [Macbeth, I.vi.1–9.]

5 [This "learned critick" has never been identified.]

of this nature, we can best explain what is right, by shewing what is wrong; and, indeed, in this case it seems to be absolutely necessary: simplicity, being only a negative virtue, cannot be described or defined. We must therefore explain its nature, and shew the advantage and beauty which is derived from it, by shewing the deformity which proceeds from its neglect.

Though instances of this neglect might be expected to be found in practice, we should not expect to find in the works of criticks, precepts that bid defiance to simplicity and every thing that relates to it. Du Piles recommends to us portrait-painters, to add grace and dignity to the characters of those, whose pictures we draw: so far he is undoubtedly right; but, unluckily, he descends to particulars, and gives his own idea of grace and dignity. "If," says he, "you draw persons of high character and dignity, they ought to be drawn in such an attitude, that the portrait must seem to speak to us of themselves, and, as it were, to say to us, 'stop, take notice of me, I am that invincible King, surrounded by Majesty': 'I am that valiant commander, who struck terrour everywhere': 'I am that great minister who knew all the springs of politicks': 'I am that magistrate of consummate wisdom and probity.' "[6] He goes on in this manner, with all the characters he can think on. We may contrast the tumour of this presumptuous loftiness with the natural unaffected air of the portraits of Titian, where dignity seeming to be natural and inherent, draws spontaneous reverence, and instead of being thus vainly assumed, has the appearance of an unalienable adjunct; whereas such pompous and laboured insolence of grandeur is so far from creating respect, that it betrays vulgarity and meanness, and new-acquired consequence.

The painters, many of them at least, have not been backward in adopting the notions contained in these precepts. The portraits of Rigaud are perfect examples of an implicit observance of these rules of Du Piles; so that though he was a painter of great merit in many respects, yet, that merit is

[6] [Roger de Piles, *The Principles of Painting* (London, 1743), p. 169.]

entirely over-powered by a total absence of simplicity in every sense.

Not to multiply instances, which might be produced for this purpose, from the works of history-painters, I shall mention only one,—a picture which I have seen, of the Supreme Being, by Coypell.[7]

This subject the Roman Catholick painters have taken the liberty to represent, however indecent the attempt, and however obvious the impossibility of any approach to an adequate representation: but here the air and character, which the painter has given, and he has doubtless given the highest he could conceive, are so degraded by an attempt at such dignity as Du Piles has recommended, that we are enraged at the folly and presumption of the artist, and consider it as little less than profanation.

As we have passed to a neighbouring nation for instances of want of this quality, we must acknowledge, at the same time, that they have produced great examples of simplicity in Poussin and Le Sueur. But as we are speaking of the most refined and subtle notion of perfection, may we not enquire, whether a curious eye cannot discern some faults, even in those great men? I can fancy, that even Poussin, by abhorring that affectation and that want of simplicity, which he observed in his countrymen, has, in certain particulars, fallen into the contrary extreme, so far as to approach to a kind of affectation,—to what, in writing, would be called pedantry.

When simplicity, instead of being a corrector, seems to set up for herself; that is, when an artist seems to value himself solely upon this quality; such an ostentatious display of simplicity becomes then as disagreeable and nauseous as any other kind of affectation. He is however, in this case, likely enough to sit down contented with his own work; for though he finds the world look at it with indifference or dislike, as being destitute of every quality that can recreate or give pleasure to the mind, yet he consoles himself, that it has simplicity, a beauty of too pure and chaste a nature to be relished by vulgar minds.

[7] [Antoine Coypel, born 1694 in Paris; died 1722. See illustrations.]

It is in art as in morals: no character would inspire us with an enthusiastick admiration of his virtue, if that virtue consisted only in an absence of vice; something more is required; a man must do more than merely his duty, to be a hero.

Those works of the ancients, which are in the highest esteem, have something beside mere simplicity to recommend them. The "Apollo," the "Venus," the "Laocoon," the "Gladiator," have a certain composition of action, have contrasts sufficient to give grace and energy in a high degree; but it must be confessed of the many thousand antique statues which we have, that their general characteristick is bordering at least on inanimate insipidity.

Simplicity, when so very inartificial as to seem to evade the difficulties of art, is a very suspicious virtue.

I do not, however, wish to degrade simplicity from the high estimation in which it has been justly held. It is our barrier against that great enemy to truth and nature, Affectation, which is ever clinging to the pencil, and ready to drop in and poison every thing it touches.

Our love and affection to simplicity proceeds in a great measure from our aversion to every kind of affectation. There is likewise another reason why so much stress is laid upon this virtue; the propensity which artists have to fall into the contrary extreme: we therefore set a guard on that side which is most assailable. When a young artist is first told that his composition and his attitudes must be contrasted, that he must turn the head contrary to the position of the body, in order to produce grace and animation; that his outline must be undulating, and swelling, to give grandeur; and that the eye must be gratified with a variety of colours;—when he is told this, with certain animating words, of spirit, dignity, energy, grace, greatness of style, and brilliancy of tints, he becomes suddenly vain of his newly acquired knowledge, and never thinks he can carry those rules too far. It is then that the aid of simplicity ought to be called in, to correct the exuberance of youthful ardour.

The same may be said in regard to colouring, which in its

pre-eminence is particularly applied to flesh. An artist in his
first essay of imitating nature, would make the whole mass of
one colour, as the oldest painters did; till he is taught to observe not only the variety of tints, which are in the object itself, but the differences produced by the gradual decline of
light to shadow: he then immediately puts his instruction in
practice, and introduces a variety of distinct colours. He must
then be again corrected, and told, that though there is this
variety, yet the effect of the whole upon the eye must have
the union and simplicity of the colouring of nature.

And here we may observe, that the progress of an individual student bears a great resemblance to the progress and
advancement of the art itself. Want of simplicity would probably be not one of the defects of an artist who had studied
nature only, as it was not of the old masters, who lived in the
time preceding the great art of painting; on the contrary,
their works are too simple and too inartificial.

The art in its infancy, like the first work of a student, was
dry, hard, and simple. But this kind of barbarous simplicity,
would be better named penury, as it proceeds from mere want;
from want of knowledge, want of resources, want of abilities
to be otherwise: their simplicity was the offspring not of
choice, but necessity.

In the second stage they were sensible of this poverty, and
those who were the most sensible of the want, were the best
judges of the measure of the supply. There were painters
who emerged from poverty without falling into luxury. Their
success induced others, who probably never would of themselves have had strength of mind to discover the original defect, to endeavour at the remedy by an abuse; and they ran
into the contrary extreme. But however they may have
strayed, we cannot recommend to them to return to that simplicity which they have justly quitted; but to deal out their
abundance with a more sparing hand, with that dignity which
makes no parade, either of its riches, or of its art. It is not
easy to give a rule which may serve to fix this just and correct
medium; because, when we may have fixed, or nearly fixed, the

middle point, taken as a general principle, circumstances may
oblige us to depart from it, either on the side of simplicity, or
on that of variety and decoration.

I thought it necessary in a former discourse, speaking of
the difference of the sublime and ornamental style of painting,
—in order to excite your attention to the more manly, noble,
and dignified manner, to leave perhaps an impression too con-
temptuous of those ornamental parts of our art, for which
many have valued themselves, and many works are much
valued and esteemed.

I said then, what I thought it was right at that time to say;
I supposed the disposition of young men more inclinable to
splendid negligence, than perseverance in laborious application to acquire correctness; and therefore did as we do in making what is crooked straight, by bending it the contrary way,
in order that it may remain straight at last.

For this purpose then, and to correct excess or neglect of
any kind, we may here add, that it is not enough that a work
be learned; it must be pleasing: the painter must add grace to
strength, if he desires to secure the first impression in his
favour. Our taste has a kind of sensuality about it, as well as a
love of the sublime; both these qualities of the mind are to
have their proper consequence, as far as they do not counteract each other; for that is the grand error which much care
ought to be taken to avoid.

There are some rules, whose absolute authority, like that of
our nurses, continues no longer than while we are in a state of
childhood. One of the first rules, for instance, that I believe
every master would give to a young pupil, respecting his conduct and management of light and shadow, would be what
Leonardo da Vinci has actually given; that you must oppose a
light ground to the shadowed side of your figure, and a dark
ground to the light side.[8] If Leonardo had lived to see the superior splendour and effect which has been since produced by
the exactly contrary conduct,—by joining light to light, and

[8] [Leonardo da Vinci, *Treatise on Painting*, trans. A. Philip McMahon
(Princeton: Princeton University Press, 1956), I, 73.]

shadow to shadow,—though without doubt he would have admired it, yet, as it ought not, so probably it would not be the first rule with which he would have begun his instructions.

Again; in the artificial management of the figures, it is directed that they shall contrast each other according to the rules generally given; that if one figure opposes his front to the spectator, the next figure is to have his back turned, and that the limbs of each individual figure be contrasted; that is, if the right leg be put forward, the right arm is to be drawn back.

It is very proper that those rules should be given in the Academy; it is proper the young students should be informed that some research is to be made, and that they should be habituated to consider every excellence as reduceable to principles. Besides; it is the natural progress of instruction to teach first what is obvious and perceptible to the senses, and from thence proceed gradually to notions large, liberal, and complete, such as comprise the more refined and higher excellencies in art. But when students are more advanced, they will find that the greatest beauties of character and expression are produced without contrast; nay more, that this contrast would ruin and destroy that natural energy of men engaged in real action, unsolicitous of grace. St. Paul preaching at Athens in one of the cartoons, far from any affected academical contrast of limbs, stands equally on both legs, and both hands are in the same attitude: add contrast, and the whole energy and unaffected grace of the figure is destroyed. Elymas the Sorcerer stretches both hands forward in the same direction, which gives perfectly the expression intended. Indeed you never will find in the works of Raffaelle any of those school-boy affected contrasts. Whatever contrast there is, appears without any seeming agency of art, by the natural chance of things.

What has been said of the evil of excesses of all kinds, whether of simplicity, variety, or contrast, naturally suggests to the painter the necessity of a general enquiry into the true meaning and cause of rules, and how they operate on those faculties to which they are addressed: by knowing their general purpose and meaning, he will often find that he need not confine himself to the literal sense, it will be sufficient if he preserve the spirit, of the law.

Critical remarks are not always understood without examples: it may not be improper therefore to give instances where the rule itself, though generally received, is false, or where a narrow conception of it may lead the artist into great errors.

It is given as a rule by Fresnoy, that "the principal figure of a subject must appear in the midst of the picture, under the principal light, to distinguish it from the rest." [9] A painter who should think himself obliged strictly to follow this rule, would encumber himself with needless difficulties; he would be confined to great uniformity of composition, and be deprived of many beauties which are incompatible with its observance. The meaning of this rule extends, or ought to extend, no further than this;—That the principal figure should be immediately distinguished at the first glance of the eye; but there is no necessity that the principal light should fall on the principal figure, or that the principal figure should be in the middle of the picture. It is sufficient that it be distinguished by its place, or by the attention of other figures pointing it out to the spectator. So far is this rule from being indispensable, that it is very seldom practised, other considerations of greater consequence often standing in the way. Examples in opposition to this rule, are found in the cartoons, in "Christ's Charge to Peter," the "Preaching of St. Paul," and "Elymas the Sorcerer," who is undoubtedly the principal object in that picture. In none of those compositions is the principal figure in the midst of the picture. In the very admirable composition of the "Tent of Darius," by Le Brun, Alexander is not in the middle of the picture, nor does the principal light fall on him; but the attention of all the other figures immediately distinguishes him, and distinguishes him more properly; the greatest light falls on the daughter of Darius, who is in the

9 [Charles Alphonse du Fresnoy, *De Arte Graphica* (London, 1695), 129 ff.]

middle of the picture, where it is more necessary the principal light should be placed.

It is very extraordinary that Felibien,[10] who has given a very minute description of this picture, but indeed such a description as may be rather called panegyrick than criticism, thinking it necessary (according to the precept of Fresnoy) that Alexander should possess the principal light, has accordingly given it to him; he might with equal truth have said that he was placed in the middle of the picture, as he seemed resolved to give this piece every kind of excellence which he conceived to be necessary to perfection. His generosity is here unluckily misapplied, as it would have destroyed in a great measure the beauty of the composition.

An other instance occurs to me where equal liberty may be taken in regard to the management of light. Though the general practice is to make a large mass about the middle of the picture surrounded by shadow, the reverse may be practised, and the spirit of the rule may still be preserved. Examples of this principle reversed may be found very frequently in the works of the Venetian school. In the great composition of Paul Veronese, the "Marriage at Cana,"[11] the figures are for the most part in half shadow; the great light is in the sky; and indeed the general effect of this picture which is so striking, is no more than what we often see in landscapes, in small pictures of fairs and country feasts; but those principles of light and shadow being transferred to a large scale, to a space containing near a hundred figures as large as life, and conducted to all appearance, with as much facility, and with an attention as steadily fixed upon *the whole together,* as if it were a small picture immediately under the eye, the work justly excites our admiration; the difficulty being encreased as the extent is enlarged.

The various modes of composition are infinite: sometimes it shall consist of one large group in the middle of the picture,

10 [André Felibien, born in Chartres, France, in 1666; died 1719.]
11 [See illustrations.]

and the smaller groups on each side; or a plain space in the middle, and the groups of figures ranged round this vacuity.

Whether this principal broad light be in the middle space of ground, as in the "School of Athens"; or in the sky, as in the "Marriage at Cana," in the "Andromeda," and in most of the pictures of Paul Veronese; or whether the light be on the groups; whatever mode of composition is adopted, every variety and licence is allowable: this only is indisputably necessary, that to prevent the eye from being distracted and confused by a multiplicity of objects of equal magnitude, those objects, whether they consist of lights, shadows, or figures, must be disposed in large masses and groups properly varied and contrasted; that to a certain quantity of action a proportioned space of plain ground is required; that light is to be supported by sufficient shadow; and, we may add, that a certain quantity of cold colours is necessary to give value and lustre to the warm colours: what those proportions are cannot be so well learnt by precept as by observation on pictures, and in this knowledge bad pictures will instruct as well as good. Our enquiry why pictures have a bad effect, may be as advantageous as the enquiry why they have a good effect; each will corroborate the principles that are suggested by the other.

Though it is not my *business* to enter into the detail of our art, yet I must take this opportunity of mentioning one of the means of producing that great effect which we observe in the works of the Venetian painters, as I think it is not generally known or observed. It ought, in my opinion, to be indispensably observed, that the masses of light in a picture be always of a warm mellow colour, yellow, red, or a yellowish-white; and that the blue, the grey, or the green colours be kept almost entirely out of these masses, and be used only to support and set off these warm colours; and for this purpose, a small proportion of cold colours will be sufficient.

Let this conduct be reversed; let the light be cold, and the surrounding colours warm, as we often see in the works of the Roman and Florentine painters, and it will be out of the power of art, even in the hands of Rubens or Titian, to make a picture splendid and harmonious.

Le Brun and Carlo Maratti were two painters of great merit, and particularly what may be called academical merit, but were both deficient in this management of colours; the want of observing this rule is one of the causes of that heaviness of effect which is so observable in their works. The principal light in the picture of Le Brun, which I just now mentioned, falls on Statira, who is dressed very injudiciously in a pale blue drapery; it is true, he has heightened this blue with gold, but that is not enough; the whole picture has a heavy air, and by no means answers the expectation raised by the print. Poussin often made a spot of blue drapery, when the general hue of the picture was inclinable to brown or yellow; which shews sufficiently, that harmony of colouring was not a part of the art that had much engaged the attention of that great painter.

The conduct of Titian in the picture of "Bacchus and Ariadne," has been much celebrated, and justly, for the harmony of colouring. To Ariadne is given (say the criticks) a red scarf, to relieve the figure from the sea which is behind her. It is not for that reason, alone, but for another of much greater consequence; for the sake of the general harmony and effect of the picture. The figure of Ariadne is separated from the great group, and is dressed in blue, which added to the colour of the sea, makes that quantity of cold colour which Titian thought necessary for the support and brilliancy of the great group; which group is composed, with very little exception, entirely of mellow colours. But as the picture in this case would be divided into two distinct parts, one half cold, and the other warm, it was necessary to carry some of the mellow colours of the great group into the cold part of the picture, and a part of the cold into the great group; accordingly Titian gave Ariadne a red scarf, and to one of the Bacchante a little blue drapery.

The light of the picture, as I observed, ought to be of a

warm colour; for though white may be used for the principal
light, as was the practice of many of the Dutch and Flemish
painters, yet it is better to suppose *that white* illumined by the
yellow rays of the setting sun, as was the manner of Titian.
The superiority of which manner is never more striking, than
when in a collection of pictures we chance to see a portrait of
Titian's hanging by the side of a Flemish picture, (even
though that should be of the hand of Vandyck,) which, however admirable in other respects, becomes cold and grey in
the comparison.

The illuminated parts of objects are in nature of a warmer
tint than those that are in the shade: what I have recommended therefore is no more, than that the same conduct be
observed in the whole, which is acknowledged to be necessary
in every individual part. It is presenting to the eye the same
effects as that which it has been *accustomed* to feel, which in
this case, as in every other, will always produce beauty; no
principle therefore in our art can be more certain, or is derived from a higher source.

What I just now mentioned of the supposed reason why
Ariadne has part of her drapery red, gives me occasion here
to observe, that this favourite quality of giving objects relief,
and which Du Piles and all the criticks have considered as a
requisite of the utmost importance, was not one of those objects which much engaged the attention of Titian: painters of
an inferior rank have far exceeded him in producing this
effect. This was a great object of attention when art was in its
infant state, as it is at present with the vulgar and ignorant,
who feel the highest satisfaction in seeing a figure, which, as
they say, looks as if they could walk round it. But however
low I may rate this pleasure of deception, I should not oppose
it, did it not oppose itself to a quality of a much higher
kind, by counteracting entirely that fulness of manner which
is so difficult to express in words, but which is found in
perfection in the best works of Correggio, and we may add, of
Rembrandt. This effect is produced by melting and losing the
shadows in a ground still darker than those shadows; whereas

that relief is produced by opposing and separating the ground from the figure either by light, or shadow, or colour. This conduct of in-laying, as it may be called, figures on their ground, in order to produce relief, was the practice of the old painters, such as Andrea Mantegna, Pietro Perugino, and Albert Durer; and to these we may add, the first manner of Leonardo da Vinci, Giorgione, and even Correggio; but these three were among the first who began to correct themselves in this dryness of style, by no longer considering relief as a principal object. As those two qualities, relief, and fulness of effect, can hardly exist together, it is not very difficult to determine to which we ought to give the preference. An artist is obliged for ever to hold a balance in his hand, by which he must determine the value of different qualities; that, when *some* fault must be committed, he may choose the least. Those painters who have best understood the art of producing a good effect, have adopted one principle that seems perfectly conformable to reason; that a part may be sacrificed for the good of the whole. Thus, whether the masses consist of light or shadow, it is necessary that they should be compact and of a pleasing shape; to this end, some parts may be made darker and some lighter, and reflexions stronger than nature would warrant. Paul Veronese took great liberties of this kind. It is said, that being once asked, why certain figures were painted in shade, as no cause was seen in the picture itself; he turned off the enquiry by answering, *"una nuevola che passa,"* a cloud is passing which has overshadowed them.

But I cannot give a better instance of this practice than a picture which I have of Rubens: it is a representation of a moon-light. Rubens has not only diffused more light over the picture than is in nature, but has bestowed on it those warm glowing colours by which his works are so much distinguished. It is so unlike what any other painters have given us of moonlight, that it might be easily mistaken, if he had not likewise added stars, for a fainter setting sun.—Rubens thought the eye ought to be satisfied in this case, above all other considerations: he might indeed have made it more natural, but it

would have been at the expence of what he thought of much
greater consequence,—the harmony proceeding from the contrast and variety of colours.

This same picture will furnish us with another instance,
where we must depart from nature for a greater advantage.
The moon in this picture does not preserve so great a superiority in regard to its lightness over the object which it
illumines, as it does in nature; this is likewise an intended
deviation, and for the same reason. If Rubens had preserved
the same scale of gradation of light between the moon and
the objects, which is found in nature, the picture must have
consisted of one small spot of light only, and at a little distance from the picture nothing but this spot would have been
seen. It may be said indeed, that this being the case, it is a
subject that ought not to be painted: but then, for the same
reason, neither armour, nor any thing shining, ought ever to
be painted; for though pure white is used in order to represent
the greatest light of shining objects, it will not in the picture
preserve the same superiority over flesh, as it has in nature,
without keeping that flesh-colour of a very low tint. Rembrandt, who thought it of more consequence to paint light
than the objects that are seen by it, has done this in a picture
of Achilles which I have. The head is kept down to a very low
tint, in order to preserve this due gradation and distinction
between the armour and the face; the consequence of which
is, that upon the whole the picture is too black. Surely too
much is sacrificed here to this narrow conception of nature:
allowing the contrary conduct a fault, yet it must be acknowledged a less fault than making a picture so dark that it cannot
be seen without a peculiar light, and then with difficulty. The
merit or demerit of the different conduct of Rubens and Rembrandt in those instances which I have given, is not to be
determined by the narrow principles of nature, separated from
its effect on the human mind. Reason and common sense tell
us, that before, and above all other considerations, it is necessary that the work should be seen, not only without difficulty
or inconvenience, but with pleasure and satisfaction; and every

obstacle which stands in the way of this pleasure and convenience must be removed.

The tendency of this discourse, with the instances which have been given, is not so much to place the artist above rules, as to teach him their reason; to prevent him from entertaining a narrow confined conception of art; to clear his mind from a perplexed variety of rules and their exceptions, by directing his attention to an intimate acquaintance with the passions and affections of the mind, from which all rules arise, and to which they are all referable. Art effects its purpose by their means; an accurate knowledge therefore of those passions and dispositions of the mind is necessary to him who desires to affect them upon sure and solid principles.

A complete essay or enquiry into the connexion between the rules of art, and the eternal and immutable dispositions of our passions, would be indeed going at once to the foundation of criticism; [12] but I am too well convinced what extensive knowledge, what subtle and penetrating judgment would be required, to engage in such an undertaking: it is enough for me, if, in the language of painters, I have produced a slight sketch of a part of this vast composition, but that sufficiently distinct to shew the usefulness of such a theory, and its practicability.

Before I conclude, I cannot avoid making one observation on the pictures now before us. I have observed, that every candidate has copied the celebrated invention of Timanthes in hiding the face of Agamemnon in his mantle; indeed such lavish encomiums have been bestowed on this thought, and that too by men of the highest character in critical knowledge, —Cicero, Quintilian, Valerius Maximus, and Pliny,—and have been since re-echoed by almost every modern that has written on the arts, that your adopting it can neither be wondered at nor blamed. It appears now to be so much connected with the subject, that the spectator would perhaps be disappointed in not finding united in the picture what he always united in his

[12] This was inadvertently said. I did not recollect the admirable treatise *On the Sublime and Beautiful* [by Edmund Burke].

mind, and considered as indispensably belonging to the subject. But it may be observed, that those who praise this circumstance were not painters. They use it as an illustration only of their own art; it served their purpose, and it was certainly not their business to enter into the objections that lie against it in another art. I fear *we* have but very scanty means of exciting those powers over the imagination which make so very considerable and refined a part of poetry. It is a doubt with me, whether we should even make the attempt. The chief, if not the only occasion which the painter has for this artifice, is, when the subject is improper to be more fully represented, either for the sake of decency, or to avoid what would be disagreeable to be seen; and this is not to raise or encrease the passions, which is the reason that is given for this practice, but on the contrary to diminish their effect.

It is true, sketches, or such drawings as painters generally make for their works, give this pleasure of imagination to a high degree. From a slight undetermined drawing, where the ideas of the composition and character are, as I may say, only just touched upon, the imagination supplies more than the painter himself, probably, could produce; and we accordingly often find that the finished work disappoints the expectation that was raised from the sketch; and this power of the imagination is one of the causes of the great pleasure we have in viewing a collection of drawings by great painters. These general ideas, which are expressed in sketches, correspond very well to the art often used in poetry. A great part of the beauty of the celebrated description of Eve in Milton's *Paradise Lost*,[13] consists in using only general indistinct expressions, every reader making out the detail according to his own particular imagination,—his own idea of beauty, grace, expression, dignity, or loveliness: but a painter, when he represents Eve on a canvas, is obliged to give a determined form, and his own idea of beauty distinctly expressed.

We cannot on this occasion, nor indeed on any other, recommend an undeterminate manner, or vague ideas of any

13 [Book IV, ll. 304 ff.]

kind, in a complete and finished picture. This notion, therefore, of leaving any thing to the imagination, opposes a very
fixed and indispensable rule in our art,—that every thing shall
be carefully and distinctly expressed, as if the painter knew,
with correctness and precision, the exact form and character
of whatever is introduced into the picture. This is what with
us is called science, and learning; which must not be sacrificed and given up for an uncertain and doubtful beauty,
which, not naturally belonging to our art, will probably be
sought for without success.

Mr. Falconet has observed, in a note on this passage in his
translation of Pliny,[14] that the circumstance of covering the face
of Agamemnon was probably not in consequence of any fine
imagination of the painter; which he considers as a discovery
of the criticks; but merely copied from the description of the
sacrifice, as it is found in Euripides.

The words from which the picture is supposed to be taken,
are these: "Agamemnon saw Iphigenia advance towards the
fatal altar; he groaned, he turned aside his head, he shed tears,
and covered his face with his robe."

Falconet does not at all acquiesce in the praise that is bestowed on Timanthes; not only because it is not his invention,
but because he thinks meanly of this trick of concealing, except in instances of blood, where the objects would be too
horrible to be seen; but says he, "in an afflicted father, in a
King, in Agamemnon, you, who are a painter, conceal from
me the most interesting circumstance, and then put me off
with sophistry and a veil. You are (he adds) a feeble painter,
without resources; you do not know even those of your art: I
care not what veil it is, whether closed hands, arms raised, or
any other action that conceals from me the countenance of the
hero. You think of veiling Agamemnon; you have unveiled
your own ignorance. A painter who represents Agamemnon
veiled, is as ridiculous as a poet would be, who in a pathetick
situation, in order to satisfy my expectations, and rid himself
of the business, should say, that the sentiments of his hero are

14 [Etienne Falconet, *Oeuvres*, V, 62.]

so far above whatever can be said on the occasion, that he shall say nothing."

To what Falconet has said, we may add, that supposing this method of leaving the expression of grief to the imagination, to be, as it was thought to be, the invention of the painter, and that it deserves all the praise that has been given it, still it is a trick that will serve but once; whoever does it a second time, will not only want novelty, but be justly suspected of using artifice to evade difficulties. If difficulties overcome make a great part of the merit of art, difficulties evaded can deserve but little commendation.

⊸ Discourse 9

October 16, 1780

GENTLEMEN,

THE honour which the arts acquire by being permitted to take possession of this noble habitation,[1] is one of the most considerable of the many instances we have received of his Majesty's protection; and the strongest proof of his desire to make the Academy respectable.

Nothing has been left undone that might contribute to excite our pursuit, or to reward our attainments. We have already the happiness of seeing the arts in a state to which they never before arrived in this nation. This building, in which we are now assembled, will remain to many future ages an illustrious specimen of the architect's abilities. It is our duty to endeavour that those who gaze with wonder at the structure, may not be disappointed when they visit the apartments. It will be no small addition to the glory which this nation has already acquired from having given birth to eminent men in every part of science, if it should be enabled to produce, in consequence of this institution, a school of English artists. The estimation in which we stand in respect to our neighbours, will be in proportion to the degree in which we excel or are inferior to them in the acquisition of intellectual excellence, of which trade and its consequential riches must be acknowledged to give the means; but a people whose whole

[1] [This discourse was given at the opening of the Royal Academy in its new quarters in Somerset Place. Note also the change in date to October rather than the usual December.]

141

attention is absorbed in those means, and who forget the end, can aspire but little above the rank of a barbarous nation. Every establishment that tends to the cultivation of the pleasures of the mind, as distinct from those of sense, may be considered as an inferior school of morality, where the mind is polished and prepared for higher attainments.[2]

Let us for a moment take a short survey of the progress of the mind towards what is, or ought to be, its true object of attention. Man, in his lowest state, has no pleasures but those of sense, and no wants but those of appetite; afterwards, when society is divided into different ranks, and some are appointed to labour for the support of others, those whom their superiority sets free from labour, begin to look for intellectual entertainments. Thus, whilst the shepherds were attending their flocks, their masters made the first astronomical observations; so musick is said to have had its origin from a man at leisure listening to the strokes of a hammer.

As the senses, in the lowest state of nature, are necessary to direct us to our support, when that support is once secure there is danger in following them further; to him who has no rule of action but the gratification of the senses, plenty is always dangerous: it is therefore necessary to the happiness of individuals, and still more necessary to the security of society, that the mind should be elevated to the idea of general beauty, and the contemplation of general truth; by this pursuit the mind is always carried forward in search of something more excellent than it finds, and obtains its proper superiority over the common senses of life, by learning to feel itself capable of higher aims and nobler enjoyments. In this gradual exaltation of human nature, every art contributes its contingent towards the general supply of mental pleasure. Whatever abstracts the thoughts from sensual gratifications, whatever teaches us

---

[2] [The general state of English painting at the time is discussed in the Introduction, p. xix. Reynolds' flattering attention to political power, his care for national pride, and his conviction that its arts are the final standard by which a nation is judged should be noted.]

to look for happiness within ourselves, must advance in some measure the dignity of our nature.

Perhaps there is no higher proof of the excellency of man than this,—that to a mind properly cultivated whatever is bounded is little. The mind is continually labouring to advance, step by step, through successive gradations of excellence, towards perfection, which is dimly seen, at a great though not hopeless distance, and which we must always follow because we never can attain; but the pursuit rewards itself: one truth teaches another, and our store is always encreasing, though nature can never be exhausted. Our art, like all arts which address the imagination, is applied to somewhat a lower faculty of the mind, which approaches nearer to sensuality; but through sense and fancy it must make its way to reason; for such is the progress of thought, that we perceive by sense, we combine by fancy, and distinguish by reason: and without carrying our art out of its natural and true character, the more we purify it from every thing that is gross in sense, in that proportion we advance its use and dignity; and in proportion as we lower it to mere sensuality, we pervert its nature, and degrade it from the rank of a liberal art; and this is what every artist ought well to remember. Let him remember also, that he deserves just so much encouragement in the state as he makes himself a member of it virtuously useful, and contributes in his sphere to the general purpose and perfection of society.

The art which we profess has beauty for its object; this it is our business to discover and to express; but the beauty of which we are in quest is general and intellectual; it is an idea that subsists only in the mind; the sight never beheld it, nor has the hand expressed it: it is an idea residing in the breast of the artist, which he is always labouring to impart, and which he dies at last without imparting; but which he is yet so far able to communicate, as to raise the thoughts, and extend the views of the spectator; and which, by a succession of art, may be so far diffused, that its effects may extend themselves imperceptibly into publick benefits, and be among the means of bestowing on whole nations refinement of taste: which, if it does not lead directly to purity of manners, obviates at least their greatest depravation, by disentangling the mind from appetite, and conducting the thoughts through successive stages of excellence, till that contemplation of universal rectitude and harmony which began by taste, may, as it is exalted and refined, conclude in virtue.[3]

[3] [In the last three paragraphs in this discourse, Reynolds' moral psychology is based on the thesis that good is dependent on cultivation of the mind, especially its rational faculties. Hence anything that gives cause for thought tends toward the good.]

·≋ Discourse 10

December 11, 1780

GENTLEMEN,

I SHALL now, as it has been customary on this day, and on this occasion, communicate to you such observations as have occurred to me on the theory of art.

If these observations have hitherto referred principally to painting, let it be remembered that this art is much more extensive and complicated than sculpture, and affords therefore a more ample field for criticism; and as the greater includes the less, the leading principles of sculpture are comprised in those of painting.

However, I wish now to make some remarks with particular relation to sculpture; to consider wherein, or in what manner, its principles and those of painting agree or differ; what is within its power of performing, and what it is vain or improper to attempt; that it may be clearly and distinctly known what ought to be the great purpose of the sculptor's labours.

Sculpture is an art of much more simplicity and uniformity than painting; it cannot with propriety, and the best effect, be applied to many subjects. The object of its pursuit may be comprised in two words, form and character; and those qualities are presented to us but in one manner, or in one style only; whereas the powers of painting, as they are more various and extensive, so they are exhibited in as great a variety of manners. The Roman, Lombard, Florentine, Venetian, and Flemish schools, all pursue the same end by different means. But sculpture having but one style, can only to one style of painting have any relation; and to this (which is indeed the highest and most dignified that painting can boast,) it has a relation so close, that it may be said to be almost the same art operating upon different materials. The sculptors of the last age, from not attending sufficiently to this discrimination of the different styles of painting, have been led into many errors. Though they well knew that they were allowed to imitate, or take ideas for the improvement of their own art from the grand style of painting, they were not aware that it was not permitted to borrow in the same manner from the ornamental. When they endeavour to copy the picturesque effects, contrasts, or petty excellencies of whatever kind, which not improperly find a place in the inferior branches of painting, they doubtless imagine themselves improving and extending the boundaries of their art by this imitation; but they are in reality violating its essential character, by giving a different direction to its operations, and proposing to themselves either what is unattainable, or at best a meaner object of pursuit. The grave and austere character of sculpture requires the utmost degree of formality in composition; picturesque contrasts have here no place; every thing is carefully weighed and measured, one side making almost an exact equipoise to the other: a child is not a proper balance to a full-grown figure, nor is a figure sitting or stooping a companion to an upright figure.

The excellence of every art must consist in the complete accomplishment of its purpose; and if by a false imitation of nature, or mean ambition of producing a picturesque effect or illusion of any kind, all the grandeur of ideas which this art endeavours to excite, be degraded or destroyed, we may boldly oppose ourselves to any such innovation. If the producing of a deception is the summit of this art, let us at once give to statues the addition of colour; which will contribute more towards accomplishing this end, than all those artifices which have been introduced and professedly defended, on no other principle but that of rendering the work more natural. But as colour is universally rejected, every practice liable to the same objection must fall with it. If the business of sculpture were to administer pleasure to ignorance, or a mere entertainment to the senses, the Venus of Medicis might certainly receive much improvement by colour; [1] but the character of sculpture makes it her duty to afford delight of a different and, perhaps, of a higher kind; the delight resulting from the contemplation of perfect beauty: and this, which is in truth an intellectual pleasure, is in many respects incompatible with what is merely addressed to the senses, such as that with which ignorance and levity contemplate elegance of form.

The sculptor may be safely allowed to practise every means within the power of his art to produce a deception, provided this practice does not interfere with or destroy higher excellencies; on these conditions he will be forced, however loth, to acknowledge that the boundaries of his art have long been fixed, and that all endeavours will be vain that hope to pass beyond the best works which remain of ancient sculpture.

Imitation is the means, and not the end, of art; it is employed by the sculptor as the language by which his ideas are presented to the mind of the spectator. Poetry and elocution of every sort make use of signs, but those signs are arbitrary and conventional. The sculptor employs the representation of the thing itself; but still as a means to a higher end,—as a gradual ascent always advancing towards faultless form and perfect beauty. It may be thought at the first view, that even this form, however perfectly represented, is to be valued and take its rank only for the sake of still a higher object, that of conveying sentiment and character, as they are exhibited by attitude, and expression of the passions. But we are sure from experience, that the beauty of form alone, without the assistance of any other quality, makes of itself a great work, and justly claims our esteem and admiration. As a proof of the high value we set on the mere excellence of form, we may produce the greatest part of the works of Michael Angelo, both in painting and sculpture; as well as most of the antique statues, which are justly esteemed in a very high degree,

1 [Reynolds seems not to know that most ancient statues were painted.]

though no very marked or striking character or expression of any kind is represented.

But, as a stronger instance that this excellence alone inspires sentiment, what artist ever looked at the "Torso" [2] without feeling a warmth of enthusiasm, as from the highest efforts of poetry? From whence does this proceed? What is there in this fragment that produces this effect, but the perfection of this science of abstract form?

A mind elevated to the contemplation of excellence perceives in this defaced and shattered fragment, *disjecti membra poetæ*,[3] the traces of superlative genius, the reliques of a work on which succeeding ages can only gaze with inadequate admiration.

It may be said that this pleasure is reserved only to those who have spent their whole life in the study and contemplation of this art; but the truth is, that all would feel its effects, if they could divest themselves of the expectation of *deception*, and look only for what it really is, a *partial* representation of nature. The only impediments of their judgment must then proceed from their being uncertain to what rank, or rather kind of excellence, it aspires; and to what sort of approbation it has a right. The state of darkness is, without doubt, irksome to every mind; but by attention to works of this kind, the knowledge of what is aimed at comes of itself, without being taught, and almost without being perceived.

The sculptor's art is limited in comparison of others, but it has its variety and intricacy within its proper bounds. Its essence is correctness: and when to correct and perfect form is added the ornament of grace, dignity of character, and appropriated expression, as in the "Apollo," the "Venus," the "Laocoon," the "Moses" of Michael Angelo, and many others, this art may be said to have accomplished its purpose.

What grace is, how it is to be acquired or conceived, are in speculation difficult questions; but *causa latet, res est notis-*

[2] [The Torso Belvedere, an ancient sculpture now in the Vatican.]

[3] ["Shattered parts of a poet" (Horace, *Satires* I. 4. 62).]

sima: [4] without any perplexing enquiry, the effect is hourly perceived. I shall only observe, that its natural foundation is correctness of design; and though grace may be sometimes united with incorrectness, it cannot proceed from it.

But to come nearer to our present subject. It has been said that the grace of the "Apollo" depends on a certain degree of incorrectness; that the head is not anatomically placed between the shoulders; and that the lower half of the figure is longer than just proportion allows.

I know that Correggio and Parmegiano are often produced as authorities to support this opinion; but very little attention will convince us, that the incorrectness of some parts which we find in their works, does not contribute to grace, but rather tends to destroy it. The "Madonna, with the Sleeping Infant," [5] and beautiful group of "Angels," by Parmegiano, in the Palazzo Piti, would not have lost any of its excellence, if the neck, fingers, and indeed the whole figure of the Virgin, instead of being so very long and incorrect, had preserved their due proportion.

In opposition to the first of these remarks I have the authority of a very able sculptor of this Academy, who has copied that figure, consequently measured and carefully examined it, to declare, that the criticism is not true. In regard to the last, it must be remembered, that Apollo is here in the exertion of one of his peculiar powers, which is swiftness; he has therefore that proportion which is best adapted to that character. This is no more incorrectness, than when there is given to an Hercules an extraordinary swelling and strength of muscles.

The art of discovering and expressing grace is difficult enough of itself, without perplexing ourselves with what is incomprehensible. A supposition of such a monster as Grace,

4 ["The cause is hidden, but the thing itself is most obvious" (Ovid, *Metamorphoses* IV. 287).]

5 [Reynolds refers to Parmigiano's "The Madonna of the Long Neck" (1535).]

begot by Deformity, is poison to the mind of a young artist, and may make him neglect what is essential to his art, correctness of design, in order to pursue a phantom which has no existence but in the imagination of affected and refined speculators.

I cannot quit the Apollo, without making one observation on the character of this figure. He is supposed to have just discharged his arrow at the Python; and, by the head retreating a little towards the right shoulder, he appears attentive to its effect. What I would remark, is the difference of this attention from that of the Discobolus, who is engaged in the same purpose, watching the effect of his discus. The graceful, negligent, though animated air of the one, and the vulgar eagerness of the other, furnish a signal instance of the judgment of the ancient sculptors in their nice discrimination of character. They are both equally true to nature, and equally admirable.

It may be remarked, that grace, character, and expression, though words of different sense and meaning, and so understood when applied to the works of painters, are indiscriminately used when we speak of sculpture. This indecision we may suspect to proceed from the undetermined effects of the art itself: those qualities are exhibited in sculpture rather by form and attitude than by the features, and can therefore be expressed but in a very general manner.

Though the Laocoon and his two sons have more expression in the countenance than perhaps any other antique statues, yet it is only the general expression of pain; and this passion is still more strongly expressed by the writhing and contortion of the body than by the features.

It has been observed in a late publication, that if the attention of the father in this group had been occupied more by the distress of his children, than by his own sufferings, it would have raised a much greater interest in the spectator. Though this observation comes from a person whose opinion, in every thing relating to the arts, carries with it the highest authority, yet I cannot but suspect that such refined expression is scarce within the provinces of this art; and in attempting it, the artist will run great risk of enfeebling expression and making it less intelligible to the spectator.

As the general figure presents itself in a more conspicuous manner than the features, it is there we must principally look for expression or character; *patuit in corpore vultus;* [6] and, in this respect, the sculptor's art is not unlike that of dancing, where the attention of the spectator is principally engaged by the attitude and action of the performer; and it is there he must look for whatever expression that art is capable of exhibiting. The dancers themselves acknowledge this, by often wearing masks, with little diminution in the expression. The face bears so very inconsiderable a proportion to the effect of the whole figure, that the ancient sculptors neglected to animate the features, even with the general expression of the passions. Of this the group of the boxers [7] is a remarkable instance; they are engaged in the most animated action with the greatest serenity of countenance. This is not recommended for imitation, (for there can be no reason why the countenance should not correspond with the attitude and expression of the figure,) but is mentioned in order to infer from hence, that this frequent deficiency in ancient sculpture could proceed from nothing but a habit of inattention to what was considered as comparatively immaterial.

Those who think sculpture can express more than we have allowed, may ask, by what means we discover, at the first glance, the character that is represented in a bust, cameo, or intaglio? I suspect it will be found, on close examination, by him who is resolved not to see more than he really does see, that the figures are distinguished by their *insignia* more than by any variety of form or beauty. Take from Apollo his lyre, from Bacchus his thirsus and vine-leaves, and from Meleager the

[6] ["The face is made apparent in the body" (source unidentified).]

[7] [Reynolds may refer here to a group of wrestlers in the Uffizi Gallery, Florence, whose heads are not original but come from an earlier period. His general point, however, is still sound concerning much ancient sculpture.]

boar's head, and there will remain little or no difference in their characters. In a Juno, Minerva, or Flora, the idea of the artist seems to have gone no further than representing perfect beauty, and afterwards adding the proper attributes, with a total indifference to which they gave them. Thus John De Bologna, after he had finished a group of a young man holding up a young woman in his arms, with an old man at his feet, called his friends together, to tell him what name he should give it, and it was agreed to call it "The Rape of the Sabines";[8] and this is the celebrated group which now stands before the old Palace at Florence. The figures have the same general expression which is to be found in most of the antique sculpture; and yet it would be no wonder if future criticks should find out delicacy of expression which was never intended; and go so far as to see, in the old man's countenance, the exact relation which he bore to the woman, who appears to be taken from him.

Though painting and sculpture are, like many other arts, governed by the same general principles, yet in the detail, or what may be called the by-laws of each art, there seems to be no longer any connexion between them. The different materials upon which those two arts exert their powers, must infallibly create a proportional difference in their practice. There are many petty excellencies which the painter attains with ease but which are impracticable in sculpture; and which, even if it could accomplish them, would add nothing to the true value and dignity of the work.

Of the ineffectual attempts which the modern sculptors have made by way of improvement, these seem to be the principal: The practice of detaching drapery from the figure, in order to give the appearance of flying in the air;—

Of making different plans in the same bas-relievos;—

Of attempting to represent the effects of perspective:—

To these we may add the ill effect of figures cloathed in a modern dress.

8 See *Il reposo di Raffaelle Borghini.*

The folly of attempting to make stone sport and flutter in the air, is so apparent, that it carries with it its own reprehension; and yet to accomplish this, seemed to be the great ambition of many modern sculptors, particularly Bernini: [9] his heart was so much set on overcoming this difficulty, that he was for ever attempting it, though by that attempt he risked every thing that was valuable in the art.

Bernini stands in the first class of modern sculptors, and therefore it is the business of criticism to prevent the ill effects of so powerful an example.

From his very early work of "Apollo," and "Daphne," the world justly expected he would rival the best productions of ancient Greece; but he soon strayed from the right path. And though there is in his works something which always distinguishes him from the common herd, yet he appears in his latter performances to have lost his way. Instead of pursuing the study of that ideal beauty with which he had so successfully begun, he turned his mind to an injudicious quest of novelty; attempted what was not within the province of the art, and endeavoured to overcome the hardness and obstinacy of his materials; which even supposing he had accomplished, so far as to make this species of drapery appear natural, the ill effect and confusion occasioned by its being detached from the figure to which it belongs, ought to have been alone a sufficient reason to have deterred him from that practice.

We have not, I think, in our Academy, any of Bernini's works, except a cast of the head of his "Neptune"; this will be sufficient to serve us for an example of the mischief produced by this attempt of representing the effects of the wind. The locks of the hair are flying abroad in all directions, insomuch that it is not a superficial view that can discover what the object is which is represented, or distinguish those flying locks from the features, as they are all of the same colour, of equal solidity, and consequently project with equal force.

The same entangled confusion which is here occasioned by

[9] [Giovanni Lorenzo Bernini, born in 1598 at Naples, Italy; died 1680.]

the hair, is produced by drapery flying off; which the eye must, for the same reason, inevitably mingle and confound with the principal parts of the figure.

It is a general rule, equally true in both arts, that the form and attitude of the figure should be seen clearly, and without any ambiguity, at the first glance of the eye. This the painter can easily do by colour, by losing parts in the ground, or keeping them so obscure as to prevent them from interfering with the more principal objects. The sculptor has no other means of preventing this confusion than by attaching the drapery for the greater part close to the figure; the folds of which following the order of the limbs, whenever the drapery is seen, the eye is led to trace the form and attitude of the figure at the same time.

The drapery of the "Apollo," though it makes a large mass, and is separated from the figure, does not affect the present question, from the very circumstance of its being so completely separated; and from the regularity and simplicity of its form, it does not in the least interfere with a distinct view of the figure. In reality, it is no more a part of it than a pedestal, a trunk of a tree, or an animal, which we often see joined to statues.

The principal use of those appendages is to strengthen and preserve the statue from accidents; and many are of opinion, that the mantle which falls from the Apollo's arm is for the same end; but surely it answers a much greater purpose, by preventing that dryness of effect which would inevitably attend a naked arm, extended almost at full length; to which we may add, the disagreeable effect which would proceed from the body and arm making a right angle.

The "Apostles," in the church of St. John Lateran,[10] appear to me to fall under the censure of an injudicious imitation of the manner of the painters. The drapery of those figures, from being disposed in large masses, gives undoubtedly that air of grandeur which magnitude or quantity is sure to produce. But though it should be acknowledged, that it is managed

10 [In Rome.]

with great skill and intelligence, and contrived to appear as light as the materials will allow, yet the weight and solidity of stone was not to be overcome.

Those figures are much in the style of Carlo Maratti,[11] and such as we may imagine he would have made if he had attempted sculpture; and when we know he had the superintendance of that work, and was an intimate friend of one of the principal sculptors, we may suspect that his taste had some influence, if he did not even give the designs. No man can look at those figures without recognizing the manner of Carlo Maratti. They have the same defect which his works so often have, of being overloaded with drapery, and that too artificially disposed. I cannot but believe, that if Ruscono, Le Gros, Monot, and the rest of the sculptors employed in that work, had taken for their guide the simple dress, such as we see in the antique statues of the philosophers, it would have given more real grandeur to their figures, and would certainly have been more suitable to the characters of the Apostles.

Though there is no remedy for the ill effect of those solid projections which flying drapery in stone must always produce in statues, yet in bas-relievos it is totally different; those detached parts of drapery the sculptor has here as much power over as the painter, by uniting and losing it in the ground, so that it shall not in the least entangle and confuse the figure.

But here again the sculptor, not content with this successful imitation, if it may be so called, proceeds to represent figures, or groups of figures, on different plans; that is, some on the fore-ground, and some at a greater distance, in the manner of painters in historical compositions. To do this he has no other means than by making the distant figures of less dimensions, and relieving them in a less degree from the surface; but this is not adequate to the end; they will still appear only as figures on a less scale, but equally near the eye with those in the front of the piece.

Nor does the mischief of this attempt, which never accomplishes its intention, rest here: by this division of the work

---

[11] [Carlo Maratti, born near Ancona, Italy, 1625; died 1713.]

into many minute parts, the grandeur of its general effect is inevitably destroyed.

Perhaps the only circumstance in which the modern have excelled the ancient sculptors, is the management of a single group in bas-relievo; the art of gradually raising the group from the flat surface, till it imperceptibly emerges into alto-relievo. Of this there is no ancient example remaining that discovers any approach to the skill which Le Gros [12] has shewn in an altar in the Jesuits Church at Rome. Different plans or degrees of relief in the same group have, as we see in this instance, a good effect, though the contrary happens when the groups are separated, and are at some distance behind each other.

This improvement in the art of composing a group in bas-relievo was probably first suggested by the practice of the modern painters, who relieve their figures, or groups of figures from their ground, by the same gentle gradation; and it is accomplished in every respect by the same general principles; but as the marble has no colour, it is the composition itself that must give it its light and shadow. The ancient sculptors could not borrow this advantage from their painters, for this was an art with which they appear to have been entirely unacquainted; and in the bas-relievos of Lorenzo Ghiberti,[13] the casts of which we have in the Academy, this art is no more attempted than it was by the painters of his age.

The next imaginary improvement of the moderns, is the representing the effects of perspective in bas-relievo. Of this little need be said; all must recollect how ineffectual has been the attempt of modern sculptors to turn the buildings which they have introduced as seen from their angle, with a view to make them appear to recede from the eye in perspective. This, though it may shew indeed their eager desire to encounter difficulties, shews at the same time how inadequate their materials are even to this their humble ambition.

The ancients, with great judgment, represented only the

[12] [Pierre Le Gros, born in 1666 at Paris; died 1719.]
[13] [Lorenzo Ghiberti, born at Florence, Italy, about 1378; died 1455.]

elevation of whatever architecture they introduced into their bas-relievos, which is composed of little more than horizontal or perpendicular lines; whereas the interruption of crossed lines or whatever causes a multiplicity of subordinate parts, destroys that regularity and firmness of effect on which grandeur of style so much depends.

We come now to the last consideration; in what manner statues are to be dressed, which are made in honour of men, either now living, or lately departed.

This is a question which might employ a long discourse of itself: I shall at present only observe, that he who wishes not to obstruct the artist, and prevent his exhibiting his abilities to their greatest advantage, will certainly not desire a modern dress.

The desire of transmitting to posterity the shape of modern dress must be acknowledged to be purchased at a prodigious price, even the price of every thing that is valuable in art.

Working in stone is a very serious business; and it seems to be scarce worth while to employ such durable materials in conveying to posterity a fashion of which the longest existence scarce exceeds a year.

However agreeable it may be to the antiquary's principles of equity and gratitude, that as he has received great pleasure from the contemplation of the fashions of dress of former ages, he wishes to give the same satisfaction to future antiquaries; yet, methinks pictures of an inferior style, or prints, may be considered as quite sufficient, without prostituting this great art to such mean purposes.

In this town may be seen an equestrian statue in a modern dress, which may be sufficient to deter future artists from any such attempt: even supposing no other objection, the familiarity of the modern dress by no means agrees with the dignity and gravity of sculpture.

Sculpture is formal, regular, and austere; disdains all familiar objects, as incompatible with its dignity; and is an enemy to every species of affectation, or appearance of academical art. All contrast, therefore, of one figure to another, or of the limbs of a single figure, or even in the folds of the drapery, must be sparingly employed. In short, whatever partakes of fancy or caprice, or goes under the denomination of picturesque, (however to be admired in its proper place,) is incompatible with that sobriety and gravity which is peculiarly the characteristick of this art.

There is no circumstance which more distinguishes a well regulated and sound taste, than a settled uniformity of design, where all the parts are compact, and fitted to each other, every thing being of a piece. This principle extends itself to all habits of life, as well as to all works of art. Upon this general ground therefore we may safely venture to pronounce, that the uniformity and simplicity of the materials on which the sculptor labours, (which are only white marble,) prescribes bounds to his art, and teaches him to confine himself to a proportionable simplicity of design.

◆ Discourse 11

December 10, 1782

GENTLEMEN,

THE highest ambition of every artist is to be thought a man of genius. As long as this flattering quality is joined to his name, he can bear with patience the imputation of carelessness, incorrectness, or defects of whatever kind.

So far indeed is the presence of genius from implying an absence of faults, that they are considered by many as its inseparable companions. Some go such lengths as to take indications from them, and not only excuse faults on account of genius, but presume genius from the existence of certain faults.

It is certainly true, that a work may justly claim the character of genius, though full of errors; and it is equally true, that it may be faultless, and yet not exhibit the least spark of genius. This naturally suggests an enquiry, a desire at least of enquiring, what qualities of a work and of a workman may justly entitle a painter to that character.

I have in a former discourse [1] endeavoured to impress you with a fixed opinion, that a comprehensive and critical knowledge of the works of nature is the only source of beauty and grandeur. But when we speak to painters we must always consider this rule, and all rules, with a reference to the mechanical practice of their own particular art. It is not properly in the learning, the taste, and the dignity of the ideas, that genius appears as belonging to a painter. There is a genius

[1] Discourse 3.

159

particular and appropriated to his own trade, (as I may call it,) distinguished from all others. For that power, which enables the artist to conceive his subject with dignity, may be said to belong to general education; and is as much the genius of a poet, or the professor of any other liberal art, or even a good critick in any of those arts, as of a painter. Whatever sublime ideas may fill his mind, he is a painter only as he can put in practice what he knows, and communicate those ideas by visible representation.

If my expression can convey my idea, I wish to distinguish excellence of this kind by calling it the genius of mechanical performance. This genius consists, I conceive, in the power of expressing that which employs your pencil, whatever it may be, *as a whole;* so that the general effect and power of the whole may take possession of the mind, and for a while suspend the consideration of the subordinate and particular beauties or defects.

The advantage of this method of considering objects, is what I wish now more particularly to enforce. At the same time I do not forget, that a painter must have the power of contracting as well as dilating his sight; because, he that does not at all express particulars, expresses nothing; yet it is certain, that a nice discrimination of minute circumstances, and a punctilious delineation of them, whatever excellence it may have, (and I do not mean to detract from it,) never did confer on the artist the character of genius.

Beside those minute differences in things which are frequently not observed at all, and, when they are, make little impression, there are in all considerable objects great characteristick distinctions, which press strongly on the senses, and therefore fix the imagination. These are by no means, as some persons think, an aggregate of all the small discriminating particulars; nor will such an accumulation of particulars ever express them. These answer to what I have heard great lawyers call the leading points in a case, or the leading cases relative to those points.

The detail of particulars, which does not assist the expression of the main characteristick, is worse than useless, it is mischievous, as it dissipates the attention, and draws it from the principal point. It may be remarked, that the impression which is left on our mind, even of things which are familiar to us, is seldom more than their general effect; beyond which we do not look in recognising such objects. To express this in painting, is to express what is congenial and natural to the mind of man, and what gives him by reflection his own mode of conceiving. The other presupposes *nicety* and *research*, which are only the business of the curious and attentive, and therefore does not speak to the general sense of the whole species; in which common, and, as I may so call it, mother tongue, every thing grand and comprehensive must be uttered.

I do not mean to prescribe what degree of attention ought to be paid to the minute parts; this it is hard to settle. We are sure that it is expressing the general effect of the whole which alone can give to objects their true and touching character; and wherever this is observed, whatever else may be neglected, we acknowledge the hand of a master. We may even go further, and observe, that when the general effect only is presented to us by a skilful hand, it appears to express the object represented in a more lively manner than the minutest resemblance would do.[2]

These observations may lead to very deep questions, which I do not mean here to discuss; among others, it may lead to an enquiry, Why we are not always pleased with the most absolute possible resemblance of an imitation to its original object. Cases may exist in which such a resemblance may be even disagreeable. I shall only observe that the effect of figures in wax-work, though certainly a more exact representation than can be given by painting or sculpture, is a sufficient proof that the pleasure we receive from imitation is not encreased merely in proportion as it approaches to minute and detailed reality; we are pleased, on the contrary, by seeing ends accomplished by seemingly inadequate means.

[2] [See illustrations, Michelangelo's "Study of the Nude for a Dead Christ."]

To express protuberance by actual relief, to express the soft-ness of flesh by the softness of wax, seems rude and inartificial,[3] and creates no grateful surprise. But to express distances on a plain surface, softness by hard bodies, and particular colouring by materials which are not singly of that colour, produces that magick which is the prize and triumph of art.

Carry this principle a step further. Suppose the effect of imitation to be fully compassed by means still more inade-quate; let the power of a few well-chosen strokes, which super-sede labour by judgment and direction, produce a complete impression of all that the mind demands in an object; we are charmed with such an unexpected happiness of execution, and begin to be tired with the superfluous diligence, which in vain solicits an appetite already satiated.

The properties of all objects, as far as a painter is concerned with them, are, the outline or drawing, the colour, and the light and shade. The drawing gives the form, the colour its visible quality, and the light and shade its solidity.

Excellence in any one of these parts of art will never be acquired by an artist, unless he has the habit of looking upon objects at large, and observing the effect which they have on the eye when it is dilated, and employed upon the whole, with-out seeing any one of the parts distinctly. It is by this that we obtain the ruling characteristick, and that we learn to imitate it by short and dexterous methods. I do not mean by dexterity a trick or mechanical habit, formed by guess, and established by custom; but that science, which, by a profound knowledge of ends and means, discovers the shortest and surest way to its own purpose.

If we examine with a critical view the manner of those painters whom we consider as patterns, we shall find that their great fame does not proceed from their works being more highly finished than those of other artists, or from a more minute attention to details, but from that enlarged comprehension which sees the whole object at once, and that

---

[3] ["Inartificial," as used here, means inartistic.]

energy of art which gives its characteristick effect by adequate
expression.

Raffaelle and Titian are two names which stand the
highest in our art; one for drawing, the other for painting.
The most considerable and the most esteemed works of Raffaelle are the cartoons, and his fresco works in the Vatican;
those, as we all know, are far from being minutely finished:
his principal care and attention seems to have been fixed upon
the adjustment of the whole, whether it was the general composition, or the composition of each individual figure; for
every figure may be said to be a lesser whole, though in regard
to the general work to which it belongs, it is but a part;
the same may be said of the head, of the hands, and feet.
Though he possessed this art of seeing and comprehending
the whole, as far as form is concerned, he did not exert the
same faculty in regard to the general effect, which is presented
to the eye by colour, and light and shade. Of this the deficiency
of his oil pictures, where this excellence is more expected than
in fresco, is a sufficient proof.

It is to Titian we must turn our eyes to find excellence with
regard to colour, and light and shade, in the highest degree.
He was both the first and the greatest master of this art. By a
few strokes he knew how to mark the general image and
character of whatever object he attempted; and produced, by
this alone, a truer representation than his master Giovanni
Bellino, or any of his predecessors, who finished every hair.
His great care was to express the general colour, to preserve
the masses of light and shade, and to give by opposition the
idea of that solidity which is inseparable from natural objects.
When those are preserved, though the work should possess no
other merit, it will have in a proper place its complete effect;
but where any of these are wanting, however minutely laboured the picture may be in the detail, the whole will have a
false and even unfinished appearance, at whatever distance,
or in whatever light, it can be shewn.

It is vain to attend to the variation of tints, if, in that attention, the general hue of flesh is lost; or to finish ever so minutely the parts, if the masses are not observed, or the whole not well put together.

Vasari seems to have had no great disposition to favour the Venetian painters, yet he every where justly commends *il modo di fare, la maniera, la bella pratica;* that is, the admirable manner and practice of that school. On Titian, in particular, he bestows the epithets of *giudicioso, bello, e stupendo.*[4]

This manner was then new to the world, but that unshaken truth on which it is founded, has fixed it as a model to all succeeding painters; and those who will examine into the artifice, will find it to consist in the power of generalising, and in the shortness and simplicity of the means employed.

Many artists, as Vasari likewise observes, have ignorantly imagined they are imitating the manner of Titian, when they leave their colours rough, and neglect the detail; but, not possessing the principles on which he wrought, they have produced what he calls *goffe pitture,* absurd foolish pictures; for such will always be the consequence of affecting dexterity without science, without selection, and without fixed principles.

Raffaelle and Titian seem to have looked at nature for different purposes; they both had the power of extending their view to the whole; but one looked only for the general effect as produced by form the other as produced by colour.

We cannot entirely refuse to Titian the merit of attending to the general *form* of his object, as well as colour; but his deficiency lay, a deficiency at least when he is compared with Raffaelle, in not possessing the power, like him, of correcting the form of his model by any general idea of beauty in his own mind. Of this his "St. Sebastian"[5] is a particular instance. This figure appears to be a most exact representation both of the form and the colour of the model, which he then happened to have before him; it has all the force of nature, and

4 ["Judicious, beautiful, and stupendous."]

5 [What Reynolds has in mind is not clear; perhaps the "Madonna with Six Saints," now in the Vatican.]

the colouring is flesh itself; but, unluckily, the model was of a bad form, especially the legs. Titian has with as much care preserved these defects, as he has imitated the beauty and brilliancy of the colouring. In his colouring he was large and general, as in his design he was minute and partial; in the one he was a genius, in the other not much above a copier. I do not, however, speak now of all his pictures; instances enough may be produced in his works, where those observations on his defects could not with any propriety be applied: but it is in the manner, or language, as it may be called, in which Titian and others of that school express themselves, that their chief excellence lies. This manner is in reality, in painting, what language is in poetry; we are all sensible how differently the imagination is affected by the same sentiment expressed in different words, and how mean or how grand the same object appears when presented to us by different painters. Whether it is the human figure, an animal, or even inanimate objects, there is nothing, however unpromising in appearance, but may be raised into dignity, convey sentiment, and produce emotion, in the hands of a painter of genius. What was said of Virgil,[6] that he threw even the dung about the ground with an air of dignity, may be applied to Titian: whatever he touched, however naturally mean, and habitually familiar, by a kind of magick he invested with grandeur and importance.

I must here observe, that I am not recommending a neglect of the detail; indeed it would be difficult, if not impossible, to prescribe *certain* bounds, and tell how far, or when it is to be observed or neglected; much must, at last, be left to the taste and judgment of the artist. I am well aware that a judicious detail will sometimes give the force of truth to the work, and consequently interest the spectator. I only wish to impress on your minds the true distinction between essential and subordinate powers; and to shew what qualities in the art claim your *chief* attention, and what may, with the least injury to your reputation, be neglected. Something, perhaps, always must be neglected; the lesser ought then to give way to the greater; and

6 [By Joseph Addison in "An Essay on Virgil's *Georgics*."]

since every work can have but a limited time allotted to it, (for even supposing a whole life to be employed about one picture, it is still limited,) it appears more reasonable to employ that time to the best advantage, in contriving various methods of composing the work,—in trying different effect of light and shadow,—and employing the labour of correction in heightening by a judicious adjustment of the parts the effects of the whole,—than that the time should be taken up in minutely finishing those parts.

But there is another kind of high finishing which may safely be condemned, as it seems to counteract its own purpose; that is, when the artist, to avoid that hardness which proceeds from the outline cutting against the ground, softens and blends the colours to excess: this is what the ignorant call high finishing, but which tends to destroy the brilliancy of colour, and the true effect of representation; which consists very much in preserving the same proportion of sharpness and bluntness that is found in natural objects. This extreme softning, instead of producing the effect of softness, gives the appearance of ivory, or some other hard substance, highly polished.

The portraits of Cornelius Jansen appear to have this defect, and consequently want that suppleness which is the characteristick of flesh; whereas, in the works of Vandyck we find that true mixture of softness and hardness perfectly observed. The same defect may be found in the manner of Vanderwerf, in opposition to that of Teniers; and such also, we may add, is the manner of Raffaelle in his oil pictures, in comparison with that of Titian.

The name which Raffaelle has so justly maintained as the first of painters, we may venture to say was not acquired by this laborious attention. His apology may be made by saying that it was the manner of his country; but if he had expressed his ideas with the facility and eloquence, as it may be called, of Titian, his works would certainly now have been less excellent; and that praise, which ages and nations have poured out upon him, for possessing genius in the higher attainments of art, would have been extended to them all.

Those who are not conversant in works of art, are often surprised at the high value set by connoisseurs on drawings which appear careless, and in every respect unfinished; but they are truly valuable; and their value arises from this, that they give the idea of an whole; and this whole is often expressed by a dexterous facility which indicates the true power of a painter, even though roughly exerted: whether it consists in the general composition, or the general form of each figure, or the turn of the attitude which bestows grace and elegance. All this we may see fully exemplified in the very skilful drawings of Parmegiano and Correggio. On whatever account we value these drawings, it is certainly not for high finishing or a minute attention to particulars.

Excellence in every part, and in every province of our art, from the highest style of history down to the resemblances of still-life, will depend on this power of extending the attention at once to the whole, without which the greatest diligence is vain.

I wish you to bear in mind, that when I speak of an whole, I do not mean simply an *whole* as belonging to composition, but an *whole* with respect to the general style of colouring; an *whole* with regard to the light and shade; an *whole* of every thing which may separately become the main object of a painter.

I remember a landscape-painter in Rome, who was known by the name of Studio, from his patience in high finishing, in which he thought the whole excellence of art consisted; so that he once endeavoured, as he said, to represent every individual leaf on a tree. This picture I never saw; but I am very sure that an artist, who looked only at the general character of the species, the order of the branches, and the masses of the foliage, would in a few minutes produce a more true resemblance of trees, than this painter in as many months.

A landscape-painter certainly ought to study anatomically (if I may use the expression) all the objects which he paints; but when he is to turn his studies to use, his skill, as a man of genius, will be displayed in shewing the general effect, preserving the same degree of hardness and softness which the objects have in nature; for he applies himself to the imagination, not to the curiosity, and works not for the virtuoso [7] or the naturalist, but for the common observer of life and nature. When he knows his subject, he will know not only what to describe, but what to omit; and this skill in leaving out, is, in all things, a great part of knowledge and wisdom.

The same excellence of manner which Titian displayed in history or portrait-painting, is equally conspicuous in his landscapes, whether they are professedly such, or serve only as backgrounds. One of the most eminent of this latter kind is to be found in the picture of "St. Pietro Martire." [8] The large trees, which are here introduced, are plainly distinguished from each other by the different manner with which the branches shoot from their trunks as well as by their different foliage; and the weeds in the fore-ground are varied in the same manner, just as much as variety requires, and no more. When Algarotti, speaking of this picture, praises it for the minute discriminations of the leaves and plants, even, as he says, to excite the admiration of a botanist, his intention was undoubtedly to give praise even at the expence of truth; for he must have known, that this is not the character of the picture; but connoisseurs will always find in pictures what they think they ought to find: he was not aware that he was giving a description injurious to the reputation of Titian.

Such accounts may be very hurtful to young artists, who never have had an opportunity of seeing the work described; and they may possibly conclude, that this great artist acquired the name of the divine Titian from his eminent attention to such trifling circumstances, which, in reality, would not raise him above the level of the most ordinary painter.

We may extend these observations even to what seems to have but a single, and that an individual, object. The excellence of portrait-painting, and we may add even the likeness,

[7] ["Virtuoso" here means amateur scientist.]
[8] [This picture was burned in 1867 and is now known only in copies.]

the character, and countenance, as I have observed in another place, depend more upon the general effect produced by the painter, than on the exact expression of the peculiarities, or minute discrimination of the parts. The chief attention of the artist is therefore employed in planting the features in their proper places, which so much contributes to giving the effect and true impression of the whole. The very peculiarities may be reduced to classes and general descriptions; and there are therefore large ideas to be found even in this contracted subject. He may afterwards labour single features to what degree he thinks proper, but let him not forget continually to examine, whether in finishing the parts he is not destroying the general effect.

It is certainly a thing to be wished, that all excellence were applied to illustrate subjects that are interesting and worthy of being commemorated; whereas, of half the pictures that are in the world, the subject can be valued only as an occasion which set the artist to work; and yet, in our high estimation of such pictures, without considering or perhaps without knowing the subject, shews how much our attention is engaged by the art alone.

Perhaps nothing that we can say will so clearly shew the advantage and excellence of this faculty, as that it confers the character of genius on works that pretend to no other merit; in which is neither expression, character, or dignity, and where none are interested in the subject. We cannot refuse the character of genius to the "Marriage" of Paul Veronese, without opposing the general sense of mankind, (great authorities have called it the triumph of painting), or, to the altar of St. Augustine at Antwerp, by Rubens, which equally deserves that title, and for the same reason. Neither of those pictures have any interesting story to support them. That of Paul Veronese, is only a representation of a great concourse of people at a dinner; and the subject of Rubens, if it may be called a subject where nothing is doing, is an assembly of various saints that lived in different ages. The whole excellence of

those pictures consists in mechanical dexterity, working however under the influence of that comprehensive faculty which I
have so often mentioned.

It is by this, and this alone, that the mechanical power is
ennobled, and raised much above its natural rank. And it
appears to me, that with propriety it acquires this character,
as an instance of that superiority with which mind predomi-
nates over matter, by contracting into one whole what nature
has made multifarious.

The great advantage of this idea of a whole is, that a greater
quantity of truth may be said to be contained and expressed
in a few lines or touches, than in the most laborious finishing
of the parts, where this is not regarded. It is upon this foundation that it stands; and the justness of the observation would
be confirmed by the ignorant in art, if it were possible to take
their opinions unseduced by some false notion of what they
imagine they ought to see in a picture. As it is an art, they
think they ought to be pleased in proportion as they see that
art ostentatiously displayed; they will, from this supposition
prefer neatness, high-finishing, and gaudy colouring to the
truth, simplicity, and unity of nature. Perhaps too, the totally
ignorant beholder, like the ignorant artist, cannot comprehend
a whole, nor even what it means. But if false notions do not
anticipate their perceptions, they who are capable of observation, and who, pretending to no skill, look only straight forward, will praise and condemn in proportion as the painter
has succeeded in the effect of the whole. Here general satisfaction, or general dislike, though perhaps despised by the
painter, as proceeding from the ignorance of the principles of
art, may help to regulate his conduct, and bring back his attention to that which ought to be his principal object, and
from which he has deviated for the sake of minuter beauties.

An instance of this right judgment I once saw in a child, in
going through a gallery where there were many portraits of
the last ages, which though neatly put out of hand, were very
ill put together. The child paid no attention to the neat finishing or naturalness of any bit of drapery, but appeared to ob-

serve only the ungracefulness of the persons represented, and put herself in the posture of every figure which she saw in a forced and awkward attitude. The censure of nature, uninformed, fastened upon the greatest fault that could be in a picture, because it related to the character and management of the whole.

I should be sorry, if what has been said should be understood to have any tendency to encourage that carelessness which leaves work in an unfinished state. I commend nothing for the want of exactness; I mean to point out that kind of exactness which is the best, and which is alone truly to be so esteemed.

So far is my disquisition from giving countenance to idleness, that there is nothing in our art which enforces such continual exertion and circumspection, as an attention to the general effect of the whole. It requires much study and much practice; it requires the painter's entire mind; whereas the parts may be finished by nice touches, while his mind is engaged on other matters; he may even hear a play or a novel read without much disturbance. The artist who flatters his own indolence, will continually find himself evading the active exertion, and applying his thoughts to the ease and laziness of highly finishing the parts; producing at last what Cowley calls "laborious effects of idleness." [9]

No work can be too much finished, provided the diligence employed be directed to its proper object; but I have observed that an excessive labour in the detail has, nine times in ten, been pernicious to the general effect, even when it has been the labour of great masters. It indicates a bad choice, which is an ill setting out in any undertaking.

To give a right direction to your industry has been my principal purpose in this discourse. It is this, which I am confident often makes the difference between two students of equal capacities, and of equal industry. While the one is employing his labour on minute objects of little consequence, the other is acquiring the art, and perfecting the habit, of seeing nature

[9] [Abraham Cowley, "Davideis," I, 714.]

in an extensive view, in its proper proportions, and its due subordination of parts.

Before I conclude, I must make one observation sufficiently connected with the present subject.

The same extension of mind which gives the excellence of genius to the theory and mechanical practice of the art, will direct him likewise in the method of study, and give him the superiority over those who narrowly follow a more confined track of partial imitation. Whoever, in order to finish his education, should travel to Italy, and spend his whole time there only in copying pictures, and measuring statues or buildings, (though these things are not to be neglected,) would return with little improvement. He that imitates the Iliad, says Dr. Young,[10] is not imitating Homer. It is not by laying up in the memory the particular details of any of the great works of art, that any man becomes a great artist, if he stops without making himself master of the general principles on which these works are conducted. If he even hopes to rival those whom he admires, he must consider their works as the means of teaching him the true art of seeing nature. When this is acquired, he then may be said to have appropriated their powers, or at least the foundation of their powers to himself; the rest must depend upon his own industry and application. The great business of study is, to form a *mind,* adapted and adequate to all times and all occasions; to which all nature is then laid open, and which may be said to possess the key of her inexhaustible riches.

10 [Edward Young, *Conjectures on Original Composition* (London, 1759), p. 21. Young continues, saying, "Imitate, but imitate not the Composition, but the Man."]

~~~~ Discourse 12

December 10, 1784

GENTLEMEN,

IN consequence of the situation in which I have the honour
to be placed in this Academy, it has often happened, that I
have been consulted by the young students who intend to
spend some years in Italy, concerning the method of regulat-
ing their studies. I am, as I ought to be, solicitously desirous
to communicate the entire result of my experience and observation; and though my openness and facility in giving my
opinions might make some amends for whatever was defective
in them, yet I fear my answers have not often given satisfaction. Indeed, I have never been sure, that I understood perfectly what they meant, and was not without some suspicion
that they had not themselves very distinct ideas of the object
of their enquiry.

If the information required was, by what means the path
that leads to excellence could be discovered; if they wished to
know whom they were to take for their guides; what to adhere
to, and what to avoid; where they were to bait, and where they
were to take up their rest; what was to be tasted only, and
what should be their diet; such general directions are certainly
proper for a student to ask, and for me, to the best of my
capacity, to give; but these rules have been already given: they
have in reality been the subject of almost all my discourses
from this place. But I am rather inclined to think, that by
method of study, it was meant (as several do mean,) that the
times and the seasons should be prescribed, and the order

173

settled, in which every thing was to be done: that it might be useful to point out to what degree of excellence one part of the art was to be carried, before the student proceeded to the next; how long he was to continue to draw from the ancient statues, when to begin to compose, and when to apply to the study of colouring.

Such a detail of instruction might be extended with a great deal of plausible and ostentatious amplification. But it would at best be useless. Our studies will be for ever, in a very great degree, under the direction of chance; like travellers we must take what we can get, and when we can get it; whether it is, or is not administered to us in the most commodious manner, in the most proper place, or at the exact minute when we would wish to have it.

Treatises on education and method of study, have always appeared to me to have one general fault. They proceed upon a false supposition of life; as if we possessed not only a power over events and circumstances, but had a greater power over ourselves than I believe any of us will be found to possess. Instead of supposing ourselves to be perfect patterns of wisdom and virtue, it seems to me more reasonable to treat ourselves (as I am sure we must now and then treat others) like humoursome children, whose fancies are often to be indulged in order to keep them in good-humour with themselves and their pursuits. It is necessary to use some artifice of this kind in all processes which by their very nature are long, tedious, and complex, in order to prevent our taking that aversion to our studies, which the continual shackles of methodical restraint are sure to produce.

I would rather wish a student, as soon as he goes abroad, to employ himself upon whatever he has been incited to by any immediate impulse, than to go sluggishly about a prescribed task: whatever he does in such a state of mind, little advantage accrues from it, as nothing sinks deep enough to leave any lasting impression; and it is impossible that any thing should be well understood, or well done, that is taken into a reluctant understanding, and executed with a servile hand.

It is desirable, and indeed is necessary to intellectual health, that the mind should be recreated and refreshed with a variety in our studies; that in the irksomeness of uniform pursuit we should be relieved, (and if I may so say, deceived,) as much as possible. Besides; the minds of men are so very differently constituted, that it is impossible to find one method which shall be suitable to all. It is of no use to prescribe to those who have no talents; and those who have talents will find methods for themselves, methods dictated to them by their own particular dispositions, and by the experience of their own particular necessities.

However, I would not be understood to extend this doctrine to the younger students: the first part of the life of a student, like that of other school-boys, must necessarily be a life of restraint. The grammar, the rudiments, however unpalatable, must at all events be mastered. After a habit is acquired of drawing correctly from the model (whatever it may be) which he has before him, the rest, I think, may be safely left to chance; always supposing that the student is *employed,* and that his studies are directed to the proper object.

A passion for his art, and an eager desire to excel, will more than supply the place of method. By leaving a student to himself he may possibly indeed be led to undertake matters above his strength: but the trial will at least have this advantage, it will discover to himself his own deficiencies; and this discovery alone, is a very considerable acquisition. One inconvenience, I acknowledge, may attend bold and arduous attempts; frequent failure may discourage. This evil however, is not more pernicious than the slow proficiency which is the natural consequence of too easy tasks.

Whatever advantages method may have in dispatch of business, (and there it certainly has many,) I have but little confidence of its efficacy in acquiring excellence in any art whatever. Indeed, I have always strongly suspected, that this love of method, on which some persons appear to place so great dependence, is, in reality, at the bottom, a love of idleness; a want of sufficient energy to put themselves into immediate action: it is a sort of an apology to themselves for doing nothing. I have known artists who may truly be said to have spent their whole lives, or at least the most precious part of their lives, in planning methods of study, without ever beginning; resolving, however, to put it all in practice at some time or other,—when a certain period arrives,—when proper conveniences are procured,—or when they remove to a certain place better calculated for study. It is not uncommon for such persons to go abroad with the most honest and sincere resolution of studying hard, when they shall arrive at the end of their journey. The same want of exertion, arising from the same cause which made them at home put off the day of labour until they had found a proper scheme for it, still continues in Italy, and they consequently return home with little, if any, improvement.

In the practice of art, as well as in morals, it is necessary to keep a watchful and jealous eye over ourselves; idleness, assuming the specious disguise of industry, will lull to sleep all suspicion of our want of an active exertion of strength. A provision of endless apparatus, a bustle of infinite enquiry and research, or even the mere mechanical labour of copying, may be employed, to evade and shuffle off real labour,—the real labour of thinking.

I have declined for these reasons to point out any particular method and course of study to young artists on their arrival in Italy. I have left it to their own prudence, a prudence which will grow and improve upon them in the course of unremitted, ardent industry, directed by a real love of their profession, and an unfeigned admiration of those who have been universally admitted as patterns of excellence in the art.

In the exercise of that general prudence, I shall here submit to their consideration such miscellaneous observations as have occurred to me on considering the mistaken notions or evil habits which have prevented that progress towards excellence which the natural abilities of several artists might otherwise have enabled them to make.

False opinions and vicious habits have done far more mischief to students, and to professors too, than any wrong methods of study.

Under the influence of sloth, or of some mistaken notion, is that disposition which always wants to lean on other men. Such students are always talking of the prodigious progress they should make if they could but have the advantage of being taught by some particular eminent master. To him they would wish to transfer that care which they ought and must take of themselves. Such are to be told, that after the rudiments are past, very little of our art can be taught by others. The most skilful master can do little more than put the end of the clue into the hands of his scholar, by which he must conduct himself.

It is true, the beauties and the defects of the works of our predecessors may be pointed out; the principles on which their works are conducted, may be explained; the great examples of ancient art may be spread out before them; but the most sumptuous entertainment is prepared in vain, if the guests will not take the trouble of helping themselves.

Even the Academy itself, where every convenience for study is procured, and laid before them, may, from that very circumstance, from leaving no difficulties to be encountered in the pursuit, cause a remission of their industry. It is not uncommon to see young artists whilst they are struggling with every obstacle in their way, exert themselves with such success as to outstrip competitors possessed of every means of improvement. The promising expectation which was formed, on so much being done with so little means, has recommended them to a patron who has supplied them with every convenience of study; from that time their industry and eagerness of pursuit has forsaken them; they stand still, and see others rush on before them.

Such men are like certain animals, who will feed only when there is but little provender, and that got at with difficulty through the bars of a rack, but refuse to touch it when there is an abundance before them.

Perhaps, such a falling off may proceed from the faculties being overpowered by the immensity of the materials; as the traveller despairs ever to arrive at the end of his journey when the whole extent of the road which he is to pass is at once displayed to his view.

Among the first moral qualities therefore, which a student ought to cultivate, is a just and manly confidence in himself or rather in the effects of that preserving industry which he is resolved to possess.

When Raffaelle, by means of his connection with Bramante, the Pope's architect, was fixed upon to adorn the Vatican with his works, he had done nothing that marked in him any great superiority over his contemporaries; though he was then but young, he had under his direction the most considerable artists of his age; and we know what kind of men those were: a lesser mind would have sunk under such a weight; and if we should judge from the meek and gentle disposition which we are told was the character of Raffaelle, we might expect this would have happened to him; but his strength appeared to encrease in proportion as exertion was required; and it is not improbable that we are indebted to the good fortune which first placed him in that conspicuous situation, for those great examples of excellence which he has left us.

The observations to which I formerly wished, and now desire, to point your attention, relate not to errors which are committed by those who have no claim to merit, but to those inadvertencies into which men of parts only can fall by the over-rating or the abuse of some real, though perhaps subordinate, excellence. The errors last alluded to are those of backward, timid characters; what I shall now speak of, belong to another class; to those artists who are distinguished for the readiness and facility of their invention. It is undoubtedly a splendid and desirable accomplishment to be able to design instantaneously any given subject. It is an excellence that I believe every artist would wish to possess; but unluckily, the

manner in which this dexterity is acquired, habituates the mind
to be contented with first thoughts without choice or selection.
The judgment, after it has been long passive, by degrees, loses
its power of becoming active when exertion is necessary.

Whoever, therefore, has this talent, must in some measure
undo what he has had the habit of doing, or at least give a new
turn to his mind: great works, which are to live and stand the
criticism of posterity, are not performed at a heat. A proportionable time is required for deliberation and circumspection.
I remember when I was at Rome looking at the "Fighting
Gladiator," [1] in company with an eminent sculptor, and I expressed my admiration of the skill with which the whole is
composed, and the minute attention of the artist to the change
of every muscle in that momentary exertion of strength, he
was of opinion that a work so perfect required nearly the
whole life of man to perform.

I believe, if we look around us, we shall find, that in the
sister art of poetry, what has been soon done, has been as soon
forgotten. The judgment and practice of a great poet on this
occasion is worthy attention. Metastasio, who has so much
and so justly distinguished himself throughout Europe, at his
outset was an *improvvisatore*, or *extempore* poet, a description of men not uncommon in Italy: it is not long since he
was asked by a friend, if he did not think the custom of in-
venting and reciting *extempore*, which he practised when a
boy in his character of an *improvvisatore*, might not be considered as a happy beginning of his education; he thought it,
on the contrary, a disadvantage to him: he said that he had
acquired by that habit, a carelessness and incorrectness, which
it cost him much trouble to overcome, and to substitute in the
place of it a totally different habit, that of thinking with selection, and of expressing himself with correctness and precision.

However extraordinary it may appear, it is certainly true,
that the inventions of the *pittori improvvisatori*,[2] as they may

---

[1] [The "Fighting Gladiator," probably the statue now known as the
"Borghese Warrior."]

[2] ["Improvisatory painters."]

be called, have,—notwithstanding the common boast of their
authors that all is spun from their own brain,—very rarely any
thing that has in the least the air of originality: their compositions are generally commonplace; uninteresting, without
character of expression; like those flowery speeches that we
sometimes hear, which impress no new ideas on the mind.

I would not be thought, however, by what has been said,
to oppose the use, the advantage, the necessity there is, of a
painter's being readily able to express his ideas by sketching.
The further he can carry such designs, the better. The evil to
be apprehended is, his resting there, and not correcting them
afterwards from nature, or taking the trouble to look about
him for whatever assistance the works of others will afford him.

We are not to suppose, that when a painter sits down to
deliberate on any work, he has all his knowledge to seek; he
must not only be able to draw *extempore* the human figure in
every variety of action, but he must be acquainted likewise
with the general principles of composition, and possess a habit
of foreseeing, while he is composing, the effect of the masses
of light and shadow, that will attend such a disposition. His
mind is entirely occupied by his attention to the whole. It is a
subsequent consideration to determine the attitude and expression of individual figures. It is in this period of his work
that I would recommend to every artist to look over his
porto-folio, or pocket-book, in which he has treasured up all
the happy inventions, all the extraordinary and expressive
attitudes that he has met with in the course of his studies; not
only for the sake of borrowing from those studies whatever may
be applicable to his own work, but likewise on account of
the great advantage he will receive by bringing the ideas of
great artists more distinctly before his mind, which will teach
him to invent other figures in a similar style.

Sir Francis Bacon speaks with approbation of the pro-
visionary methods Demosthenes and Cicero employed to assist
their invention; and illustrates their use by a quaint comparison after his manner. These particular *Studios* being not im-

mediately connected with our art, I need not cite the passage I allude to, and shall only observe that such preparation totally opposes the general received opinions that are floating in the world, concerning genius and inspiration. The same great man in another place speaking of his own essays, remarks, that they treat of "those things, wherein both men's lives and persons are most conversant, whereof a man shall find much in experience, but little in books": [3] they are then what an artist would naturally call invention; and yet we may suspect that even the genius of Bacon, great as it was, would never have been enabled to have made those observations, if his mind had not been trained and disciplined by reading the observations of others. Nor could he without such reading have known that those opinions were not to be found in other books. I know there are many artists of great fame, who appear never to have looked · out of themselves, and who probably would think it derogatory to their character, to be supposed to borrow from any other painter. But when we recollect, and compare the works of such men with those who took to their assistance the inventions of others, we shall be convinced of the great advantage of this latter practice.

The two men most eminent for readiness of invention, that occur to me, are Luca Giordano and La Fage; one in painting and the other in drawing.

To such extraordinary powers as were possessed by both of those artists, we cannot refuse the character of genius; at the same time, it must be acknowledged, that it was that kind of mechanick genius which operates without much assistance of the head. In all their works, which are (as might be expected) very numerous, we may look in vain for any thing that can be said to be original and striking; and yet, according to the ordinary ideas of originality, they have as good pretensions as most painters; for they borrowed very little from others, and still less will any artist, that can distinguish between excellence and insipidity, ever borrow from them.

To those men, and all such, let us oppose the practice of the

[3] [The passage comes from the dedication to the *Essays*.]

first of painters. I suppose we shall all agree, that no man
ever possessed a greater power of invention, and stood less in
need of foreign assistance, than Raffaelle; and yet, when he
was designing one of his greatest as well as latest works, the
cartoons, it is very apparent that he had the studies which
he had made from Masaccio [4] before him. Two noble figures
of St. Paul, which he found there, he adopted in his own work:
one of them he took for St. Paul preaching at Athens; and the
other for the same saint, when chastising the sorcerer Elymas.
Another figure in the same work, whose head is sunk in his
breast, with his eyes shut, appearing deeply wrapt up in
thought, was introduced amongst the listeners to the preaching
of St. Paul. The most material alteration that is made in those
two figures of St. Paul, is the addition of the left hands, which
are not seen in the original. It is a rule that Raffaelle observed,
(and indeed ought never to be dispensed with,) in a principal
figure, to shew both hands, that it should never be a question,
what is become of the other hand. For the "Sacrifice at Listra,"
he took the whole ceremony much as it stands in an ancient
bas-relievo, since published in the Admiranda.[5]

I have given examples from those pictures only of Raffaelle
which we have among us, though many other instances might
be produced of this great painter's not disdaining assistance:
indeed his known wealth was so great, that he might borrow
where he pleased without loss of credit.

It may be remarked, that this work of Masaccio, from
which he has borrowed so freely, was a publick work, and at
no farther distance from Rome, than Florence; so that if he
had considered it a disgraceful theft, he was sure to be de-
tected; but he was well satisfied that his character for invention
would be little affected by such a discovery; nor is it, except in
the opinion of those who are ignorant of the manner in which
great works are built.

Those who steal from mere poverty; who, having nothing

4 [Tommaso Masaccio (1401–1428), an important influence on Raphael.]
5 [Pietro S. Bartoli and Giovanni P. Bellori, *Admiranda Romanarum
Antiquitatum* (Rome, 1693), plate 10.]

of their own, cannot exist a minute without making such depredations; who are so poor that they have no place in which they can even deposit what they have taken; to men of this description nothing can be said: but such artists as those to whom I suppose myself now speaking, men whom I consider as competently provided with all the necessaries and conveniences of art, and who do not desire to steal baubles and common trash, but wish only to possess peculiar rarities which they select to ornament their cabinets, and take care to enrich the general store with materials of equal or of greater value than what they have taken; such men surely need not be ashamed of that friendly intercourse which ought to exist among artists, of receiving from the dead and giving to the living, and perhaps to those who are yet unborn.

The daily food and nourishment of the mind of an artist is found in the great works of his predecessors. There is no other way for him to become great himself. *Serpens nisi serpentem comederit, non fit draco,*[6] is a remark of a whimsical natural history, which I have read, though I do not recollect its title; however false as to dragons, it is applicable enough to artists.

Raffaelle, as appears from what has been said, had carefully studied the works of Masaccio; and indeed there was no other, if we except Michael Angelo, (whom he likewise imitated,) so worthy of his attention; and though his manner was dry and hard, his compositions formal, and not enough diversified, according to the custom of painters in that early period, yet his works possess that grandeur and simplicity which accompany, and even sometimes proceed from, regularity and hardness of manner. We must consider the barbarous state of the arts before his time, when skill in drawing was so little understood, that the best of the painters could not even foreshorten the foot, but every figure appeared to stand upon his toes; and what served for drapery, had, from the hardness and smallness of the folds, too much the appearance of cords clinging round the body. He first introduced large drapery, flowing

6 ["Unless a serpent eats a serpent, it will never become a dragon" (quoted from Bacon's *Essays*).]

in an easy and natural manner: indeed he appears to be the first who discovered the path that leads to every excellence to which the art afterwards arrived, and may therefore be justly considered as one of the great fathers of modern art.

Though I have been led on to a longer digression respecting this great painter than I intended, yet I cannot avoid mentioning another excellence which he possessed in a very eminent degree; he was as much distinguished among his contemporaries for his diligence and industry, as he was for the natural facilities of his mind. We are told, that his whole attention was absorbed in the pursuit of his art, and that he acquired the name of Masaccio,[7] from his total disregard to his dress, his person, and all the common concerns of life. He is indeed a signal instance of what well-directed diligence will do in a short time; he lived but twenty-seven years; yet in that short space carried the art so far beyond what it had before reached, that he appears to stand alone as a model for his successors. Vasari gives a long catalogue of painters and sculptors, who formed their taste, and learned their art, by studying his works; among those, he names Michael Angelo, Leonardo da Vinci, Pietro Perugino, Raffaelle, Bartolomeo, Andrea del Sarto, Il Rosso, and Pierino del Vaga.

The habit of contemplating and brooding over the ideas of great geniuses, till you find yourself warmed by the contact, is the true method of forming an artist-like mind; it is impossible, in the presence of those great men, to think, or invent in a mean manner; a state of mind is acquired that receives those ideas only which relish of grandeur and simplicity.

Beside the general advantage of forming the taste by such an intercourse, there is another of a particular kind, which was suggested to me by the practice of Raffaelle, when imitating the work of which I have been speaking. The figure of the proconsul Sergius Paulus is taken from the "Felix" of Masaccio, though one is a front figure, and the other seen in profile; the action is likewise somewhat changed; but it is plain Raffaelle

---

[7] The addition of *accio* denotes some deformity or imperfection attending that person to whom it is applied.

had that figure in his mind. There is a circumstance indeed, which I mention by the bye, which marks it very particularly; Sergius Paulus wears a crown of laurel; this is hardly reconcileable to strict propriety, and the *costume,* of which Raffaelle was in general a good observer; but he found it so in Masaccio, and he did not bestow so much pains in disguise as to change it. It appears to me to be an excellent practice thus to suppose the figures which you wish to adopt in the works of those great painters to be statues; and to give, as Raffaelle has here given, another view, taking care to preserve all the spirit and grace you find in the original.

I should hope, from what has been lately said, that it is not necessary to guard myself against any supposition of recommending an entire dependence upon former masters. I do not desire that you should get other people to do your business, or to think for you; I only wish you to consult with, to call in, as counsellors, men the most distinguished for their knowledge and experience, the result of which counsel must ultimately depend upon yourself. Such conduct in the commerce of life has never been considered as disgraceful, or in any respect to imply intellectual imbecility; it is a sign rather of that true wisdom, which feels individual imperfection; and is conscious to itself how much collective observation is necessary to fill the immense extent, and to comprehend the infinite variety, of nature. I recommend neither self-dependence nor plagiarism. I advise you only to take that assistance which every human being wants, and which, as appears from the examples that have been given, the greatest painters have not disdained to accept. Let me add, that the diligence required in the search, and the exertion subsequent in accommodating those ideas to your own purpose, is a business which idleness will not, and ignorance cannot, perform. But in order more distinctly to explain what kind of borrowing I mean, when I recommend so anxiously the study of the works of great masters, let us for a minute return again to Raffaelle, consider his method of practice, and endeavour to imitate him, in his manner of imitating others.

The two figures of St. Paul which I lately mentioned, are so
nobly conceived by Masaccio, that perhaps it was not in the
power even of Raffaelle himself to raise and improve them,
nor has he attempted it; but he has had the address to change
in some measure without diminishing the grandeur of their
character; he has substituted, in the place of a serene composed dignity, that animated expression which was necessary
to the more active employment he has assigned them.

In the same manner he has given more animation to the
figure of Sergius Paulus, and to that which is introduced in the
picture of St. Paul preaching, of which little more than hints
are given by Masaccio, which Raffaelle has finished. The
closing the eyes of this figure, which in Masaccio might be
easily mistaken for sleeping, is not in the least ambiguous
in the cartoon: his eyes indeed are closed, but they are
closed with such vehemence, that the agitation of a mind
"perplexed in the extreme" [8] is seen at the first glance; but what
is most extraordinary, and I think particularly to be admired
is, that the same idea is continued through the whole figure,
even to the drapery, which is so closely muffled about him,
that even his hands are not seen; by this happy correspondence
between the expression of the countenance, and the disposition
of the parts, the figure appears to think from head to foot.
Men of superior talents alone are capable of thus using and
adapting other men's minds to their own purposes, or are able
to make out and finish what was only in the original a hint or
imperfect conception. A readiness in taking such hints, which
escape the dull and ignorant, makes in my opinion no inconsiderable part of that faculty of the mind which is called
genius.

It often happens that hints may be taken and employed in
a situation totally different from that in which they were originally employed. There is a figure of a Bacchante leaning backward, her head thrown quite behind her, which seems to be a
favourite invention, as it is so frequently repeated in bas-
relievos, cameos and intaglios; it is intended to express an

8 [*Othello*, V.ii.345.]

enthusiastick frantick kind of joy. This figure Baccio Bandi-
nelli, in a drawing that I have of that master, of the "Descent
from the Cross," has adopted, (and he knew very well what
was worth borrowing,) for one of the Marys, to express frantick agony of grief. It is curious to observe, and it is certainly
true, that the extremes of contrary passions are with very little
variation expressed by the same action.

If I were to recommend method in any part of the study of
a painter, it would be in regard to invention; that young students should not presume to think themselves qualified to
invent, till they were acquainted with those stores of invention the world already possesses, and had by that means
accumulated sufficient materials for the mind to work with.
It would certainly be no improper method of forming the mind
of a young artist, to begin with such exercises as the Italians
call a *Pasticcio* [9] composition of the different excellencies which
are dispersed in all other works of the same kind. It is not
supposed that he is to stop here, but that he is to acquire by
this means the art of selecting, first what is truly excellent in
art, and then what is still more excellent in nature; a task,
which, without this previous study, he will be but ill qualified
to perform.

The doctrine which is here advanced, is acknowledged to be
new, and to many may appear strange. But I only demand for
it the reception of a stranger; a favourable and attentive consideration, without that entire confidence which might be
claimed under authoritative recommendation.

After you have taken a figure, or any idea of a figure, from
any of those great painters, there is another operation still
remaining, which I hold to be indispensably necessary, that is,
never to neglect finishing from nature every part of the work.
What is taken from a model, though the first idea may have
been suggested by another, you have a just right to consider
as your own property. And here I cannot avoid mentioning a
circumstance in placing the model, though to some it may
appear trifling. It is better to possess the model with the attri-

9 [*Pasticcio* is a pastiche.]

tude you require, than to place him with your own hands: by this means it happens often that the model puts himself in an action superior to your own imagination. It is a great matter to be in the way of accident, and to be watchful and ready to take advantage of it: besides; when you fix the position of a model, there is danger of putting him in an attitude into which no man would naturally fall. This extends even to drapery. We must be cautious in touching and altering a fold of the stuff, which serves as a model, for fear of giving it inadvertently a forced form; and it is perhaps better to take the chance of another casual throw, than to alter the position in which it was at first accidentally cast.

Rembrandt, in order to take the advantage of accident, appears often to have used the pallet-knife to lay his colours on the canvass, instead of the pencil. Whether it is the knife or any other instrument, it suffices if it is something that does not follow exactly the will. Accident in the hands of an artist who knows how to take the advantage of its hints, will often produce bold and capricious beauties of handling and facility, such as he would not have thought of, or ventured, with his pencil, under the regular restraint of his hand. However, this is fit only on occasions where no correctness of form is required, such as clouds, stumps of trees, rocks, or broken ground. Works produced in an accidental manner, will have the same free unrestrained air as the works of nature, whose particular combinations seem to depend upon accident.

I again repeat, you are never to lose sight of nature; the instant you do, you are all abroad, at the mercy of every gust of fashion, without knowing or seeing the point to which you ought to steer. Whatever trips you make, you must still have nature in your eye. Such deviations as art necessarily requires, I hope in a future discourse to be able to explain. In the mean time, let me recommend to you, not to have too great dependence on your practice of memory, however strong those impressions may have been which are there deposited. They are for ever wearing out, and will be at last obliterated, unless they are continually refreshed and repaired.

It is not uncommon to meet with artists who from a long neglect of cultivating this necessary intimacy with nature, do not even know her when they see her; she appearing a stranger to them, from their being so long habituated to their own representation of her. I have heard painters acknowledge, though in that acknowledgment no degradation of themselves was intended, that they could do better without nature than with her; or as they expressed it themselves, "that it only put them out." A painter with such ideas and such habits, is indeed in a most hopeless state. *The art of seeing nature,* or in other words, the art of using models, is in reality the great object, the point to which all our studies are directed. As for the power of being able to do tolerably well, from practice alone, let it be valued according to its worth. But I do not see in what manner it can be sufficient for the production of correct, excellent, and finished pictures. Works deserving this character never were produced, nor ever will arise, from memory alone; and I will venture to say, that an artist who brings to his work a mind tolerably furnished with the general principles of art, and a taste formed upon the works of good artists, in short who knows in what excellence consists, will, with the assistance of models, which we will likewise suppose he has learnt the art of using, be an over-match for the greatest painter that ever lived who should be debarred such advantages.

Our neighbours, the French, are much in this practice of *extempore* invention, and their dexterity is such as even to excite admiration, if not envy; but how rarely can this praise be given to their finished pictures!

The late Director of their Academy, Boucher,[10] was eminent in this way. When I visited him some years since, in France, I found him at work on a very large picture, without drawings or models of any kind. On my remarking this particular circumstance, he said, when he was young, studying his art, he found it necessary to use models; but he had left off them for many years.

10 [François Boucher (1703–1770).]

Such pictures as this was, and such as I fear always will be produced by those who work solely from practice or memory, may be a convincing proof of the necessity of the conduct which I have recommended. However, in justice I cannot quit this painter without adding, that in the former part of his life, when he was in the habit of having recourse to nature, he was not without a considerable degree of merit,—enough to make half the painters of his country his imitators; he had often grace and beauty, and good skill in composition; but I think, all under the influence of a bad taste: his imitators are indeed abominable.

Those artists who have quitted the service of nature, (whose service, when well understood, is *perfect freedom)* and have put themselves under the direction of I know not what capricious fantastical mistress, who fascinates and overpowers their whole mind, and from whose dominion there are no hopes of their being ever reclaimed, (since they appear perfectly satisfied, and not at all conscious of their forlorn situation,) like the transformed followers of Comus,—

"Not once perceive their foul disfigurement;
But boast themselves more comely than before." 11

Methinks, such men, who have found out so short a path, have no reason to complain of the shortness of life, and the extent of art; since life is so much longer than is wanted for their improvement, or indeed is necessary for the accomplishment of their idea of perfection. On the contrary, he who recurs to nature, at every recurrence renews his strength. The rules of art he is never likely to forget; they are few and simple; but nature is refined, subtle, and infinitely various, beyond the power of retention of memory; it is necessary, therefore, to have continual recourse to her. In this intercourse, there is no end of his improvement; the longer he lives, the nearer he approaches to the true and perfect idea of art.

11 [John Milton, "Comus," 74–75.]

❧ Discourse 13

December 11, 1786

GENTLEMEN,

To discover beauties, or to point out faults, in the works of celebrated masters, and to compare the conduct of one artist with another, is certainly no mean or inconsiderable part of criticism; but this is still no more than to know the art through the artist. This test of investigation must have two capital defects; it must be narrow, and it must be uncertain. To enlarge the boundaries of the art of painting, as well as to fix its principles, it will be necessary, that, *that* art, and *those* principles, should be considered in their correspondence with the principles of the other arts, which like this, address themselves primarily and principally to the imagination. When those connected and kindred principles are brought together to be compared, another comparison will grow out of this; that is the comparison of them all with those of human nature, from whence arts derive the materials upon which they are to produce their effects.

When this comparison of art with art, and of all arts with the nature of man, is once made with success, our guiding lines are well ascertained and established, as they can be in matters of this description.

This, as it is the highest style of criticism, is at the same time the soundest; for it refers to the eternal and immutable nature of things.

You are not to imagine that I mean to open to you at large, or to recommend to your research, the whole of this vast field of science.[1] It is certainly much above my faculties to reach it; and though it may not be above yours, to comprehend it fully, if it were fully and properly brought before you, yet perhaps the most perfect criticism requires habits of speculation and abstraction, not very consistent with the employment which ought to occupy, and the habits of mind which ought to prevail in a practical artist. I only point out to you these things, that when you do criticise, (as all who work on a plan, will criticise more or less,) your criticism may be built on the foundation of true principles; and that though you may not always travel a great way, the way that you do travel, may be the right road.

I observe, as a fundamental ground, common to all the arts with which we have any concern in this discourse, that they address themselves only to two faculties of the mind, its imagination and its sensibility.

All theories which attempt to direct or control the art, upon any principles falsely called rational, which we form to ourselves upon a supposition of what ought in reason to be the end or means of art, independent of the known first effect produced by objects on the imagination, must be false and delusive. For though it may appear bold to say it, the imagination is here the residence of truth. If the imagination be affected, the conclusion is fairly drawn; if it be not affected, the reasoning is erroneous, because the end is not obtained; the effect itself being the test, and the only test, of the truth and efficacy of the means.

There is in the commerce of life, as in art, a sagacity which is far from being contradictory to right reason, and is superior to any occasional exercise of that faculty, which supersedes it; and does not wait for the slow progress of deduction, but goes at once, by what appears a kind of intuition, to the conclusion. A man endowed with this faculty, feels and acknowledges the truth, though it is not always in his power, perhaps, to give a reason for it; because he cannot recollect and bring before him all the materials that gave birth to his opinion; for very

1 ["Science," as used here, means knowledge in general.]

many and very intricate considerations may unite to form the principle, even of small and minute parts, involved in, or dependent on, a great system of things: though these in process of time are forgotten, the right impression still remains fixed in his mind.

This impression is the result of the accumulated experience of our whole life, and has been collected, we do not always know how, or when. But this mass of collective observation, however acquired, ought to prevail over that reason, which however powerfully exerted on any particular occasion, will probably comprehend but a partial view of the subject; and our conduct in life as well as in the arts, is, or ought to be, generally governed by this habitual reason: it is our happiness that we are enabled to draw on such funds. If we were obliged to enter into a theoretical deliberation on every occasion, before we act, life would be at a stand, and art would be impracticable.[2]

It appears to me therefore, that our first thoughts, that is, the effect which any thing produces on our minds on its first appearance, is never to be forgotten; and it demands for that reason because it is the first, to be laid up with care. If this be not done, the artist may happen to impose on himself by partial reasoning; by a cold consideration of those animated thoughts which proceed, not perhaps from caprice or rashness, (as he may afterwards conceit,)[3] but from the fullness of his mind, enriched with the copious stores of all the various inventions which he had ever seen, or had ever passed in his mind. These ideas are infused into his design, without any conscious effort; but if he be not on his guard, he may reconsider and correct them, till the whole matter is reduced to a common-place invention.

[2] [In these first paragraphs, Reynolds is seeking, not always with success, to defend an intuitive approach to art on objective grounds. His rationalism is, of course, typical of his age; his imagination, however, points toward theories of art more commonly associated with a later period.]

[3] ["Conceit" here means believe or rationalize.]

This is sometimes the effect of what I mean to caution you against; that is to say, an unfounded distrust of the imagination and feeling, in favour of narrow, partial, confined, argumentative theories; and of principles that seem to apply to the design in hand; without considering those general impressions on the fancy in which real principles of *sound reason,* and of much more weight and importance, are involved, and, as it were, lie hid, under the appearance of a sort of vulgar sentiment.

Reason, without doubt, must ultimately determine every thing; at this minute it is required to inform us when that very reason is to give way to feeling.

Though I have often spoke of that mean conception of our art which confines it to mere imitation, I must add, that it may be narrowed to such a mere matter of experiment, as to exclude from it the application of science, which alone gives dignity and compass to any art. But to find proper foundations for science is neither to narrow or to vulgarise it; and this is sufficiently exemplified in the success of experimental philosophy. It is the false system of reasoning grounded on a partial view of things, against which I would most earnestly guard you. And I do it the rather, because those narrow theories, so coincident with the poorest and most miserable practice, and which are adopted to give it countenance, have not had their origin in the poorest minds, but in the mistakes, or possibly in the mistaken interpretations, of great and commanding authorities. We are not therefore in this case misled by feeling, but by false speculation.

When such a man as Plato speaks of painting [4] as only an imitative art, and that our pleasure proceeds from observing and acknowledging the truth of the imitation, I think he misleads us by a partial theory.[5] It is in this poor, partial, and so

[4] [*Republic* **X**, *passim.*]

[5] [The reference to Plato is part of one of the major eighteenth-century controversies in which Plato and his "ideal" theory of art (cf. "Ion") and knowledge came in conflict with the tradition of Locke, Berkeley, and Hume, with which Reynolds was much more in sympathy.]

far, false, view of the art, that Cardinal Bembo has chosen to distinguish even Raffaelle himself, whom our enthusiasm honours with the name of Divine. The same sentiment is adopted by Pope in his "Epitaph on Sir Godfrey Kneller"; [6] and he turns the panegyrick solely on imitation, as it is a sort of deception.

I shall not think my time misemployed, if by any means I may contribute to confirm your opinion of what ought to be the object of your pursuit; because, though the best criticks must always have exploded this strange idea, yet I know that there is a disposition towards a perpetual recurrence to it, on account of its simplicity and superficial plausibility. For this reason I shall beg leave to lay before you a few thoughts on this subject; to throw out some hints that may lead your minds to an opinion, (which I take to be the truth,) that painting is not only to be considered as an imitation, operating by deception, but that it is, and ought to be, in many points of view, and strictly speaking, no imitation at all of external nature. Perhaps it ought to be as far removed from the vulgar idea of imitation, as the refined civilized state in which we live, is removed from a gross state of nature; and those who have not cultivated their imaginations, which the majority of mankind certainly have not, may be said, in regard to arts, to continue in this state of nature. Such men will always prefer imitation to that excellence which is addressed to another faculty that they do not possess; but these are not the persons to whom a painter is to look, any more than a judge of morals and manners ought to refer controverted points upon those subjects to the opinions of people taken from the banks of the Ohio, or from New Holland.

It is the lowest style only of arts, whether of painting, poetry, or musick, that may be said, in the vulgar sense, to be naturally pleasing. The higher efforts of those arts, we know by experience, do not affect minds wholly uncultivated. This refined taste is the consequence of education and habit; we are born only with a capacity of entertaining this refinement,

6 [Living, great Nature fear'd he might outvie
  Her works; and dying, fears herself may die.]

as we are born with a disposition to receive and obey all the rules and regulations of society; and so far it may be said to be natural to us, and no further.

What has been said, may shew the artist how necessary it is, when he looks about him for the advice and criticism of his friends, to make some distinction of the character, taste, experience, and observation in this art, of those, from whom it is received. An ignorant uneducated man may, like Apelles's critick,[7] be a competent judge of the truth of the representation of a sandal; or to go somewhat higher, like Moliere's old woman, may decide upon what is nature, in regard to comick humour; but a critick in the higher style of art, ought to possess the same refined taste, which directed the artist in his work.

To illustrate this principle by a comparison with other arts, I shall now produce some instances to shew, that they, as well as our own art, renounce the narrow idea of nature, and the narrow theories derived from that mistaken principle, and apply to that reason only which informs us not what imitation is, a natural representation of a given object, but what it is natural for the imagination to be delighted with. And perhaps there is no better way of acquiring this knowledge, than by this kind of analogy: each art will corroborate and mutually reflect the truth on the other. Such a kind of juxtaposition may likewise have this use, that whilst the artist is amusing himself in the contemplation of other arts, he may habitually transfer the principles of those arts to that which he professes; which ought to be always present to his mind, and to which every thing is to be referred.

So far is art from being derived from, or having any immediate intercourse with, particular nature as its model, that there are many arts that set out with a professed deviation from it.

This is certainly not so exactly true in regard to painting

---

[7] [A shoemaker corrected the Greek sculptor Apelles for his inaccurate representation of a sandal. Pliny, *Historia naturalis* XXXV. 36, 85.]

and sculpture. Our elements are laid in gross common nature, an exact imitation of what is before us: but when we advance to the higher state, we consider this power of imitation, though first in the order of acquisition, as by no means the highest in the scale of perfection.

Poetry addresses itself to the same faculties and the same dispositions as painting, though by different means. The object of both is to accommodate itself to all the natural propensities and inclinations of the mind. The very existence of poetry depends on the licence it assumes of deviating from actual nature, in order to gratify natural propensities by other means, which are found by experience full as capable of affording such gratification. It sets out with a language in the highest degree artificial, a construction of measured words, such as never is, nor ever was used by man. Let this measure be what it may, whether hexameter or any other metre used in Latin or Greek,—or rhyme, or blank verse varied with pauses and accents, in modern languages,—they are all equally removed from nature, and equally a violation of common speech. When this artificial mode has been established as the vehicle of sentiment, there is another principle in the human mind, to which the work must be referred, which still renders it more artificial, carries it still further from common nature, and deviates only to render it more perfect. That principle is the sense of congruity, coherence, and consistency, which is a real existing principle in man; and it must be gratified. Therefore having once adopted a style and a measure not found in common discourse, it is required that the sentiments also should be in the same proportion elevated above common nature, from the necessity of there being an agreement of the parts among themselves, that one uniform whole may be produced.

To correspond therefore with this general system of deviation from nature, the manner in which poetry is offered to the ear, the tone in which it is recited, should be as far removed from the tone of conversation, as the words of which that poetry is composed. This naturally suggests the idea of modulating the voice by art, which I suppose may be considered as accomplished to the highest degree of excellence in the recitative of the Italian opera; as we may conjecture it was in the chorus that attended the ancient drama. And though the most violent passions, the highest distress, even death itself, are expressed in singing or recitative, I would not admit as sound criticism the condemnation of such exhibitions on account of their being unnatural.

If it is natural for our senses, and our imaginations, to be delighted with singing, with instrumental musick, with poetry, and with graceful action, taken separately; (none of them being in the vulgar sense natural, even in that separate state;) it is conformable to experience, and therefore agreeable to reason as connected with and referred to experience, that we should also be delighted with this union of musick, poetry, and graceful action, joined to every circumstance of pomp and magnificence calculated to strike the senses of the spectator. Shall reason stand in the way, and tell us we ought not to like what we know we do like, and prevent us from feeling the full effect of this complicated exertion of art? This is what I would understand by poets and painters being allowed to dare every thing; for what can be more daring, than accomplishing the purpose and end of art, by a complication of means, none of which have their archetypes in actual nature?

So far therefore is servile imitation from being necessary, that whatever is familiar, or in any way reminds us of what we see and hear every day, perhaps does not belong to the higher provinces of art, either in poetry or painting. The mind is to be transported, as Shakspeare expresses it, "beyond the ignorant present," [8] to ages past. Another and a higher order of beings is supposed; and to those beings every thing which is introduced into the work must correspond. Of this conduct, under these circumstances, the Roman and Florentine schools afford sufficient examples. Their style by this means is raised and elevated above all others; and by the same means the compass of art itself is enlarged.

We often see grave and great subjects attempted by artists

[8] [*Macbeth*, I.v.57–58.]

of another school; who, though excellent in the lower class of art, proceeding on the principles which regulate that class, and not recollecting, or not knowing, that they were to address themselves to another faculty of the mind, have become perfectly ridiculous.

The picture which I have at present in my thoughts is a sacrifice of Iphigenia, painted by Jean Steen, a painter of whom I have formerly had occasion to speak with the highest approbation; and even in this picture, the subject of which is by no means adapted to his genius, there is nature and expression; but it is such expression, and the countenances are so familiar, and consequently so vulgar, and the whole accompanied with such finery of silks and velvet, that one would be almost tempted to doubt, whether the artist did not purposely intend to burlesque his subject.

Instances of the same kind we frequently see in poetry. Parts of Hobbes's translation of Homer are remembered and repeated merely for the familiarity and meanness of their phraseology, so ill corresponding with the ideas which ought to have been expressed, and, as I conceive, with the style of the original.[9]

We may proceed in the same manner through the comparatively inferior branches of art. There are in works of that class, the same distinction of a higher and a lower style; and they take their rank and degree in proportion as the artist departs more, or less, from common nature, and makes it an object of his attention to strike the imagination of the spectator by ways belonging specially to art,—unobserved and untaught out of the school of its practice.

If our judgments are to be directed by narrow, vulgar, untaught or rather ill-taught reason, we must prefer a portrait by Denner or ony other high finisher, to those of Titian or Vandyck; and a landscape of Vanderhyde to those of Titian or Rubens; for they are certainly more exact representations of nature.

If we suppose a view of nature represented with all the

[9] [The philosopher Thomas Hobbes translated the *Odyssey* (London, 1673) and the *Iliad* (London, 1676).]

truth of the *camera obscura*,[10] and the same scene represented
by a great artist, how little and mean will the one appear in
comparison of the other, where no superiority is supposed
from the choice of the subject. The scene shall be the same,
the difference only will be in the manner in which it is presented to the eye. With what additional superiority then will
the same artist appear when he has the power of selecting his
materials, as well as elevating his style? Like Nicolas Poussin,
he transports us to the environs of ancient Rome, with all the
objects which a literary education make so precious and interesting to man: or, like Sebastian Bourdon, he leads us to the
dark antiquity of the pyramids of Egypt; or, like Claude Lorrain, he conducts us to the tranquillity of Arcadian scenes and
fairy land.

Like the history-painter, a painter of landscapes in this style
and with this conduct, sends the imagination back into antiquity; and, like the poet, he makes the elements sympathise
with his subject: whether the clouds roll in volumes like those
of Titian or Salvator Rosa,—or, like those of Claude, are
gilded with the setting sun; whether the mountains have sudden or bold projections, or are gently sloped; whether the
branches of his trees shoot out abruptly in right angles from
their trunks, or follow each other with only a gentle inclination. All these circumstances contribute to the general character of the work whether it be of the elegant, or of the more
sublime kind. If we add to this the powerful materials of
lightness and darkness, over which the artist has complete
dominion, to vary and dispose them as he pleases; to diminish,
or encrease them as will best suit his purpose, and correspond
to the general idea of his work: a landscape thus conducted,
under the influence of a poetical mind, will have the same superiority over the more ordinary and common views, as Milton's "Allegro" and "Penseroso" have over a cold prosaick

10 [The "camera obscura" was a device which produced an exact
image on the wall of a darkened room. Were Reynolds writing today,
he would use either the photograph as his example, or some comparable method of exact, mechanical reproduction of reality.]

narration or description; and such a picture would make a more forcible impression on the mind than the real scenes, were they presented before us.

If we look abroad to other arts, we may observe the same distinction, the same division into two classes, each of them acting under the influence of two different principles, in which the one follows nature, the other varies it, and sometimes departs from it.

The theatre, which is said "to hold the mirrour up to nature," [11] comprehends both those ideas. The lower kind of comedy, or farce, like the inferior style of painting, the more naturally it is represented, the better; but the higher appears to me to aim no more at imitation, so far as it belongs to any thing like deception, or to expect that the spectators should think that the events there represented are really passing before them, than Raffaelle in his cartoons, or Poussin in his sacraments, expected it to be believed, even for a moment, that what they exhibited were real figures.

For want of this distinction, the world is filled with false criticism. Raffaelle is praised for naturalness and deception, which he certainly has not accomplished, and as certainly never intended; and our late great actor, Garrick, has been as ignorantly praised by his friend Fielding; who doubtless imagined he had hit upon an ingenious device, by introducing in one of his novels, (otherwise a work of the highest merit,) an ignorant man, mistaking Garrick's representation of a scene in Hamlet, for reality.[12] A very little reflection will convince us, that there is not one circumstance in the whole scene that is of the nature of deception. The merit and excellence of Shakspeare, and of Garrick, when they were engaged in such scenes, is of a different and much higher kind. But what adds to the falsity of this intended compliment, is, that the best stage-representation appears even more unnatural to a person of such a character, who is supposed never to have seen a play

11 [*Hamlet,* III.ii.24.]

12 [*Tom Jones,* Book XVI, chap. 5.]

before, than it does to those who have had a habit of allowing for those necessary deviations from nature which the art requires.

In theatrick representation, great allowances must always be made for the place in which the exhibition is represented; for the surrounding company, the lighted candles, the scenes visibly shifted in your sight; and the language of blank verse, so different from common English; which merely as English must appear surprising in the mouths of Hamlet, and all the court and natives of Denmark. These allowances are made; but their being made puts an end to all manner of deception: and further; we know that the more low, illiterate, and vulgar any person is, the less he will be disposed to make these allowances, and of course to be deceived by any imitation; the things in which the trespass against nature and common probability is made in favour of the theatre, being quite within the sphere of such uninformed men.

Though I have no intention of entering into all the circumstances of unnaturalness in theatrical representations, I must observe, that even the expression of violent passion, is not always the most excellent in proportion as it is the most natural: so great terror and such disagreeable sensations may be communicated to the audience, that the balance may be destroyed by which pleasure is preserved, and holds its predominancy in the mind: violent distortion of action, harsh screamings of the voice, however great the occasion, or however natural on such occasion, are therefore not admissible in the theatrick art. Many of these allowed deviations from nature arise from the necessity which there is, that every thing should be raised and enlarged beyond its natural state; that the full effect may come home to the spectator, which otherwise would be lost in the comparatively extensive space of the theatre. Hence the deliberate and stately step, the studied grace of action, which seems to enlarge the dimensions of the actor, and alone to fill the stage. All this unnaturalness, though right and proper in its place, would appear affected and ridiculous in a private room; *quid enim deformius, quam scenam in vitam transferre?* [13]

And here I must observe, and I believe it may be considered as a general rule, that no art can be engrafted with success on another art. For though they all profess the same origin, and to proceed from the same stock, yet each has its own peculiar modes both of imitating nature, and of deviating from it, each for the accomplishment of its own particular purpose. These deviations, more especially, will not bear transplantation to another soil.

If a painter should endeavour to copy the theatrical pomp and parade of dress and attitude, instead of that simplicity, which is not a greater beauty in life, than it is in painting, we should condemn such pictures as painted in the meanest style.

So also gardening, as far as gardening is an art, or entitled to that appellation, is a deviation from nature; for if the true taste consists, as many hold, in banishing every appearance of art, or any traces of the footsteps of man, it would then be no longer a garden. Even though we define it, "Nature to advantage dress'd," [14] and in some sense it is such, and much more beautiful and commodious for the recreation of man; it is however, when so dress'd, no longer a subject for the pencil of a landscape-painter, as all landscape-painters know, who love to have recourse to nature herself, and to dress her according to the principles of their own art; which are far different from those of gardening, even when conducted according to the most approved principles, and such as a landscape-painter himself would adopt in the disposition of his own grounds, for his own private satisfaction. [15]

---

[13] ["For what is more unsightly than a theatrical scene brought over into life?" (probably from Francis Bacon's *Advancement of Learning*).]

[14] [Alexander Pope, "Essay on Criticism," 297: "True art is Nature to advantage dress'd."]

[15] [During the eighteenth century, large-scale landscape gardening was an English passion and great efforts were made to introduce various kinds of illusions. Fake ruins, bridges, and streams were common, as were extensive plantings and earthworks. Many such gardens did not come to maturity for nearly a century after the death of their originators.]

I have brought together as many instances as appear necessary, to make out the several points which I wished to suggest to your consideration in this discourse; that your own thoughts may lead you further in the use that may be made of the analogy of the arts, and of the restraint which a full understanding of the diversity of many of their principles ought to impose on the employment of that analogy.

The great end of all those arts is, to make an impression on the imagination and the feeling. The imitation of nature frequently does this. Sometimes it fails, and something else succeeds. I think therefore the true test of all the arts, is not solely whether the production is a true copy of nature, but whether it answers the end of art, which is to produce a pleasing effect upon the mind.

It remains only to speak a few words of architecture, which does not come under the denomination of an imitative art. It applies itself, like musick (and I believe we may add poetry,) directly to the imagination, without the intervention of any kind of imitation.

There is in architecture, as in painting, an inferior branch of art, in which the imagination appears to have no concern. It does not however acquire the name of a polite and liberal art, from its usefulness, or administering to our wants or necessities, but from some higher principle: we are sure that in the hands of a man of genius it is capable of inspiring sentiment,[16] and of filling the mind with great and sublime ideas.

It may be worth the attention of artists, to consider what materials are in their hands, that may contribute to this end; and whether this art has it not in its power to address itself to the imagination with effect, by more ways than are generally employed by architects.

To pass over the effect produced by that general symmetry and proportion, by which the eye is delighted, as the ear is with musick, architecture certainly possesses many principles in common with poetry and painting. Among those which

---

[16] ["Sentiment" has any number of critical meanings in this period, but as Reynolds uses it here it seems simply to mean "feeling."]

may be reckoned as the first, is, that of affecting the imagination by means of association of ideas. Thus, for instance, as we have naturally a veneration for antiquity, whatever building brings to our remembrance ancient customs and manners, such as the castles of the barons of ancient chivalry, is sure to give this delight. Hence it is that "towers and battlements" [17] are so often selected by the painter and the poet, to make a part of the composition of their ideal landscape; and it is from hence in a great degree, that in the buildings of Vanbrugh, who was a poet as well as an architect, there is a greater display of imagination, than we shall find perhaps in any other; and this is the ground of the effect which we feel in many of his works, notwithstanding the faults with which many of them are justly charged. For this purpose, Vanbrugh appears to have had recourse to some principles of the Gothick architecture; which, though not so ancient as the Grecian, is more so to our imagination, with which the artist is more concerned than with absolute truth.

The barbarick splendour of those Asiatick buildings, which are now publishing by a member of this Academy,[18] may possibly, in the same manner, furnish an architect, not with models to copy, but with hints of composition and general effect, which would not otherwise have occurred.

It is, I know, a delicate and hazardous thing, (and as such I have already pointed it out,) to carry the principles of one art to another, or even to reconcile in one object the various modes of the same art, when they proceed on different principles. The sound rules of the Grecian architecture are not to be lightly sacrificed. A deviation from them, or even an addition to them, is like a deviation or addition to, or from, the rules of other arts, fit only for a great master, who is thoroughly conversant in the nature of man, as well as all combinations in his own art.

[17] Towers and Battlements it sees
   Bosm'd high in tufted trees. Milton, "L'Allegro."
[18] Mr. [William] Hodges [who was then publishing *Select Views of India* (London, 1786)].

It may not be amiss for the architect to take advantage *sometimes* of that to which I am sure the painter ought always to have his eyes open, I mean the use of accidents; to follow when they lead, and to improve them, rather than always to trust to a regular plan. It often happens that additions have been made to houses, at various times, for use or pleasure. As such buildings depart from regularity, they now and then acquire something of scenery by this accident, which I should think might not unsuccessfully be adopted by an architect, in an original plan, if it does not too much interfere with convenience. Variety and intricacy is a beauty and excellence in every other of the arts which address the imagination; and why not in architecture?

The forms and turnings of the streets of London, and other old towns, are produced by accident, without any original plan or design; but they are not always the less pleasant to the walker or spectator, on that account. On the contrary, if the city had been built on the regular plan of Sir Christopher Wren, the effect might have been, as we know it is in some new parts of the town, rather unpleasing; the uniformity might have produced weariness, and a slight degree of disgust.

I can pretend to no skill in the detail of architecture. I judge now of the art, merely as a painter. When I speak of Vanbrugh, I mean to speak of him in the language of our art. To speak then of Vanbrugh in the language of a painter, he had originality of invention, he understood light and shadow, and had great skill in composition. To support his principal object, he produced his second and third groups or masses; he perfectly understood in *his* art what is the most difficult in ours, the conduct of the background, by which the design and invention is set off to the greatest advantage. What the background is in painting, in architecture is the real ground on which the building is erected; and no architect took greater care than he that his work should not appear crude and hard: that is, it did not abruptly start out of the ground without expectation or preparation.

This is a tribute, which a painter owes to an architect who

composed like a painter; and was defrauded of the due reward of his merit by the wits of his time, who did not understand the principles of composition in poetry better than he;
and who knew little, or nothing, of what he understood perfectly, the general ruling principles of architecture and painting. His fate was that of the great Perrault; both were the
objects of the petulant sarcasms of factious men of letters; and
both have left some of the fairest ornaments which to this day
decorate their several countries; the façade of the Louvre,
Blenheim, and castle Howard.

Upon the whole, it seems to me, that the object and intention of all the arts is to supply the natural imperfection of
things, and often to gratify the mind by realising and embodying what never existed but in the imagination.

It is allowed on all hands, that facts, and events, however
they may bind the historian, have no dominion over the poet
or the painter. With us, history is made to bend and conform
to this great idea of art. And why? Because these arts, in
their highest province, are not addressed to the gross senses,
but to the desires of the mind, to that spark of divinity which
we have within, impatient of being circumscribed and pent up
by the world which is about us. Just so much as our art has
of this, just so much of dignity, I had almost said of divinity,
it exhibits; and those of our artists who possessed this mark
of distinction in the highest degree, acquired from thence the
glorious appellation of Divine.

‑‑✒ Discourse 14

December 10, 1788

GENTLEMEN,

IN THE study of our art, as in the study of all arts, something is the result of *our own* observation of nature; something, and that not little, the effect of the example of those who have studied the same nature before us, and who have cultivated before us the same art, with diligence and success. The less we confine ourselves in the choice of those examples, the more advantage we shall derive from them; and the nearer we shall bring our performances to a correspondence with nature and the great general rules of art. When we draw our examples from remote and revered antiquity,—with some advantage undoubtedly in that selection, we subject ourselves to some inconveniences. We may suffer ourselves to be too much led away by great names, and to be too much subdued by overbearing authority. Our learning, in that case, is not so much an exercise of our judgment, as a proof of our docility. We find ourselves, perhaps, too much overshadowed; and the character of our pursuits is rather distinguished by the tameness of the follower, than animated by the spirit of emulation. It is sometimes of service, that our examples should be *near* us; and such as raise a reverence, sufficient to induce us carefully to observe them, yet not so great as to prevent us from engaging with them in something like a generous contention.

We have lately lost Mr. Gainsborough,[1] one of the greatest

1 [Thomas Gainsborough, born in Suffolk, 1727, died in 1788, was one of Reynolds' most important rivals. After an unimpressive early career, he

ornaments of our Academy. It is not our business here, to make panegyricks on the living, or even on the dead who were of our body. The praise of the former might bear the appearance of adulation; and the latter, of untimely justice; perhaps of envy of those whom we have still the happiness to enjoy, by an oblique suggestion of invidious comparisons. In discoursing therefore on the talents of the late Mr. Gainsborough, my object is, not so much to praise or to blame him, as to draw from his excellencies and defects, matter of instruction to the students in our Academy. If ever this nation should produce genius sufficient to acquire to us the honourable distinction of an English school, the name of Gainsborough will be transmitted to posterity, in the history of the art, among the very first of that rising name. That our reputation in the arts is now only rising, must be acknowledged; and we must expect our advances to be attended with old prejudices, as adversaries, and not as supporters, standing in this respect in a very different situation from the late artists of the Roman school to whose reputation ancient prejudices have certainly contributed: the way was prepared for them, and they may be said rather to have lived in the reputation of their country than to have contributed to it; whilst whatever celebrity is obtained by the English artists, can arise only from the operation of a fair and true comparison. And when they communicate to their country a share of their reputation, it is a portion of fame not borrowed from others, but solely acquired by their own labour and talents. As Italy has undoubtedly a prescriptive right to an admiration bordering on prejudice, as a soil peculiarly adapted, congenial, and, we may add, destined to the production of men of great genius in our art, we may not unreasonably suspect that a portion of the great fame of some of their late artists has been owing to the general readiness and disposition of mankind, to acquiesce in their original prepossessions in favour of the productions of the Roman school.

---

went to the fashionable resort town of Bath in 1760, where he won fame for his portraits. He returned to London in 1774 and was one of the founding members of the Royal Academy.]

On this ground, however unsafe, I will venture to prophecy, that two of the last distinguished painters of that country, I mean Pompeio Battoni, and Raffaelle Mengs, however great their names may at present sound in our ears, will very soon fall into the rank of Imperiale, Sebastian Concha, Placido Constanza, Massuccio, and the rest of their immediate predecessors; whose names, though equally renowned in their lifetime, are now fallen into what is little short of total oblivion. I do not say that those painters were not superior to the artist I allude to, and whose loss we lament, in a certain routine of practice which, to the eyes of common observers, has the air of a learned composition, and bears a sort of superficial resemblance to the manner of the great men who went before them. I know this perfectly well; but I know likewise, that a man, looking for real and lasting reputation, must unlearn much of the common-place method so observable in the works of the artists whom I have named. For my own part, I confess, I take more interest in, and am more captivated with the powerful impression of nature, which Gainsborough exhibited in his portraits and in his landscapes, and the interesting simplicity and elegance of his little ordinary beggar-children, than with any of the works of that school, since the time of Andrea Sacchi, or perhaps, we may say Carlo Maratti; two painters who may truly be said to be *Ultimi Romanorium.*[2]

I am well aware how much I lay myself open to the censure and ridicule of the academical professors of other nations, in preferring the humble attempts of Gainsborough to the works of those regular graduates in the great historical style. But we have the sanction of all mankind in preferring genius in a lower rank of art, to feebleness and insipidity in the highest.

It would not be to the present purpose, even if I had the means and materials, which I have not, to enter into the private life of Mr. Gainsborough. The history of his gradual advancement and the means by which he acquired such excellence in his art, would come nearer to our purpose and wishes, if

---

[2] [The last of the Romans.]

it were by any means attainable; but the slow progress of advancement is in general imperceptible to the man himself who makes it; it is the consequence of an accumulation of various ideas which his mind has received he does not perhaps know how or when. Sometimes indeed it happens, that he may be able to mark the time when, from the sight of a picture, a passage in an author, or a hint in conversation, he has received, as it were, some new and guiding light, something like inspiration, by which his mind has been expanded; and is morally sure that his whole life and conduct has been affected by that accidental circumstance. Such interesting accounts we may however sometimes obtain from a man who has acquired an uncommon habit of self-examination, and has attended to the progress of his own improvement.

It may not be improper to make mention of some of the customs and habits of this extraordinary man; points which come more within the reach of an observer; I however mean such only as are connected with his art, and indeed were, as I apprehend, the causes of his arriving to that high degree of excellence, which we see and acknowledge in his works. Of these causes we must state, as the fundamental, the love which he had to his art; to which, indeed, his whole mind appears to have been devoted, and to which every thing was referred; and this we may fairly conclude from various circumstances of his life, which were known to his intimate friends. Among others he had a habit of continually remarking to those who happened to be about him, whatever peculiarity of countenance, whatever accidental combination of figures, or happy effects of light and shadow, occurred in prospects, in the sky, in walking the streets, or in company. If, in his walks, he found a character that he liked, and whose attendance was to be obtained, he ordered him to his house: and from the fields he brought into his painting-room, stumps of trees, weeds, and animals of various kinds; and designed them, not from memory, but immediately from the objects. He even framed a kind of model of landscapes, on his table; composed of broken stones, dried herbs, and pieces of looking glass, which he magnified and improved into rocks, trees, and water. How far this latter practice may be useful in giving hints, the professors of landscape can best determine. Like every other technical practice it seems to me wholly to depend on the general talent of him who uses it. Such methods may be nothing better than contemptible and mischievous trifling; or they may be aids. I think upon the whole, unless we constantly refer to real nature, that practice may be more likely to do harm than good. I mention it only, as it shews the solicitude and extreme activity which he had about every thing that related to his art; that he wished to have his objects embodied as it were, and distinctly before him; that he neglected nothing which could keep his faculties in exercise, and derived hints from every sort of combination.[3]

We must not forget whilst we are on this subject, to make some remarks on his custom of painting by night, which confirms what I have already mentioned, his great affection to his art; since he could not amuse himself in the evenings by any other means so agreeable to himself. I am indeed much inclined to believe that it is a practice very advantageous and improving to an artist; for by this means he will acquire a new and a higher perception of what is great and beautiful in nature. By candle-light, not only objects appear more beautiful, but from their being in a greater breadth of light and shadow, as well as having a greater breadth and uniformity of colour, nature appears in a higher style; and even the flesh seems to take a higher and richer tone of colour. Judgment is to direct us in the use to be made of this method of study; but the method itself is, I am very sure, advantageous. I have often imagined that the two great colourists, Titian and Correggio, though I do not know that they painted effects of objects by this artificial light: but I am more assured that whoever attentively studies the first and best manner of Guercino,[4] will be convinced that he either painted by this light,

3 [See illustrations, Gainsborough's "Portrait of Mrs. David Garrick," and "Gainsborough's Forest."]

4 [Il Guercino (Giovanni Francesco Barbieri), born in Cento, Italy, 1591; died 1666.]

or formed his manner on this conception.

Another practice Gainsborough had, which is worth mentioning as it is certainly worthy of imitation; I mean his manner of forming all the parts of his picture together; the whole going on at the same time, in the same manner as nature creates her works. Though this method is not uncommon to those who have been regularly educated, yet probably it was suggested to him by his own natural sagacity. That this custom is not universal appears from the practice of a painter whom I have just mentioned, Pompeio Battoni, who finished his historical pictures part after part; and in his portraits completely finished one feature before he proceeded to another. The consequence was, as might be expected; the countenance was never well expressed; and, as the painters say, the whole was not well put together.

The first thing required to excel in our art, or I believe in any art, is, not only a love for it, but even an enthusiastick ambition to excel in it. This never fails of success proportioned to the natural abilities with which the artist has been endowed by Providence. Of Gainsborough, we certainly know, that his passion was not the acquirement of riches, but excellence in his art; and to enjoy that honourable fame which is sure to attend it.—That "he felt this ruling passion strong in death," [5] I am myself a witness. A few days before he died, he wrote me a letter, to express his acknowledgements for the good opinion I entertained of his abilities, and the manner in which (he had been informed) I always spoke of him; and desired he might see me, once more, before he died. I am aware how flattering it is to myself to be thus connected with the dying testimony which this excellent painter bore to his art. But I cannot prevail on myself to suppress that I was not connected with him by any habits of familiarity; if any little jealousies had subsisted between us, they were forgotten, in those moments of sin-

[5] [Alexander Pope, *Moral Essays*, Epistle I, 262–263:
And you! brave Cobham, to the latest breath
Shall feel your ruling passion strong in death:]

cerity; and he turned towards me as one, who was engrossed by the same pursuits, and who deserved his good opinion, by being sensible of his excellence. Without entering into a detail of what passed at this last interview, the impression of it upon my mind was, that his regret at losing life, was principally the regret of leaving his art; and more especially as he now began, he said, to see what his deficiencies were; which, he said, he flattered himself in his last works were in some measure applied.

When such a man as Gainsborough arrives to great fame, without the assistance of an academical education, without travelling to Italy, or any of those preparatory studies which have been so often recommended, he is produced as an instance, how little such studies are necessary; since so great excellence may be acquired without them. This is an inference not warranted by the success of any individual; and I trust it will not be thought that I wish to make this use of it.

It must be remembered that the style and department of art which Gainsborough chose, and in which he so much excelled, did not require that he should go out of his own country for the objects of his study; they were every where about him; he found them in the streets, and in the fields; and from the models thus accidentally found, he selected with great judgment such as suited his purpose. As his studies were directed to the living world principally, he did not pay a general attention to the works of the various masters, though they are, in my opinion, always of great use, even when the character of our subject requires us to depart from some of their principles. It cannot be denied, that excellence in the department of the art which he professed may exist without them; that in such subjects, and in the manner that belongs to them, the want of them is supplied, and more than supplied, by natural sagacity, and a minute observation of particular nature. If Gainsborough did not look at nature with a poet's eye, it must be acknowledged that he saw her with the eye of a painter; and gave a faithful, if not a poetical, representation of what he had before him.

Though he did not much attend to the works of the great historical painters of former ages, yet he was well aware, that the language of the art, the art of imitation, must be learned somewhere; and as he knew that he could not learn it in an equal degree from his contemporaries, he very judiciously applied himself to the Flemish school, who are undoubtedly the greatest masters of one necessary branch of art; and he did not need to go out of his own country for examples of that school: from that he learnt the harmony of colouring, the management and disposition of light and shadow, and every means which the masters of it practised, to ornament and give splendour to their works. And to satisfy himself as well as others, how well he knew the mechanism and artifice which they employed to bring out that tone of colour which we so much admire in their works, he occasionally made copies from Rubens, Teniers, and Vandyck, which it would be no disgrace to the most accurate connoisseur to mistake, at the first sight, for the works of those masters. What he thus learned, he applied to the originals of nature, which he saw with his own eyes; and imitated, not in the manner of those masters, but in his own.

Whether he most excelled in portraits, landscapes, or fancy-pictures, it is difficult to determine: whether his portraits were most admirable for exact truth of resemblance, or his landscapes for a portrait-like representation of nature, such as we see in the works of Rubens, Ruysdaal, and others of those schools. In his fancy-pictures, when he had fixed on his object of imitation, whether it was the mean and vulgar form of a wood-cutter, or a child of an interesting character, as he did not attempt to raise the one, so neither did he lose any of the natural grace and elegance of the other; such a grace, and such an elegance, as are more frequently found in cottages than in courts. This excellence was his own, the result of his particular observation and taste; for this he was certainly not indebted to the Flemish school, nor indeed to any school; for his grace was not academical, or antique, but selected by himself from the great school of nature; and there are yet a thousand modes of grace, which are neither theirs, nor his, but lie open in the multiplied scenes and figures of life, to be brought out by skilful and faithful observers.

Upon the whole, we may justly say, that whatever he attempted he carried to a high degree of excellence. It is to the credit of his good sense and judgment that he never did attempt that style of historical painting, for which his previous studies had made no preparation.

And here it naturally occurs to oppose the sensible conduct of Gainsborough in this respect, to that of our late excellent Hogarth,[6] who, with all his extraordinary talents, was not blessed with this knowledge of his own deficiency; or of the bounds which were set to the extent of his own powers. After this admirable artist had spent the greatest part of his life in an active, busy, and we may add, successful attention to the ridicule of life; after he had invented a new species of dramatick painting, in which probably he will never be equalled, and had stored his mind with infinite materials to explain and illustrate the domestick and familiar scenes of common life, which were generally, and ought to have been always, the subject of his pencil; he very imprudently, or rather presumptuously, attempted the great historical style, for which his previous habits had by no means prepared him: he was indeed so entirely unacquainted with the principles of this style, that he was not even aware, that any artificial preparation was at all necessary. It is to be regretted, that any part of the life of such a genius should be fruitlessly employed. Let his failure teach us not to indulge ourselves in the vain imagination, that by a momentary resolution we can give either dexterity to the hand, or a new habit to the mind.

I have, however, little doubt, but that the same sagacity, which enabled those two extraordinary men to discover their

6 [William Hogarth, born in London, 1697, died 1794, is best known today for his "Marriage à la Mode" (six pictures) and "The Rake's Progress" (eight pictures). His portraits met with varied success. His critical work *The Analysis of Beauty* (1753) is a significant document in the eighteenth-century English theory of art.]

true object, and the peculiar excellence of that branch of art which they cultivated, would have been equally effectual in discovering the principles of the higher style; if they had investigated those principles with the same eager industry, which they exerted in their own department. As Gainsborough never attempted the heroick style, so neither did he destroy the character and uniformity of his own style, by the idle affectation of introducing mythological learning in any of his pictures. Of this boyish folly we see instances enough, even in the works of great painters. When the Dutch school attempt this poetry of our art in their landscapes, their performances are beneath criticism; they become only an object of laughter. This practice is hardly excusable, even in Claude Lorrain, who had shewn more discretion, if he had never meddled with such subjects.

Our late ingenious academician, Wilson,[7] has, I fear, been guilty, like many of his predecessors, of introducing gods and goddesses, ideal beings, into scenes which were by no means prepared to receive such personages. His landscapes were in reality too near common nature to admit supernatural objects. In consequence of this mistake, in a very admirable picture of a storm, which I have seen of his hand, many figures are introduced in the fore-ground, some in apparent distress, and some struck dead, as a spectator would naturally suppose, by the lightning; had not the painter, injudiciously (as I think) rather chosen that their death should be imputed to a little Apollo, who appears in the sky, with his bent bow, and that those figures should be considered as the children of Niobe.

To manage a subject of this kind, a peculiar style of art is required; and it can only be done without impropriety, or even without ridicule, when we adapt the character of the

[7] [Richard Wilson, born in Montgomeryshire, England, in 1713, died 1782, was an unsuccessful landscape painter. He was librarian of the Academy (1776) and one of its original members. Although disappointed during his life, he is now regarded as one of the best of English landscape painters.]

landscape and that too, in all its parts, to the historical or
poetical representation. This is a very difficult adventure, and
it requires a mind thrown back two thousand years, and as
it were naturalized in antiquity, like that of Nicolas Poussin,
to achieve it. In the picture alluded to, the first idea that
presents itself, is that of wonder, at seeing a figure in so uncommon a situation as that in which the Apollo is placed; for
the clouds on which he kneels, have not the appearance of
being able to support him; they have neither the substance
nor the form, fit for the receptacle of a human figure; and
they do not possess in any respect that romantick character
which is appropriated to such a subject, and which alone can
harmonize with poetical stories.

It appears to me, that such conduct is no less absurd than
if a plain man, giving a relation of a real distress, occasioned
by an inundation accompanied with thunder and lightning,
should, instead of simply relating the event, take it into his
head, in order to give a grace to his narration, to talk of
Jupiter Pluvius, or Jupiter and his thunder-bolts, or any other
figurative idea; an intermixture which, though in poetry,
with its proper preparations and accompaniments, it might
be managed with effect, yet in the instance before us would
counteract the purpose of the narrator, and instead of being
interesting, would be only ridiculous.

The Dutch and Flemish style of landscape, not even ex-
cepting those of Rubens, is unfit for poetical subjects; but to
explain in what this inaptitude consists, or to point out all the
circumstances that give nobleness, grandeur, and the poetick
character, to style, in landscape, would require a long discourse of itself; and the end would be then perhaps but
imperfectly attained. The painter who is ambitious of this
perilous excellence, must catch his inspiration from those
who have cultivated with success the poetry, as it may be
called, of the art; and they are few indeed.

I cannot quit this subject without mentioning two examples
which occur to me at present, in which the poetical style of
landscape may be seen happily executed; the one is "Jacob's

Dream" by Salvator Rosa, and the other the "Return of the Arc from Captivity," by Sebastian Bourdon. With whatever dignity those histories are presented to us in the language of Scripture, this style of painting possesses the same power of inspiring sentiments of grandeur and sublimity, and is able to communicate them to subjects which appear by no means adapted to receive them. A ladder against the sky has no very promising appearance of possessing a capacity to excite any heroick ideas; and the Arc, in the hands of a second-rate master, would have little more effect than a common waggon on the highway; yet those subjects are so poetically treated throughout, the parts have such a correspondence with each other, and the whole and every part of the scene is so visionary, that it is impossible to look at them, without feeling, in some measure, the enthusiasm which seems to have inspired the painters.

By continual contemplation of such works, a sense of the higher excellencies of art will by degrees dawn on the imagination; at every review that sense will become more and more assured, until we come to enjoy a sober certainty of the real existence (if I may so express myself) of those almost ideal beauties; and the artist will then find no difficulty in fixing in his mind the principles by which the impression is produced; which he will feel, and practice, though they are perhaps too delicate and refined, and too peculiar to the imitative art, to be conveyed to the mind by any other means.

To return to Gainsborough: the peculiarity of his manner, or style, or we may call it—the language in which he expressed his ideas, has been considered by many, as his greatest defect. But without altogether wishing to enter into the discussion whether this peculiarity was a defect or not, intermixed, as it was, with great beauties, of some of which it was probably the cause, it becomes a proper subject of criticism and enquiry to a painter.

A novelty and peculiarity of manner, as it is often a cause of our approbation, so likewise it is often a ground of censure; as being contrary to the practice of other painters, in whose manner we have been initiated, and in whose favour we have perhaps been prepossessed from our infancy; for, fond as we are of novelty, we are upon the whole creatures of habit. However, it is certain, that all those odd scratches and marks, which, on a close examination, are so observable in Gainsborough's pictures, and which even to experienced painters appear rather the effect of accident than design; this chaos, this uncouth and shapeless appearance, by a kind of magick, at a certain distance assumes form, and all the parts seem to drop into their proper places; so that we can hardly refuse acknowledging the full effect of diligence, under the appearance of chance and hasty negligence. That Gainsborough himself considered this peculiarity in his manner and the power it possesses of exciting surprise, as a beauty in his works, I think may be inferred from the eager desire which we know he always expressed, that his pictures, at the Exhibition, should be seen near, as well as at a distance.

The slightness which we see in his best works, cannot always be imputed to negligence. However they may appear to superficial observers, painters know very well that a steady attention to the general effect, takes up more time, and is much more laborious to the mind, than any mode of high finishing or smoothness, without such attention. His *handling, the manner of leaving the colours,* or in other words, the methods he used for producing the effect, had very much the appearance of the work of an artist who had never learned from others the usual and regular practice belonging to the art; but still, like a man of strong intuitive perception of what was required, he found out a way of his own to accomplish his purpose.

It is no disgrace to the genius of Gainsborough, to compare him to such men as we sometimes meet with, whose natural eloquence appears even in speaking a language, which they can scarce be said to understand; and who, without knowing the appropriate expression of almost any one idea, contrive to communicate the lively and forcible impressions of an energetick mind.

I think some apology may reasonably be made for his manner, without violating truth, or running any risk of poisoning the minds of the younger students, by propagating false criticism, for the sake of raising the character of a favourite artist. It must be allowed, that this hatching [8] manner of Gainsborough did very much contribute to the lightness of effect which is so eminent a beauty in his pictures; as on the contrary, much smoothness, and uniting the colours, is apt to produce heaviness. Every artist must have remarked, how often that lightness of hand which was in his dead-colour,[9] or first painting, escaped in the finishing, when he had determined the parts with more precision; and another loss he often experiences, which is of greater consequence; whilst he is employed in the detail, the effect of the whole together is either forgotten or neglected. The likeness of a portrait, as I have formerly observed, consists more in preserving the general effect of the countenance, than in the most minute finishing of the features, or any of the particular parts. Now Gainsborough's portraits were often little more, in regard to finishing, or determining the form of the features, than what generally attends a dead-colour; but as he was always attentive to the general effect, or whole together, I have often imagined that this unfinished manner contributed even to that striking resemblance for which his portraits are so remarkable. Though this opinion may be considered as fanciful, yet I think a plausible reason may be given, why such a mode of painting should have such an effect. It is presupposed that in this undetermined manner there is the general effect; enough to remind the spectator of the original; the imagination supplies the rest, and perhaps more satisfactorily to himself, if not more exactly, than the artist, with all his care, could possibly have done. At the same time it must be acknowledged there is one evil attending this mode; that if the portrait were seen, previous to any knowledge of the original, different persons would

[8] [Crosshatching of lines.]
[9] [The preliminary layer of color in a painting.]

form different ideas, and all would be disappointed at not finding the original correspond with their own conceptions; under the great latitude which indistinctness gives to the imagination, to assume almost what character or form it pleases.

Every artist has some favourite part on which he fixes his attention, and which he pursues with such eagerness, that it absorbs every other consideration; and he often falls into the opposite error of that which he would avoid, which is always ready to receive him. Now Gainsborough having truly a painter's eye for colouring, cultivated those effects of the art which proceed from colours; and sometimes appears to be indifferent to or to neglect other excellencies. Whatever defects are acknowledged, let him still experience from us the same candour that we so freely give upon similar occasions to the ancient masters; let us not encourage that fastidious disposition, which is discontented with every thing short of perfection, and unreasonably require, as we sometimes do, a union of excellencies, not perhaps quite compatible with each other.—We may, on this ground, say even of the divine Raffaelle, that he might have finished his picture as highly and as correctly as was his custom, without heaviness of manner; and that Poussin might have preserved all his precision without hardness or dryness.

To shew the difficulty of uniting solidity with lightness of manner, we may produce a picture of Rubens in the Church of St. Judule, at Brussels, as an example; the subject is, "Christ's Charge to Peter" which, as it is the highest, and smoothest, finished picture I remember to have seen of that master, so it is by far the heaviest; and if I had found it in any other place, I should have suspected it to be a copy; for painters know very well, that it is principally by this air of facility, or the want of it, that originals are distinguished from copies.—A lightness of effect, produced by colour, and that produced by facility of handling, are generally united; a copy may preserve something of the one, it is true, but hardly ever of the other; a connoisseur therefore finds it often necessary to look carefully into the picture before he determines on its originality. Gainsborough possessed this quality of lightness of manner and effect, I think, to an unexampled degree of excellence; but, it must be acknowledged, at the same time, that the sacrifice which he made to this ornament of our art, was too great; it was, in reality, preferring the lesser excellencies to the greater.

To conclude. However, we may apologize for the deficiencies of Gainsborough, (I mean particularly his want of precision and finishing,) who so ingeniously contrived to cover his defects by his beauties; and who cultivated that department of art, where such defects are more easily excused; you are to remember, that no apology can be made for this deficiency, in that style which this Academy teaches, and which ought to be the object of your pursuit. It will be necessary for you, in the first place, never to lose sight of the great rules and principles of the art, as they are collected from the full body of the best general practice, and the most constant and uniform experience; this must be the ground-work of all your studies: afterwards you may profit, as in this case I wish you to profit, by the peculiar experience and personal talents of artists living and dead; you may derive lights, and catch hints from their practice; but the moment you turn them into models, you fall infinitely below them; you may be corrupted by excellencies, not so much belonging to the art as personal and appropriated to the artist; and become bad copies of good painters, instead of excellent imitators of the great universal truth of things.

~ Discourse 15

December 10, 1790

GENTLEMEN,

THE intimate connection which I have had with the Royal
Academy ever since its establishment, the social duties in
which we have all mutually engaged for so many years, make
any profession of attachment to this institution, on my part,
altogether superfluous; the influence of habit alone in such a
connexion would naturally have produced it.

Among men united in the same body, and engaged in the
same pursuit, along with permanent friendship occasional differences will arise. In these disputes men are naturally too
favourable to themselves, and think perhaps too hardly of
their antagonists. But composed and constituted as we are,
those little contentions will be lost to others, and they ought
certainly to be lost amongst ourselves, in mutual esteem for
talents and acquirements: every controversy ought to be, and
I am persuaded will be, sunk in our zeal for the perfection of
our common art.

In parting with the Academy, I shall remember with pride,
affection, and gratitude, the support with which I have almost
uniformly been honoured from the commencement of our intercourse. I shall leave you, gentlemen, with unaffected cordial
wishes for your future concord, and with a well-founded hope,
that in that concord, the auspicious and not obscure origin of
our Academy may be forgotten in the splendour of your succeeding prospects.

My age, and my infirmities still more than my age, make it

224

probable that this will be the last time I shall have the honour of addressing you from this place. Excluded as I am, *spatiis iniquis*,[1] from indulging my imagination with a distant and forward perspective of life, I may be excused if I turn my eyes back on the way which I have passed.

We may assume to ourselves, I should hope, the credit of having endeavoured, at least, to fill with propriety that middle station which we hold in the general connexion of things, Our predecessors have laboured for our advantage, we labour for our successors; and though we have done no more in this mutual intercourse and reciprocation of benefits, than has been effected by other societies formed in this nation for the advancement of useful and ornamental knowledge, yet there is one circumstance which appears to me to give *us* an higher claim than the credit of merely doing our duty. What I at present allude to, is the honour of having been, some of us, the first contrivers, and all of us the promoters and supporters, of the annual Exhibition. This scheme could only have originated from artists already in possession of the favour of the publick, as it would not have been so much in the power of others to have excited curiosity. It must be remembered, that for the sake of bringing forward into notice concealed merit, they incurred the risk of producing rivals to themselves; they voluntarily entered the lists, and ran the race a second time for the prize which they had already won.

When we take a review of the several departments of the institution, I think we may safely congratulate ourselves on our good fortune in having hitherto seen the chairs of our professors filled with men of distinguished abilities, and who have so well acquitted themselves of their duty in their several departments. I look upon it to be of importance, that none of them should be ever left unfilled: a neglect to provide for qualified persons, is to produce a neglect of qualifications.

In this honourable rank of professors, I have not presumed to class myself, though in the discourses which I have had the

[1] ["Because of the insufficiency of the time remaining" (to me), (Virgil, *Georgics* IV. 147).]

honour of delivering from this place, while in one respect I
may be considered as a volunteer, in another view it seems as
if I was involuntarily pressed into this service. If prizes were
to be given, it appeared not only proper, but almost indispensably necessary, that something should be said by the President
on the delivery of those prizes; and the President for his own
credit would wish to say something more than mere words of
compliment, which, by being frequently repeated, would soon
become flat and uninteresting, and by being uttered to many,
would at last become a distinction to none: I thought, therefore, if I were to preface this compliment with some instructive
observations on the art, when we crowned merit in the artist
whom we rewarded, I might do something to animate and
guide them in their future attempts.

I am truly sensible how unequal I have been to the expression of my own ideas. To develop the latent excellencies,
and draw out the interior principles, of our art, requires more
skill and practice in writing, than is likely to be possessed by
a man perpetually occupied in the use of the pencil and the
pallet. It is for that reason, perhaps, that the sister art has had
the advantage of better criticism. Poets are naturally writers
of prose. They may be said to be practising only an inferior
department of their own art, when they are explaining and
expatiating upon its most refined principles. But still such
difficulties ought not to deter artists who are not prevented by
other engagements from putting their thoughts in order as
well as they can, and from giving to the publick the result of
their experience. The knowledge which an artist has of his
subject will more than compensate for any want of elegance in
the manner of treating it, or even of perspicuity, which is still
more essential; and I am convinced that one short essay written
by a painter, will contribute more to advance the theory of
our art, than a thousand volumes such as we sometimes see;
the purpose of which appears to be rather to display the refinement of the author's own conceptions of impossible practice, than to convey useful knowledge or instruction of any
kind whatever. An artist knows what is, and what is not,

within the province of his art to perform, and is not likely to be for ever teazing the poor student with the beauties of mixed passions, or to perplex him with an imaginary union of excellencies incompatible with each other.

To this work, however, I could not be said to come totally unprovided with materials. I had seen much, and I had thought much upon what I had seen; I had something of an habit of investigation, and a disposition to reduce all that I observed and felt in my own mind, to method and system; but never having seen what I myself knew, distinctly placed before me on paper, I knew nothing correctly. To put those ideas into something like order was, to my inexperience, no easy task. The composition, the *ponere totum* [2] even of a single discourse, as well as of a single statue, was the most difficult part, as perhaps it is of every other art, and most requires the hand of a master.

For the manner, whatever deficiency there was, I might reasonably expect indulgence; but I thought it indispensably necessary well to consider the opinions which were to be given out from this place, and under the sanction of a Royal Academy; I therefore examined not only my own opinions, but likewise the opinions of others. I found in the course of this research, many precepts and rules established in our art, which did not seem to me altogether reconcileable with each other, yet each seemed in itself to have the same claim of being supported by truth and nature; and this claim, irreconcileable as they may be thought, they do in reality alike possess.

To clear away those difficulties, and reconcile those contrary opinions, it became necessary to distinguish the greater truth, as it may be called, from the lesser truth; the larger and more liberal idea of nature from the more narrow and confined; that which addresses itself to the imagination, from that which is solely addressed to the eye. In consequence of this discrimination, the different branches of our art, to which those different truths were referred, were perceived to make so wide a

[2] ["The disposition of the whole" (Horace, *Ars poetica* 35).]

separation, and put on so new an appearance, that they seemed scarcely to have proceeded from the same general stock. The different rules and regulations, which presided over each department of art, followed of course: every mode of excellence, from the grand style of the Roman and Florentine schools down to the lowest rank of still life, had its due weight and value; fitted some class or other; and nothing was thrown away. By this disposition of our art into classes, that perplexity and confusion, which I apprehend every artist has at some time experienced from the variety of styles, and the variety of excellence with which he is surrounded, is, I should hope, in some measure removed, and the student better enabled to judge for himself, what peculiarly belongs to his own particular pursuit.

In reviewing my discourses, it is no small satisfaction to be assured that I have, in no part of them, lent my assistance to foster *newly-hatched unfledged* opinions, or endeavoured to support paradoxes, however tempting may have been their novelty, or however ingenious I might, for the minute, fancy them to be; nor shall I, I hope, any where be found to have imposed on the minds of young students declamation for argument, a smooth period for a sound precept. I have pursued a plain and *honest method;* I have taken up the art simply as I found it exemplified in the practice of the most approved painters. That approbation which the world has uniformly given, I have endeavoured to justify by such proofs as questions of this kind will admit; by the analogy which painting holds with the sister arts, and consequently by the common congeniality which they all bear to our nature. And though in what has been done, no new discovery is pretended, I may still flatter myself, that from the discoveries which others have made by their own intuitive good sense and native rectitude of judgment, I have succeeded in establishing the rules and principles of our art on a more firm and lasting foundation than that on which they had formerly been placed.

Without wishing to divert the student from the practice

of his art to speculative theory, to make him a mere connoisseur instead of a painter, I cannot but remark, that he will certainly find an account in considering once for all, on what ground the fabrick of our art is built. Uncertain, confused, or erroneous opinions are not only detrimental to an artist in their immediate operation, but may possibly have very serious consequences; affect his conduct, and give a peculiar character (as it may be called) to his taste, and to his pursuits, through his whole life.

I was acquainted at Rome in the early part of my life, with a student of the French Academy, who appeared to me to possess all the qualities requisite to make a great artist, if he had suffered his taste and feelings, and I may add even his prejudices, to have fair play. He saw and felt the excellencies of the great works of art with which we were surrounded, but lamented that there was not to be found that nature which is so admirable in the inferior schools; and he supposed with Felibien, Du Piles, and other theorists, that such an union of different excellencies would be the perfection of art. He was not aware, that the narrow idea of nature, of which he lamented the absence in the works of those great artists, would have destroyed the grandeur of the general ideas which he admired, and which was indeed the cause of his admiration. My opinions being then confused and unsettled, I was in danger of being borne down by this kind of plausible reasoning, though I remember I then had a dawning of suspicion that it was not sound doctrine; and at the same time I was unwilling obstinately to refuse assent to what I was unable to confute.

That the young artist may not be seduced from the right path, by following what, at first view, he may think the light of reason, and which is indeed reason in part, but not in the whole, has been much the object of these discourses.

I have taken every opportunity of recommending a rational method of study, as of the last importance. The great, I may say the sole, use of an Academy is, to put, and for some time to keep, students in that course; that too much indulgence may not be given to peculiarity, and that a young man may not be taught to believe, that what is generally good for others is not good for him.

I have strongly inculcated in my former discourses, as I do in this my last, the wisdom and necessity of previously obtaining the appropriated instruments of the art, in a first correct design, and a plain manly colouring, before any thing more is attempted. But by this I would not wish to cramp and fetter the mind, or discourage those who follow (as most of us may at one time have followed) the suggestion of a strong inclination: something must be conceded to great and irresistible impulses: perhaps every student must not be strictly bound to general methods, if they strongly thwart the peculiar turn of his own mind. I must confess, that it is not absolutely of much consequence, whether he proceeds in the general method of seeking first to acquire mechanical accuracy, before he attempts poetical flights, provided he diligently studies to attain the full perfection of the style he pursues; whether like Parmegiano, he endeavours at grace and grandeur of manner before he has learned correctness of drawing, if like him he feels his own wants, and will labour, as that eminent artist did, to supply those wants; whether he starts from the east or from the west, if he relaxes in no exertion to arrive ultimately at the same goal. The first publick work of Parmegiano is the "St. Eustachius," in the church of St. Petronius in Bologna, and was done when he was a boy; and one of the last of his works is the "Moses Breaking the Tables" in Parma. In the former there is certainly something of grandeur in the outline, or in the conception of the figure, which discovers the dawnings of future greatness; of a young mind impregnated with the sublimity of Michael Angelo, whose style he here attempts to imitate, though he could not then draw the human figure with any common degree of correctness. But this same Parmegiano, when in his more mature age he painted the Moses, had so completely supplied his first defects, that we are here at a loss which to admire most, the correctness of drawing, or the grandeur of the conception. As a confirmation of its great excellence, and of the impression which it leaves on the minds of elegant spectators, I may observe, that our great lyrick poet, when he conceived his sublime idea of the indignant Welch bard,[3] acknowledged, that though many years had intervened, he had warmed his imagination with the remembrance of this noble figure of Parmegiano.

When we consider that Michael Angelo was the great archetype to whom Parmegiano was indebted for that grandeur which we find in his works, and from whom all his contemporaries and successors have derived whatever they have possessed of the dignified and the majestick; that he was the bright luminary, from whom painting has borrowed a new lustre; that under his hands it assumed a new appearance, and is become another and superior art; I may be excused if I take this opportunity, as I have hitherto taken every occasion, to turn your attention to this exalted founder and father of modern art, of which he was not only the inventor, but which by the divine energy of his own mind, he carried at once to its highest point of possible perfection.

The sudden maturity to which Michael Angelo brought our art, and the comparative feebleness of his followers and imitators, might perhaps be reasonably, at least plausibly explained, if we had time for such an examination. At present I shall only observe, that the subordinate parts of our art, and perhaps of other arts, expand themselves by a slow and progressive growth; but those which depend on a native vigour of imagination generally burst forth at once in fullness of beauty. Of this Homer probably, and Shakspeare more assuredly, are signal examples. Michael Angelo possessed the poetical part of our art in a most eminent degree; and the same daring spirit, which urged him first to explore the unknown regions of the imagination, delighted with the novelty, and animated by the success of his discoveries, could not have failed to stimulate and impel him forward in his career beyond those limits, which his followers destitute of the same incentives, had not strength to pass.

---

[3] [Thomas Gray (1716–1771), "The Bard."]

To distinguish between correctness of drawing, and that part which respects the imagination, we may say the one approaches to the mechanical (which in its way too may make just pretensions to genius) and the other to the poetical. To encourage a solid and vigorous course of study, it may not be amiss to suggest, that perhaps a confidence in the mechanick produces a boldness in the poetick. He that is sure of the goodness of his ship and tackle puts out fearlessly from the shore; and he who knows, that his hand can execute whatever his fancy can suggest, sports with more freedom in embodying the visionary forms of his own creation. I will not say Michael Angelo was eminently poetical, only because he was greatly mechanical; but I am sure that mechanick excellence invigorated and emboldened his mind to carry painting into the regions of poetry, and to emulate that art in its most adventurous flights. Michael Angelo equally possessed both qualifications. Yet of mechanick excellence there were certainly great examples to be found in ancient sculpture, and particularly in the fragment known by the name of the "Torso" of Michael Angelo; but of that grandeur of character, air, and attitude, which he threw into all his figures, and which so well corresponds with the grandeur of his outline, there was no example; it could therefore proceed only from the most poetical and sublime imagination.

It is impossible not to express some surprise, that the race of painters who preceded Michael Angelo, men of acknowledged great abilities, should never have thought of transferring a little of that grandeur of outline which they could not but see and admire in ancient sculpture, into their own works; but they appear to have considered sculpture as the later schools of artists look at the inventions of Michael Angelo, as something to be admired, but with which they have nothing to do: *quod super nos, nihil ad nos.*[4]—The artists of that age, even Raffaelle himself, seemed to be going on very contentedly in the dry manner of Pietro Perugino; and if Michael

[4] ["What is greater than us is nothing to us" (Minucius Felix, *Octavius* XIII. 1).]

Angelo had never appeared, the art might still have continued in the same style.

Beside Rome and Florence, where the grandeur of this style was first displayed, it was on this foundation that the Caracci built the truly great academical Bolognian school, of which the first stone was laid by Pellegrino Tibaldi. He first introduced this style amongst them; and many instances might be given in which he appears to have possessed as by inheritance, the true, genuine, noble and elevated mind of Michael Angelo. Though we cannot venture to speak of him with the same fondness as his countrymen, and call him, as the Caracci did, *Nostro Michael Angelo riformato*,[5] yet he has a right to be considered amongst the first and greatest of his followers: there are certainly many drawings and inventions of his, of which Michael Angelo himself might not disdain to be supposed the author, or that they should be, as in fact they often are, mistaken for his. I will mention one particular instance, because it is found in a book which is in every young artist's hands;—Bishop's *Ancient Statues*.[6] He there has introduced a print, representing Polyphemus, from a drawing of Tibaldi and has inscribed it with the name of Michael Angelo, to whom he has also in the same book attributed a sybil of Raffaelle. Both these figures, it is true, are professedly in Michael Angelo's style and spirit, and even worthy of his hand. But we know that the former is painted in the *Institute a Bologna* by Tibaldi, and the other in the *Pace* [7] by Raffaelle.

The Caracci, it is acknowledged, adopted the mechanical part with sufficient success. But the divine part which addresses itself to the imagination, as possessed by Michael Angelo or Tibaldi, was beyond their grasp: they formed, however, a most respectable school, a style more on the level, and calculated to please a greater number; and if excellence of this kind is to be valued according to the number, rather than

---

5 ["Our reformed (i.e., recreated) Michelangelo."]

6 [Jan de Bisschop, *Paradigmata Graphices* (Amsterdam, 1671).]

7 [The Church of Santa Maria della Pace, Rome.]

the weight and quality of admirers, it would assume even an higher rank in art. The same, in some sort, may be said of Tintoret, Paul Veronese, and others of the Venetian painters. They certainly much advanced the dignity of their style by adding to their fascinating powers of colouring something of the strength of Michael Angelo; at the same time it may still be a doubt how far their ornamental elegance would be an advantageous addition to his grandeur. But if there is any manner of painting which may be said to unite kindly with his style, it is that of Titian. His handling, the manner in which his colours are left on the canvas, appears to proceed (as far as that goes) from a congenial mind, equally disdainful of vulgar criticism.

Michael Angelo's strength thus qualified, and made more palatable to the general taste, reminds me of an observation which I heard a learned critick [8] make, when it was incidentally remarked, that our translation of Homer, however excellent, did not convey the character, nor had the grand air of the original. He replied, that if Pope had not cloathed the naked majesty of Homer with the graces and elegancies of modern fashions, though the real dignity of Homer was degraded by such a dress, his translation would not have met with such a favourable reception, and he must have been contented with fewer readers.

Many of the Flemish painters, who studied at Rome, in that great era of our art, such as Francis Floris, Hemskerk, Michael Coxis, Jerom Cock, and others, returned to their own country, with as much of this grandeur as they could carry. But like seeds falling on a soil not prepared or adapted to their nature, the manner of Michael Angelo thrived but little with them; perhaps, however, they contributed to prepare the way for that free, unconstrained, and liberal outline, which was afterwards introduced by Rubens, through the medium of the Venetian painters.

[8] Dr. Johnson [said Pope's translation of Homer was the greatest work of the kind that has ever been produced (Boswell, *Life of Johnson*, III, 257)].

This grandeur of style has been in different degrees disseminated over all Europe. Some caught it by living at the time, and coming into contact with the original author, whilst others received it at second hand; and being every where adopted, it has totally changed the whole taste and style of design, if there could be said to be any style before his time. Our art, in consequence, now assumes a rank to which it could never have dared to aspire if Michael Angelo had not discovered to the world the hidden powers which it possessed. Without his assistance we never could have been convinced, that painting was capable of producing an adequate representation of the persons and actions of the heroes of the Iliad.

I would ask any man qualified to judge of such works, whether he can look with indifference at the personification of the Supreme Being in the center of the Capella Sestina, or the figures of the sybils which surround that chapel,[9] to which we may add the statue of Moses; and whether the same sensations are not excited by those works, as what he may remember to have felt from the most sublime passages of Homer? I mention those figures more particularly, as they come nearer to a comparison with his Jupiter, his demi-gods, and heroes; those sybils and prophets being a kind of intermediate beings between men and angels. Though instances may be produced in the works of other painters, which may justly stand in competition with those I have mentioned, such as the "Isaiah," and the "Vision of Ezekiel," by Raffaelle, the "St. Mark" of Frate Bartolomeo, and many others; yet these, it must be allowed, are inventions so much in Michael Angelo's manner of thinking, that they may be truly considered as so many rays which discover manifestly the center from whence they emanated.

The sublime in painting, as in poetry, so overpowers, and takes such a possession of the whole mind, that no room is left for attention to minute criticism. The little elegancies of art in the presence of these great ideas thus greatly expressed, lose all their value, and are, for the instant at least, felt to be

9 [See illustrations, Michelangelo's "The Delphic Sybil."]

unworthy of our notice. The correct judgment, the purity of taste, which characterise Raffaelle, the exquisite grace of Correggio and Parmegiano, all disappear before them.

That Michael Angelo was capricious in his inventions, cannot be denied; and this may make some circumspection necessary in studying his works; for though they appear to become him, an imitation of them is always dangerous, and will prove sometimes ridiculous. "Within that circle none durst walk but he." [10] To me, I confess, his caprice does not lower the estimation of his genius, even though it is sometimes, I acknowledge, carried to the extreme: and however those eccentrick excursions are considered, we must at the same time recollect, that those faults, if they are faults, are such as never could occur to a mean and vulgar mind; that they flowed from the same source which produced his greatest beauties, and were therefore such as none but himself was capable of committing; they were the powerful impulses of a mind unused to subjection of any kind, and too high to be controlled by cold criticism.

Many see his daring extravagance, who can see nothing else. A young artist finds the works of Michael Angelo so totally different from those of his own master, or of those with whom he is surrounded, that he may be easily persuaded to abandon and neglect studying a style, which appears to him wild, mysterious, and above his comprehension, and which he therefore feels no disposition to admire; a good disposition, which he concludes that he should naturally have, if the style deserved it. It is necessary therefore that students should be prepared for the disappointment which they may experience at their first setting out; and they must be cautioned, that probably they will not, at first sight, approve.

It must be remembered, that as this great style itself is artificial in the highest degree, it presupposes in the spectator,

10 [Dryden, "Prologue to *The Tempest*":
But *Shakespear's* Magick could not copy'd be,
Within that circle none durst walk but he.]

a cultivated and prepared artificial state of mind. It is an absurdity therefore to suppose that we are born with this taste, though we are with the seeds of it, which, by the heat and kindly influences of his genius, may be ripened in us.

A late philosopher and critick [11] has observed, speaking of taste, that "we are on no account to expect that fine things should descend to us,"—our taste, if possible, must be made to ascend to them. The same learned writer recommends to us "even to feign a relish, till we find a relish come; and feel, that what began in fiction, terminates in reality." If there be in our art, any thing of that agreement or compact, such as I apprehend there is in musick, with which the critick is necessarily required previously to be acquainted, in order to form a correct judgment; the comparison with this art will illustrate what I have said on these points, and tend to shew the probability, we may say the certainty, that men are not born with a relish for those arts in their most refined state, which as they cannot understand, they cannot be impressed with their effects. This great style of Michael Angelo is as far removed from the simple representation of the common objects of nature, as the most refined Italian musick is from the inartificial notes of nature, from whence they both profess to originate. But without such a supposed compact, we may be very confident that the highest state of refinement in either of those arts will not be relished without a long and industrious attention.

In pursuing this great art, it must be acknowledged that we labour under greater difficulties than those who were born in the age of its discovery, and whose minds from their infancy were habituated to this style; who learnt it as language, as their mother tongue. They had no mean state to unlearn; they needed no persuasive discourse to allure them to a favourable reception of it, no abstruse investigation of its principles to convince them of the great latent truths on which it is founded. We are constrained, in these later days, to have re-

[11] James Harris, Esq. [Both passages are from "Rules Defended," *Philological Inquiries*, Part II, chap. 12, in Harris' *Works* (Oxford, 1841).]

course to a sort of grammar and dictionary, as the only means of recovering a dead language. It was by them learned by rote, and perhaps better learned that way than by precept.

The style of Michael Angelo, which I have compared to language, and which may, poetically speaking, be called the language of the gods, now no longer exists, as it did in the fifteenth century; yet, with the aid of diligence, we may in a great measure supply the deficiency which I mentioned, of not having his works so perpetually before our eyes, by having recourse to casts from his models and designs in sculpture; to drawings or even copies of those drawings; to prints, which however ill executed, still convey something by which this taste may be formed; and a relish may be fixed and established in our minds for this grand style of invention. Some examples of this kind we have in the Academy; and I sincerely wish there were more, that the younger students might in their first nourishment, imbibe this taste; whilst others, though settled in the practice of the common-place style of painters, might infuse, by this means, a grandeur into their works.

I shall now make some remarks on the course which I think most proper to be pursued in such a study. I wish you not to go so much to the derivative streams, as to the fountain-head; though the copies are not to be neglected; because they may give you hints in what manner you may copy, and how the genius of one man may be made to fit the peculiar manner of another.

To recover this lost taste, I would recommend young artists to study the works of Michael Angelo, as he himself did the works of the ancient sculptors; he began, when a child, a copy of a mutilated satyr's head, and finished in his model what was wanting in the original. In the same manner, the first exercise that I would recommend to the young artist when he first attempts invention, is to select every figure, if possible, from the inventions of Michael Angelo. If such borrowed figures will not bend to his purpose, and he is constrained to make a change to supply a figure himself, that figure will necessarily be in the same style with the rest, and his taste will by this means be naturally initiated, and nursed in the lap of grandeur. He will sooner perceive what constitutes this grand style by one practical trial than by a thousand speculations, and he will in some sort procure to himself that advantage which in these later ages has been denied him; the advantage of having the greatest of artists for his master and instructor.

The next lesson should be, to change the purpose of the figures without changing the attitude, as Tintoretto has done with the Sampson of Michael Angelo. Instead of the figure which Sampson bestrides, he has placed an eagle under him and instead of the jawbone, thunder and lightening in his right hand; and thus it becomes a Jupiter. Titian, in the same manner, has taken the figure which represents God dividing the light from the darkness in the vault of the Capella Sestina, and has introduced it in the famous battle of Cadore, so much celebrated by Vasari; and extraordinary as it may seem, it is here converted to a general, falling from his horse. A real judge who should look at this picture, would immediately pronounce the attitude of that figure to be in a greater style than any other figure of the composition. These two instances may be sufficient, though many more might be given in their works, as well as in those of other great artists.

When the student has been habituated to this grand conception of the art, when the relish for this style is established, makes a part of himself, and is woven into his mind, he will, by this time, have got a power of selecting from whatever occurs in nature that is grand, and corresponds with that taste which he has now acquired, and will pass over whatever is common-place and insipid. He may then bring to the mart such works of his own proper invention as may enrich and increase the general stock of invention in our art.

I am confident of the truth and propriety of the advice which I have recommended; at the same time I am aware, how much by this advice I have laid myself open to the sarcasms of those criticks who imagine our art to be a matter of inspiration. But I should be sorry it should appear even to my-

self that I wanted that courage which I have recommended to
the students in another way: equal courage perhaps is required in the adviser and the advised; they both must
equally dare and bid defiance to narrow criticism and vulgar opinion.

That the art has been in a gradual state of decline, from
the age of Michael Angelo to the present, must be acknowledged; and we may reasonably impute this declension to the
same cause to which the ancient cricks and philosophers
have imputed the corruption of eloquence. Indeed the same
causes are likely at all times and in all ages to produce the
same effects: indolence,—not taking the same pains as our
great predecessors took,—desiring to find a shorter way,—are
the general imputed causes. The words of Petronius [12] are
very remarkable. After opposing the natural chaste beauty
of the eloquence of former ages to the strained inflated style
then in fashion, "neither," says he, "has the art of painting
had a better fate, after the boldness of the Egyptians had
found out a compendious way to execute so great art."

By "compendious," I understand him to mean a mode of
painting, such as has infected the style of the later painters
of Italy and France; common-place, without thought, and
with as little trouble, working as by a receipt; in contra-
distinction to that style for which even a relish cannot be
acquired without care and long attention, and most certainly
the power of executing cannot be obtained without the most
laborious application.

I have endeavoured to stimulate the ambition of artists to
tread in this great path of glory, and, as well as I can, have
pointed out the track which leads to it, and have at the same
time told them the price at which it may be obtained. It is
an ancient saying, that labour is the price which the gods have
set upon every thing valuable.

The great artist, who has been so much the subject of the
present discourse, was distinguished even from his infancy for

[12] Pictura quoque non alium exitum fecit, postquam Aegyptiorum
audacia tam magnae artis compendiariam invenit. [Petronius, *Satyricon* 2.]

his indefatigable diligence; and this was continued through his whole life, till prevented by extreme old age. The poorest of men, as he observed himself, did not labour from necessity, more than he did from choice. Indeed, from all the circumstances related of his life, he appears not to have had the least conception that his art was to be acquired by any other means than by great labour; and yet he, of all men that ever lived, might make the greatest pretensions to the efficacy of native genius and inspiration. I have no doubt that he would have thought it no disgrace, that it should be said of him, as he himself said of Raffaelle, that he did not possess his art from nature, but by long study.[13] He was conscious that the great excellence to which he arrived was gained by dint of labour, and was unwilling to have it thought that any transcendent skill, however natural its effects might seem, could be purchased at a cheaper price than he had paid for it. This seems to have been the true drift of his observation. We cannot suppose it made with any intention of depreciating the genius of Raffaelle, of whom he always spoke, as Condivi says, with the greatest respect: though they were rivals, no such illiberality existed between them; and Raffaelle on his part entertained the greatest veneration for Michael Angelo, as appears from the speech which is recorded of him, that he congratulated himself, and thanked God, that he was born in the same age with that painter.

If the high esteem and veneration in which Michael Angelo has been held by all nations and in all ages, should be put to the account of prejudice, it must still be granted that those prejudices could not have been entertained without a cause: the ground of our prejudice then becomes the source of our admiration. But from whatever it proceeds, or whatever it is called, it will not I hope, be thought presumptuous in me to appear in the train, I cannot say of his imitators, but of his admirers. I have taken another course, one more suited to my abilities, and to the taste of the times in which I live. Yet however unequal I feel myself to that attempt,

[13] *Che Raffaelle non ebbe quest' arte da natura, ma per lungo studio.*

were I now to begin the world again, I would tread in the steps of that great master: to kiss the hem of his garment, to catch the slightest of his perfections, would be glory and distinction enough for an ambitious man.

I feel a self-congratulation in knowing myself capable of such sensations as he intended to excite. I reflect not without vanity, that these discourses bear testimony of my admiration of that truly divine man, and I should desire that the last words which I should pronounce in this Academy, and from this place, might be the name of—Michael Angelo.[14]

THE END OF THE DISCOURSES

[14] Unfortunately for mankind, these *were* the last words pronounced by this great painter from the Academical chair. He died about fourteen months after this discourse was delivered.

Selections from *The Idler*

⟐ Selections from *The Idler*

Number 76

I was much pleased with your ridicule of those shallow
criticks, whose judgment, though often right as far as it goes,
yet reaches only to inferior beauties, and who, unable to
comprehend the whole, judge only by parts, and from thence
determine the merit of extensive works. But there is another
kind of critick still worse, who judges by narrow rules, and
those too often false, and which, though they should be true,
and founded on nature, will lead him but a very little way
toward the just estimation of the sublime beauties in works
of genius; for whatever part of an art can be executed or
criticised by rules, that part is no longer the work of genius,
which implies excellence out of the reach of rules.

Number 79

Amongst the painters, and the writers on painting, there
is one maxim universally admitted and continually inculcated. *Imitate nature* is the invariable rule; but I know
none who have explained in what manner this rule is to be
understood; the consequence of which is, that every one
takes it in the most obvious sense, that objects are represented naturally when they have such relief that they seem
real. It may appear strange, perhaps, to hear this sense of
the rule disputed; but it must be considered, that, if the
excellency of a painter consisted only in this kind of imitation, painting must lose its rank, and be no longer considered as a liberal art, and sister to poetry, this imitation

being merely mechanical, in which the slowest intellect is always sure to succeed best: for the painter of genius cannot stoop to drudgery, in which the understanding has no part; and what pretence has the art to claim kindred with poetry, but by its powers over the imagination?

Number 82

I suppose it will be easily granted, that no man can judge whether any animal be beautiful in its kind, or deformed, who has seen only one of that species: this is as conclusive in regard to the human figure; so that if a man, born blind, was to recover his sight, and the most beautiful woman was brought before him, he could not determine whether she was handsome or not; nor, if the most beautiful and most deformed were produced, could he any better determine to which he should give the preference, having seen only those two. To distinguish beauty, then, implies the having seen many individuals of that species.

Every species of the animal, as well as the vegetable creation, may be said to have a fixed or determinate form towards which nature is continually inclining, like various lines terminating in the centre; or it may be compared to pendulums vibrating in different directions over one central point; and as they all cross the centre, though only one passes through any other point, so it will be found that perfect beauty is oftener produced by nature than deformity; I do not mean than deformity in general, but than any one kind of deformity.

Novelty is said to be one of the causes of beauty: that novelty is a very sufficient reason why we should admire, is not denied; but, because it is uncommon, is it, therefore, beautiful? The beauty that is produced by colour, as when we prefer one bird to another, though of the same form, on account of its colour, has nothing to do with this argument, which reaches only to form. I have here considered the word "beauty" as being properly applied to form alone. There is a necessity of fixing this confined sense; for there can be no argument, if the sense of the word is extended to every thing that is approved.

✒ Index

The Library of Liberal Arts

Below is a representative selection from The Library of Liberal Arts. This partial listing—taken from the more than 200 scholarly editions of the world's finest literature and philosophy—indicates the scope, nature, and concept of this distinguished series.

HOBBES, T., Leviathan, I and II

HORACE, The Odes of Horace *and* The Centennial Hymn

HUME, D., Dialogues Concerning Natural Religion
Inquiry Concerning Human Understanding
Inquiry Concerning the Principles of Morals
Of the Standard of Taste, and Other Essays
Philosophical Historian
Political Essays

KANT, I., Analytic of the Beautiful
Critique of Practical Reason
First Introduction to the Critique of Judgment
Foundations of the Metaphysics of Morals
The Metaphysical Elements of Justice, Part I of *Metaphysik der Sitten*
The Metaphysical Principles of Virtue, Part II of *Metaphysik der Sitten*
On History
Perpetual Peace
Prolegomena to Any Future Metaphysics

LEIBNIZ, G., Monadology and Other Philosophical Essays

LUCIAN, Selected Works

LUCRETIUS, On Nature

MACHIAVELLI, N., The Art of War

MILL, J. S., Autobiography
On Liberty
On the Logic of the Moral Sciences
Utilitarianism

MOLIÈRE, Tartuffe

PAINE, T., The Age of Reason

PICO DELLA MIRANDOLA, On the Dignity of Man, On Being and the One, *and* Heptaplus

PLATO, Epistles
Euthydemus
Euthyphro, Apology, Crito
Gorgias
Meno
Phaedo
Phaedrus
Protagoras
Statesman
Symposium
Theatetus
Timaeus
Commentaries:
BLUCK, R., Plato's Phaedo
CORNFORD, F., Plato and Parmenides
Plato's Cosmology
Plato's Theory of Knowledge
HACKFORTH, R., Plato's Examination of Pleasure
Plato's Phaedo
Plato's Phaedrus

POPE, A., An Essay on Man

PLAUTUS, The Menaechmi

QUINTILIAN, On the Early Education of the Citizen-Orator

REYNOLDS, J., Discourses on Art

Roman Drama, Copley and Hadas, trans.

RUSSELL, B., Philosophy of Science

Sappho, The Poems of

SCHLEGEL, J., On Imitation and Other Essays

SCHOPENHAUER, A., On the Basis of Morality

SHELLEY, P., A Defence of Poetry

Song of Roland, Terry, trans.

TERENCE, The Woman of Andros

VERGIL, Aeneid

VICO, G. B., On the Study Methods of Our Time

XENOPHON, Recollections of Socrates *and* Socrates' Defense Before the Jury

THE AMERICAN HERITAGE SERIES

THE COLONIAL PERIOD

Adams, John *The Political Writings of John Adams: Representative Selections* AHS 8 George A. Peek, Jr.

The English Libertarian Heritage: From the Writings of John Trenchard and Thomas Gordon in The Independent Whig *and* Cato's Letters AHS 32 David L. Jacobson

The Great Awakening AHS 34 Alan Heimert, Perry Miller

Puritan Political Thought AHS 33 Edmund S. Morgan

THE REVOLUTIONARY ERA

The American Revolution as a Democratic Movement AHS 36 Alfred Young

The Antifederalists AHS 38 Cecelia Kenyon

Early American Libertarian Thought: Freedom of the Press from Zenger to Jefferson AHS 41 Leonard W. Levy

Franklin, Benjamin *The Political Thought of Benjamin Franklin* AHS 64 Ralph Ketcham

Paine, Thomas *Common Sense and Other Political Writings* AHS 5 Nelson F. Adkins

THE YOUNG NATION

Calhoun, John C. *Disquisition on Government and Selections from the* Discourse AHS 10 C. Gordon Post

Channing, William Ellery *Unitarian Christianity and Other Essays* AHS 21 Irving H. Bartlett

Democracy, Liberty, and Property: The State Constitutional Conventions of the 1820's AHS 43 Merrill D. Peterson

TOPICAL VOLUMES